A Portrait of Pacifists

Religion, Theology, and the Holocaust

OTHER TITLES IN RELIGION, THEOLOGY, AND THE HOLOCAUST

Disenchantment: George Steiner and the Meaning of Western Civilization after Auschwitz
CATHERINE D. CHATTERLEY

Emil L. Fackenheim: A Jewish Philosopher's Response to the Holocaust
DAVID PATTERSON

Fiorello's Sister: Gemma La Guardia Gluck's Story
GEMMA LA GUARDIA GLUCK; ROCHELLE G. SAIDEL, ed.

Four Letters to the Witnesses of My Childhood
HELENA GANOR

Harry Haft: Survivor of Auschwitz, Challenger of Rocky Marciano
ALAN SCOTT HAFT

Murder Without Hatred: Estonians and the Holocaust
ANTON WEISS-WENDT

Nitzotz: The Spark of Resistance in Kovno Ghetto and Dachau-Kaufering Concentration Camp
LAURA M. WEINRIB, ed.; ESTEE SHAFIR WEINRIB, trans.

Obliged by Memory: Literature, Religion, Ethics
STEVEN T. KATZ and ALAN ROSEN, eds.

The Warriors: My Life as a Jewish Soviet Partisan
HAROLD ZISSMAN

When the Danube Ran Red
ZSUZSANNA OZSVATH

A Portrait of Pacifists

Le Chambon, the Holocaust, and the Lives of
André and Magda Trocmé

Richard P. Unsworth

WITH A FOREWORD BY PETER I. ROSE

SYRACUSE UNIVERSITY PRESS

Copyright © 2012 by Syracuse University Press
Syracuse, New York 13244-5290

All Rights Reserved

First Edition 2012

12 13 14 15 16 17   6 5 4 3 2 1

For images provided by the United States Holocaust Memorial Museum: The views or opinions expressed in this book, and the context in which the images are used, do not necessarily reflect the views or policy of, nor imply approval or endorsement by, the U.S. Holocaust Memorial Museum. All images and photographs, except where indicated in captions, are courtesy of the Trocmé Family Private Collection.

∞ The paper used in this publication meets the minimum requirements of the American National Standard for Information Sciences—Permanence of Paper for Printed Library Materials, ANSI Z39.48-1992.

For a listing of books published and distributed by Syracuse University Press, visit our Web site at SyracuseUniversityPress.syr.edu.

ISBN: 978-0-8156-0970-4

LIBRARY OF CONGRESS CATALOGING-IN-PUBLICATION DATA

Unsworth, Richard P.

A portrait of pacifists : Le Chambon, the Holocaust, and the lives of André and Magda Trocmé / Richard P. Unsworth ; with a foreword by Peter I. Rose. — 1st ed.

p. cm. — (Religion, theology, and the Holocaust)

Includes bibliographical references and index.

ISBN 978-0-8156-0970-4 (cloth : alk. paper) 1. Trocmé, André, 1901–1971. 2. Trocmé, Magda, 1901–1996. 3. Trocmé, André, 1901–1971—Religion. 4. Trocmé, Magda, 1901–1996—Religion. 5. Righteous Gentiles in the Holocaust—France—Le Chambon-sur-Lignon—Biography. 6. Pacifists—France—Le Chambon-sur-Lignon—Biography. 7. Holocaust, Jewish (1939–1945)—France—Le Chambon-sur-Lignon. 8. World War, 1939–1945—Jews—Rescue—France—Le Chambon-sur-Lignon. 9. World War, 1939–1945—Underground movements—France—Le Chambon-sur-Lignon. 10. Le Chambon-sur-Lignon (France)—History—20th century. I. Title.

D804.66.T76U57 2012

940.53'18092244595—dc23   2012006657

Manufactured in the United States of America

For my beloved Joy

Richard P. Unsworth is a Senior Fellow of The Kahn Liberal Arts Institute at Smith College. He earned his academic degrees at Princeton University, Yale University Divinity School, and the Harvard Divinity School. He has taught religion at Smith and at Dartmouth College as well as serving chaplaincy positions in both. A decade of his career was spent as Headmaster and President of Northfield Mount Hermon School. His years of involvement with the Collège Cévenol in France led to a friendship with André and Magda Trocmé and ultimately to writing this book.

Contents

LIST OF ILLUSTRATIONS ✦ *ix*
FOREWORD, *Peter I. Rose* ✦ *xi*
ACKNOWLEDGMENTS ✦ *xvii*
AUTHOR'S NOTE ON THE MEMOIRS ✦ *xix*
INTRODUCTION: *Pacifism in the Twentieth Century* ✦ *xxi*
ABBREVIATIONS AND TERMS ✦ *xxv*

1. Remembering: *June 1971* ✦ 1
2. Life after June 5 ✦ 16
3. Pacifism Discovered ✦ 26
4. Fathers and Sons ✦ 40
5. Out of Siberia ✦ 52
6. A Renegade Gentleman ✦ 66
7. The Military Misadventure ✦ 83
8. The Turnaround Year ✦ 101
9. Real Church, Actual Church ✦ 115
10. Le Chambon in the Thirties ✦ 134
11. Understanding Catastrophe: *1939–1941* ✦ 155
12. The War Worsens: *1942–1943* ✦ 174
13. Climax and Denouement: *1943–1944* ✦ 194
14. The Bridge from War to Peace ✦ 214
15. Versailles: *The IFOR Years* ✦ 233

16. Versailles: *Rebuilding Peace* ✢ 251
17. Geneva and Beyond ✢ 271

APPENDIX ✢ 297
A PARTIAL CHRONOLOGY OF THE TROCMÉS'
LIVES AND EVENTS ✢ 301
SUGGESTED READING ✢ 303
REFERENCES ✢ 307
INDEX ✢ 311

Illustrations

1. André Trocmé, ca. 1963 ♣ *3*
2. Jispa (Alice Reynier), 1950s ♣ *17*
3. Paula Schwerdtmann with André, 1901 ♣ *27*
4. Paul Trocmé ♣ *41*
5. The storyteller (image of a letter) ♣ *49*
6. Varia Poggio Wissotsky, ca. 1915 ♣ *53*
7. Allesandro Poggio and daughter Varia, 1864 ♣ *54*
8. Nelly Wissotsky, 1899 ♣ *58*
9. Oscar Grilli di Cortona, 1900 ♣ *61*
10. Bombed home church in St. Quentin ♣ *71*
11. Geodesic Brigade, 1921–22 ♣ *88*
12. André Trocmé, 1925 ♣ *102*
13. Magda Trocmé, 1925 ♣ *104*
14. Homes in St. Gobain and St. Quentin ♣ *117*
15. Pastors of the Église du Nord ♣ *121*
16. Four Trocmé children, July 1934 ♣ *130*
17. Le Chambon-sur-Lignon Protestant Temple ♣ *135*
18. Dining room in the presbytère ♣ *143*
19. Sanctuary, temple in Le Chambon-sur-Lignon ♣ *147*
20. Edouard and Mildred Theis ♣ *153*
21. Burns Chalmers, 1940 ♣ *165*
22. Jacob Lewin and students of La Guespy ♣ *171*
23. Auguste Bohny, 2001 ♣ *172*
24. Lamirand visits Le Chambon-sur-Lignon ♣ *181*
25. Henri and Emma Héritier, 1944 ♣ *185*
26. Prisoners in Saint-Paul d'Eyjeaux detention camp ♣ *191*
27. Trocmé, Darcissac, and Theis are released ♣ *195*
28. Hôtel des Roches ♣ *197*

29. Daniel Trocmé ✤ *199*
30. Jean-Pierre Trocmé, August 1944 ✤ *209*
31. The CFD railroad station ✤ *223*
32. Carl M. and Florence Sangree ✤ *225*
33. The Luquet, 1961 ✤ *228*
34. Work camp in action ✤ *230*
35. I. Gandhi, C. Rajagopalachari, and M. Trocmé, 1949 ✤ *242*
36. "The Tower," Maison de la Réconciliation, 1954 ✤ *245*
37. André Trocmé and Kozo Tanaka Kokutai, Hiroshima, 1958 ✤ *265*
38. André Trocmé and Lanza del Vasto, Marcoule, 1958 ✤ *267*
39. Trocmé plaque in Yad Vashem, Jerusalem ✤ *288*
40. Magda in her late eighties ✤ *292*

Foreword

PETER I. ROSE

My Dutch wife and her older sister were hidden in an Amsterdam cellar for nearly four years during World War II. They owed their lives to the selfless sacrifice of a modern-day Good Samaritan, Cathoos Koolhaas Revers-DeWitt. Known to the children as Tante Toos, their protector was later to have another sobriquet: "Righteous Christian." She was one of a courageous few who risked their lives to save Jews during the dark days of the Holocaust.

André and Magda Trocmé were also "Righteous Christians" who rescued, hid, and protected Jewish children—in their case, hundreds of refugee children. But unlike Tante Toos, whose audacious deeds were seemingly the impromptu action of a loving friend, the Trocmés' actions were an almost inevitable result of a long-time moral commitment to being their brothers' keepers, even under the most extreme conditions. Their incredibly perilous activities in the French village of Le Chambon-sur-Lignon from 1940–44 were motivated and sustained by a commitment to the principles of absolute pacifism to which they devoted their adult lives and which they sustained to the very end.

At the Smith College chapel in the early 1970s, Magda Trocmé spoke of her conviction: "There are no war crimes. The crime is war." The curt statement was a shorthand expression of her belief and that of her late husband that "Thou shalt not kill" meant never, under any circumstances. To such believers there is no such thing as a just war, not even one waged against genocide or ethnic cleansing, known today as crimes against humanity.

It is this position, perhaps more than any other, that gives pause to those most sympathetic to the basic principles of pacifism.

Like many others who decried violence and denounced bloodshed, the Trocmés were well aware how difficult it is to persuade others never to take up arms, even in defense of their countries or their families. Instead they advocated nonviolent resistance to oppression, the protection of the innocent, and reconciliation even with those who had engaged in acts of violence themselves.

While the names of the two pacifists were widely known in Europe at the end of World War II, few people knew very much about the Trocmés themselves: who they were, how they met, what they believed, how they came to their unwanted celebrity.

Now their story is told in this new detailed double biography written by Richard P. Unsworth. From his narrative we learn about the lives of two people he first came to know, admire, and work with when he became the American representative of Collège Cévenol in Le Chambon-sur-Lignon. Not long after he met them he would become a part of the inner circle of the Trocmé friends, doubtless drawn together because they found they shared a number of striking similarities in their careers and worldviews.

Like André Trocmé, Unsworth had decided to become a minister while in his teens, and like André, his subsequent intellectual, social, and political involvements were undergirded by what they both saw as core Christian virtues. Yet even though active in many campaigns of nonviolent direct action for human and civil rights, Unsworth would never call himself an absolute pacifist.

André had come to his commitment to denounce war unequivocally only after considerable study and a number of seminal experiences, some of them quite serendipitous. Among those that seemed to have had the most profound impact were an unexpected colloquy with a young German soldier billeted in the Trocmé home in 1917; his family's uprooting and flight into Belgium during the worst of the fighting in their area; the sight of German soldiers being humiliated in defeat after the Armistice in the fall of 1918, and his own very limited experience while filling his mandatory military duty in a geodesic brigade in Morocco a few years later. Equally important were his membership in the Christian Union and encounters with certain professors and fellow students in the Faculty of Theology at the Sorbonne in Paris, where he studied for an advanced degree. Among those most influential were classmates Henri Roser, Jacques Martin, Edouard Theis, and Arnold Brémond, each of whom had refused to take up arms, bucking the sentiments of the vast majority of countrymen who saw conscientious objection as tantamount to treason. But perhaps most important of all was André's increasing devotion to one of the fundamental tenets of his faith: "They will beat their swords into ploughshares, and their spears into pruning hooks. Nation will not take up sword against nation, nor will they train for war any more."

André and Magda were two persons with very different backgrounds, religious sensibilities and personalities. In many ways they were the yin and yang of the movement that became central to both of their lives. As Unsworth puts it, referring to the two of them: "Theology was André's game, not hers." Yet he also shows how much they were as one in a single, abiding concept deeply rooted in the singular phrase, "The Audacity of Believing," the title of André's unpublished manuscript re-discovered many years after the war. In its pages André addresses the reality of a world on fire with the powers of reason and conscience and faith in a loving God: an inner resolve, shared by Magda. In many ways this sentiment was their personal shibboleth.

André and Magda were both born of privilege—he of strict, conventional haute bourgeoisie French and German Protestant parentage; she, née Magda Lisa Larissa Grilli di Cortona, of more colorful upper class Russian and Italian descent, religiously a "hodgepodge of Russian Orthodox, Catholic and Protestant strains." Her Russian ancestors had been Decembrists who sought to overthrow the Tsar in 1825; her Italian ones numbered supporters of Giuseppe Mazzini's revolutionaries a few years later.

The two met and fell in love in 1925 while both were graduate students spending a year in New York, he at Union Theological Seminary, she at the New York School of Social Work. They were married in André's home town of St. Quentin in 1926 and soon moved to an industrial town in the north of France where André became an apprentice to the local pastor and first tested his skills as a preacher and his rebellious nature as an activist. Neither sat too well with his superiors. He did far better in subsequent appointments.

His full conversion to war resistance came in the turbulent early 1930s, the very period when even many peace-loving activists began to say, "If there was ever a reason for a just war. . . ." André understood the sentiment. He is reported to have felt he could "condemn no one who, in good conscience, felt a responsibility to serve the country in the military," but decided that he, himself, would have no part of it. In fact, "if forced to choose between his country's call to go to war and loyalty to God's word," Unsworth writes, "he knew he could not take up a rifle and kill an enemy soldier." But he found a way to reconcile his intense opposition to the Nazis and their Vichy lackeys by working with those who were the principal scapegoats in the war.

There is little doubt that his greatest example of acting on the basis of his abhorrence to war and his compassion for victims of war were the actions he and Magda took in Le Chambon-sur-Lignon, the site of his third parish and the place where they would stay for sixteen years.

Le Chambon and its surrounding towns were quite different from most places in France. As Unsworth explains, once a Huguenot bastion, there was already a spirit of greater open-mindedness in the villages of the plateau than elsewhere owing to three socially concerned Protestant factions. Some of these "liberals" were followers of Christianisme Social, devoted to serving just causes based on religious conviction, some were soldiers in the Armée du Salut (Salvation Army), and some were Darbyists, a group founded by renegade Irish Anglicans who were basically Judaphiles, who believed that Jews were the original People of God and that nothing could be more in keeping with the faith than caring for and supporting Jews who were being persecuted.

Early in their time in predominantly Protestant Le Chambon, high on a plateau in southern France, the Trocmés established the internationally oriented École Nouvelle Cévenole (later to be called the Collège Cévenol). Many who came to the school in the late 1930s, including some Jewish youngsters, had been sent there to escape harassment. In 1941 an American, Burns Chalmers, the Smith College chaplain on a year's leave to work with the Quakers in French internment camps, challenged Trocmé and his parish to provide shelter and education for children being released from the camps. They accepted the challenge, and soon waves of children were coming from camps like Gurs to Le Chambon. By the end of the war, more than 800 Jewish children had been hidden and educated there and in surrounding towns. Le Chambon, the City of Refuge, had also had become a way station on an underground railroad that spirited some of the most vulnerable asylum seekers into Switzerland.

After the collapse of the Third Reich and the restoration of the French Republic, the Trocmés remained in Le Chambon. The story of the sheltering of the children and their critical roles soon became known throughout Europe and then the United States. They were widely acclaimed as paragons of a particularly unique form of French resistance and often asked to speak about their exploits. While willing to describe how their charges were kept from the hands of the Gestapo and to lecture about their continued commitment to pacifism, neither André nor Magda could abide the hero label, nor did they feel they could accept the myriad awards many tried to bestow upon them. If any should get credit, they said over and over, it should be the people of Le Chambon.

These are but the bare bones of the story. In the pages of *A Portrait of Pacifists* Richard Unsworth treats readers to an intimate and detailed picture of two very human—and humane—idols of the twentieth century who spent their lives waging war against war. Albert Einstein once declared, "I am not only a pacifist but a militant pacifist. I am willing to fight for peace." André and Magda Trocmé were fighters, too. Their weapons were not slings and arrows or guns and bombs but beliefs, strong, unshakable beliefs, that there are better ways to resolve conflicts than violence.

Being nonviolent and compassionate does not mean failing to act or simply turning the other cheek. The resistance of the Trocmés, like Gandhi's and later Martin Luther King's, was never passive. Yet every action came with a price, a price paid not only by those being led but also by those dealing with internal turmoil about staying the course or altering it, as some did, in order to remain alive to continue to do the good work their consciences demanded. These dilemmas confronted the Trocmés on more than one occasion, none more wrenching than when André learned that he was targeted by the Gestapo and would likely be picked up and killed unless he went into hiding. Should he surrender, sacrificing himself to protect his charges? Would that make a difference? Should he stand firm and pray that he and the others would not be harmed, knowing the risks of endangering his family and the very real chance that the refugees he was shielding would be discovered and sent to the death camps? He chose to go into hiding—to fight, in his nonviolent way, another day. As Richard Unsworth tells us, he mused about that decision for the rest of his life: "For André, the greatest threat to his sense of integrity came with any departure from his fundamental commitment. It was both the strength and the price of his absolutism about moral essentials."

In 1989 Samuel P. Oliner, an Auschwitz survivor, and his wife, Pearl M. Oliner, published *The Altruistic Personality: Rescuers of Jews in Nazi Europe*. They interviewed individuals in six countries who had helped those deemed *Untermenschen* to sustain life when they had been stripped of their rights, aided and abetted escapes from camps and prisons, smuggled them out of Germany or conquered lands, and especially provided sanctuary and sustenance to those who lived underground. Their research provided them with a good deal of background information about the rescuers and their motivations. In the end the Oliners found four principal reasons why these individuals did what they did: they were personal, economic, political, and religious. While my wife's Tante Toos would surely be placed under the first rubric, André and Magda Trocmé definitely belong under the last one. They were doing God's work: Bringing to Life.

Acknowledgments

As with any book worth writing, help has come from many quarters. Joy Merritt Unsworth brought her sharp eye for literary potholes and her invariably useful critique to this project from the beginning. She also patiently awaited the last page being written. Our daughter Lucy Slosser's keen insight created the apt title for the book.

Nelly Trocmé Hewett, Jacques Trocmé and his wife Leslyn have all been patient and unstinting in their support of this project. They have opened the large collection of family papers and memorabilia to me and answered my many questions. Several professorial friends have constantly stressed the importance of the project and encouraged me in its pursuit: Reformation historian Miriam Chrisman, Klemens von Klemperer, historian of the German resistance, Peter I. Rose, sociologist and writer on refugees and the dispossessed, artist and renowned sculptor Elliot Offner, English professors James English and John Unsworth, and my colleagues in the Kahn Liberal Arts Institute at Smith College. Raymond Green, long-time member and chair of the American Friends of the Collège Cévenol, provided rich detail about the earliest postwar years of the Collège. Liane Hartman's technical skills and Marian Macdonald's experienced editorial eye have been indispensable in moving the book from its rough draft to its final form. So have editors Kay Steinmetz and Jennika Baines at the Syracuse University Press.

A now deceased French historian and archivist of Le Chambon, Annik Flaud, was a veritable scholarly bloodhound in the way she tracked down facts and exposed fictions. Other scholars with overlapping interests have been very helpful, especially Pierre Sauvage, Patrick G. Henry, Pierre Boismorand, and Christian Maillebouis.

I owe my thanks to all those whom I interviewed, but I want to single out a few whose conversations were exceptionally helpful: Howard Schomer, Gérard Bollon, Simone Mairesse, Rolande Lombard, Olivier Hatzfeld, Tracy Strong Jr., René Rivière, Jeanne Theis, Lydie Russier-Chave, Thomas Johnson, Pastor Cyrille Payot, Christian and Solange Mazel, Alfred Werner, Jean-Pierre and Yvonne Marchand, Auguste Bohny, and Hans-Ruedi Weber.

Author's Note on the Memoirs

Both André's and Magda's memoirs were prepared over many years. They were intended only for their children and grandchildren, and they were added to in rather haphazard fashion whenever time allowed. They both begin with comments on childhood and early family life and go on through adult life. Inevitably, their historical accuracy is more fragile the more distant the writing is from the event.

André's effort began in 1944, probably during his months in hiding in Perdyer, and consisted of sixty-six pages handwritten in a bound school notebook. It was set aside for several years and forgotten, but his project got a second start during the 1950s, when André and Magda lived in Versailles and worked for the International Fellowship of Reconciliation. This time André wrote on loose sheets which he kept in boxes. His entries in the memoir were sporadic during their ten years in Versailles, and there they ended, except for one entry, written in Perdyer in July of 1968, where he tries to help his children and grandchildren understand what shaped his Christian faith throughout his life. There are no entries about his ministry in Geneva or projects in Europe, North Africa, Japan, and Vietnam during the 1960s.

After André's death in 1971, Magda moved from Geneva to Paris in 1977. She got out the boxes and set about putting pages in chronological order and transcribing them with the help of a friend and volunteer, Gertrude Zuber. Over several years, these papers were put in typewritten form (with occasional marginal scribbles by Magda).

Magda had also kept some autobiographic notes, starting in June of 1942. She was less determined than André to keep the project going, and it was not until January of 1964 that she picked up the threads, but only briefly. Then during a visit with her daughter in the United States, she learned to use a tape recorder and, under Nelly's prodding, continued her story by dictating it on eight cassettes. This brought the narrative to the summer of 1946. Magda promised to have the tapes transcribed and said she would then pick up her pen and write the story of their years in Versailles, the decade in Geneva, and finally, after André's death, her years in Paris. The transcriptions happened, but the writing did not. For this reason, references to their memoirs are given with page numbers, but without dates.

There is a generous record of their work in the decade of the sixties, but none of it is found in their memoirs. During those last years of ministry, they wrote lengthy reports to the church in Geneva and to agencies that helped finance their projects in North Africa, India, Japan, and Vietnam. Fortunately they kept copies of virtually all those documents.

Jacques Trocmé created two successive English language versions of his parents' memoirs, intended for those grandchildren who did not speak French. I have worked from both the English and the original French versions of these two works. In this book, references to these memoirs are paginated according to the original French versions of André's *Mémoires* and Magda's *Souvenirs Autobiographiques.*

All the French and English versions of these and other Trocmé documents are in the archives of the Peace Collection at the Swarthmore College Library (which holds the copyright on the Trocmé papers), and in the archives of the library of the World Council of Churches in Geneva.

Introduction
Pacifism in the Twentieth Century

Since this is a book about two remarkable twentieth century pacifists, it will be useful to understand the complexity of pacifism as it played out in the western world during their century. Two world wars and wars in Korea and Vietnam dominated the period. Roughly one hundred and fifty million people died in those wars. This country's prolonged Cold War with the Soviet Union involved few casualties but many threats and endless tension about nuclear weapons. If you look for periods of peace, there are only twelve years of the whole twentieth century without one nation or empire being at war with another. Yet pacifism took many shapes and targets through those decades, and it was also a century whose last years saw a remarkable drop in political violence.

From the earliest days of Christian communities, peace activists were witnesses to their faith, refusing to kill for any king or emperor, a posture that often cost them their lives. But when the twentieth century began, the use of "pacifism" to describe opposition to war and violence was not common in Europe and North America. The term "pacifism" was first adopted by a group of peace activists gathered at the Universal Peace Congress in Glasgow in 1901.

Twentieth-century pacifism is best understood as a movement with many sources and forms: three centuries of Quaker peace testimony; the long-standing presence of conscientious objectors (COs), especially Jehovah's Witnesses, Mennonites, and other "peace churches"; and anti-militarism among the socialist and organized labor movements that grew up in the late nineteenth century (Brock and Young, 4–6).

The pacifism movement has had a dozen faces. Its members may be moved by their religious tradition, by a personal spiritual commitment, by the stories of international peacemakers, or by an altogether secular animosity toward war.

Four leading twentieth-century pacifists drew attention and often a following that was scattered throughout the western world and beyond: Leon Tolstoy (died 1910), Russian novelist and radical Christian pacifist; Mahatma Ghandi (died 1948), who taught millions in India to fight tyranny with strictly nonviolent civil disobedience; Pope John XIII (died 1963), the most ecumenical of popes and, while in Paris as Papal Nuncio, a personal acquaintance of André Trocmé; and Martin Luther King Jr. (died 1968), whose commitment to nonviolent direct action to bring about social change won him the Nobel Peace Prize in 1966. These four certainly brought pacifist aspirations to many more than the total membership of the world's existing peace organizations. They also instilled in those organizations a tendency to broaden their membership beyond narrow religious boundaries.

An example is the Mouvement International de la Réconciliation (MIR), a local French pacifist organization, begun in 1923 by a handful of young Protestant theologians. During the 1950s, the MIR became a branch of the International Fellowship of Reconciliation (IFOR). The MIR has remained small: less than 200 inscribed members, but its administrative council now has two co-presidents, one Catholic and the other Protestant, an arrangement unthinkable in the 1950s when the Trocmés were stationed in Versailles as European co-secretaries of the IFOR. Its work now reaches far beyond France. The French MIR sustains an active partnership with African nonviolence groups scattered over seven sub-Saharan African nations.

The IFOR parent organization, founded in 1919, now has eighty MIR branches and affiliates in forty-eight countries over every continent. It maintains permanent representatives at the United Nations and participates in meetings that deal with nonviolent alternatives in the field of human rights. It has had six Nobel Peace Prize Laureates among former and present members. Another facet of its membership is its religious diversity. Example: one African chapter, MIR Congo, produced programs broadcast over the area by members of Muslim and traditional African religions. The IFOR is now a worldwide Non-Governmental Organization (NGO) with a tight focus on training populations to accept nonviolence as the essential tool to build the basis of peace and justice.

Active pacifist groups are still to be found around the western world pursuing their challenges to the development of nuclear weapons, aggressive military actions and international commerce in weapons, as well as offering training in nonviolence programs. In recent decades, however, they are less likely to be suppressed by government forces, except in countries that require terms of military service. Hungary would be an example, where conscription is required and prison is the answer to anyone who refuses to comply (Brock, 21).

Until midcentury, most nations, like Hungary, required men to fulfill a period of military service. The assumption was that wars are bound to break out and one's country must be at the ready. But as the nature and extent of conscientious objection evolved during this period, it led to a reassessment of pacifism.

When World War I broke out, only two nations, Great Britain and the United States, made exemption for conscientious objectors. For the most part, only Quakers and other "Peace Church" members were recognized as religious objectors. Others who presented themselves as conscientious objectors were, as a rule, sent to jail. The British made earlier and broader options for their recognized objectors. When the United States joined the war in 1916, those decisions were made by local civilian boards, groups far less likely to accept the pacifist's status. Those who were offered exemption from combatant service were assigned to medical or engineering or similar work in the army. Those who refused to serve in the military were given severe jail terms (Brock and Young, 18–57).

The Second World War involved conscription throughout Europe and North America, and—as a consequence—the phenomenon of conscientious objection. This time Great Britain and the United States made more options open to COs, including noncombatant assignments. The American option was a system of 150 Civilian Public Service camps, organized and overseen as a rule by Peace Church personnel (Brock and Socknat, 312–30). Prison terms were inflicted only on pacifists who refused to cooperate with any part of the system. Religious conviction was still the general standard, but now that was recognized in more cases than those who were Quakers or members of other traditional Peace Churches.

The European countries, however, gave virtually no standing to conscientious objectors. Those who took the stance were given prison terms. When they were released, they were required to report for duty or be returned to prison. Under Hitler's regime, pacifists of whatever sort were sent to concentration camps or executed, no matter their religious background.

In the postwar years, conscription in Britain was phased out in 1961. In the United States, it continued until the end of the Vietnam War in 1973. In France in 1963 de Gaulle recognized the rights of conscientious objectors to alternate service, but like the rest of Europe, conscription continued and COs had to account for themselves.

Now that the century has turned, the whole practice of conscription is fading. Most European Union countries still carry mandatory conscription on the books, but in practice the EU nations have begun to phase it out and depend totally on volunteers to provide their armed forces.

Whatever form of pacifism might have flourished during the twentieth century, its opponents have always outnumbered its adherents, charging that pacifists evade their share of responsibility for the defense and safety of their society. They were seen as fellow citizens who lacked patriotism, or suffered from simple cowardice. André and Magda Trocmé would have profoundly disagreed.

Abbreviations and Terms

Christianisme Social: An organization of Protestant intellectuals headquartered in the village of Le Mazet-Saint-Voy, near Le Chambon-sur-Lignon. Many critically important meetings took place there during the Second World War, often resulting in developing tactics of resistance to anti-Semitic and other policies of the Vichy government.

CIMADE: *Commission Inter-Mouvements Auprès des Évacués*. A joint effort of religious and secular organizations that dealt effectively with the growing number of refugee camps, primarily in the Free Zone of France.

Collège: A private secondary school preparing for the baccalaureate examination required for admission to a French university.

Conseil d'administration: The governing board, comparable to trustees, of the Collège Cévenol.

La Croix Bleue: Founded in Switzerland in 1877 by a Protestant minister, Pasteur Louis-Lucien Rochat, its members swore to abstain from using alcohol.

ÉRF: *Église Réformée de France*. The northern and southern French Reformed churches merged into this national church in 1938 under the leadership of Pasteur Marc Boegner. André's father, Paul Trocmé, was the lay leader of the northern church who helped Boegner bring the two churches together.

FPF: *Federation Protestante de France*. The Federation of churches that would, in 1928, bring together Protestant, Lutheran, and Evangelical church groups whose cooperation was the groundwork for France's first ecumenical moves: among them, the ERF.

IFOR: *International Fellowship of Reconciliation* headquartered in New York.

MIR: *Mouvement International de la Réconciliation*, the French chapter of the IFOR.

OSE: *Oeuvres de Secour aux Enfants*. The Society for the Protection of Children was founded in 1912 by a group of leading Russian Jewish intellectuals as a means for insuring the health of children of the Eastern European ghettoes. A French chapter was established in 1933 and became a major force in providing escape routes or places of hiding for refugee children. They worked closely with Catholic and Protestant churches.

SCI: *Service Civil International.* An International Civil Service organization created by the Swiss government and active in creating homes for dispossessed children brought from concentration camps to le Chambon-sur-Lignon.

STO: *Service de Travail Obligatoire.* As Germany took men from its war industries and sent them to the Russian Front, they rounded up men from countries they had occupied. In France, the Vichy government passed the law of 16 February, 1943, which required groups of French men to do forced labor in Germany.

Temple: The name used for a Protestant church building. In France, the term Église (Church) refers only to a Catholic Church, a leftover from the days when Catholicism was the only recognized form of Christianity.

A Portrait of Pacifists

1

Remembering
June 1971

It was a fine Saturday morning in June, a time of the year when Geneva is at its most pleasant—a walking city with eight o'clock sunsets, temperatures in the 70s, and on most days a decent breeze off the Lac Léman. By now one could see how the garden would look, enjoy the languorous evenings, and be grateful that Geneva wasn't yet as noisy and humid as it would be when all the windows were open in search of fresh air.

For the last five weeks, alone in his room in the Cantonal Hospital, André Trocmé had tried to make the best of it. His mind often traveled back to momentous events in his life. He cherished the insights he gained from bringing the past forward to inform the present. His whole life was the stuff of stories, and André loved a good story.

Even his hospitalization produced stories. Paralyzed and unable to walk, he still found the energy to be a pastor to other patients. The Sunday morning Protestant worship service in the hospital, held on the top floor in a rather dismal patients' lounge, drew an odd assortment of patients in various stages of dress and undress, some still in their hospital beds.[1] André had conducted those services often. He knew intimately what the members of his congregation were experiencing because he shared that experience every day.

The evening before he died he dictated a letter that was later printed under the title "The Face of God on Earth: one sick person speaks to

---

1. From an interview with Trocmé's daughter, Nelly Trocmé Hewett.

another"[2] and made available to his fellow patients. It was not a premonitory writing, for it was in his nature to assume that he would recover and get on with his life, even though constrained by his paralysis. Both the contemplative and the activist sides of André Trocmé come to the surface in this text:

> But what do I see in the face of my God? What are the wrinkles, which crease his cheeks like the cheeks of mothers whose children are incurably ill? What is that fold which crosses his forehead . . . that slight trembling in the healing hands of Jesus? A sign of the beginning of exhaustion in him who gives himself entirely each day to others. . . . We are going to rise up and free God from what is killing him . . . because if God is killed by hatred, by agony, and by death, then the destiny of man is hopeless. All has been tried, all has failed, nothing has any meaning; evil and death triumph over all.

André's whole adult life had been a standoff with hatred, war, and death, and he knew he would never see a resolution. He could not have known that his own end was only a day away. What counted now was his enforced leisure that gave him time to think—about his medical situation, about where he was in his life and work, and about what would come next.

He had retired earlier that year after eleven years at St. Gervais, a venerable church in the old quarter of downtown Geneva, a church that had once been Catholic and after the Reformation became Protestant. At a certain age Swiss clergy were required to retire, no matter the state of their health or the vigor of their minds. So at age seventy he left the pulpit, still vigorous and active and perhaps a little frustrated by his imposed leisure. Leisure had not been a significant part of his life. He was most himself when he was generating a new project or finding a new way to approach an old issue. But at least the release from weekly meetings and sermon writing and visits with parishioners meant more time to write on projects that were important to him.

---

2. *Visage de Dieu sur la Terre: écrit d'une malade à un autre.*

1. André Trocmé, ca. 1963. Unknown photographer.

Hiding in Perdyer

As he looked back over things he had done, he remembered a neglected and unpublished book manuscript prepared in 1943–44 while he was in hiding from the Gestapo. Perhaps his retirement would permit him a chance to revisit that project, begun many years earlier during those long months of separation from his family and his community. With prodigious discipline, he had prepared the full text of a book designed as a kind of "instruction in the faith." When he returned to his church in Le Chambon-sur-Lignon and the active life to which he was committed took over his time, he had a manuscript he called "Oser Croire" (The Audacity of Believing). The book was intended to address the conflict between two realities: the world in which he lived and the things that sustained his inner life, "an enigma very difficult to decipher," he called it (A. Trocmé 1944, 1).

When he left Le Chambon-sur-Lignon in July of 1943, his world was on fire. By the best reckoning of the experts, about thirty-six million people died in the European nations that were party to this prolonged slaughter. As in every war, survival usually trumped ethics, civility, and moral purpose. And now it was André's turn to face his own conflict: whether to leave aside the tangle of obligations and purposes that dominated his daily life in Le Chambon and go into hiding.

It all began when a young member of the armed resistance, a maquisard, had come to the parsonage. He claimed to be a double agent who worked for the Germans and was able to know ahead of time some of their operational plans. He warned André that he was on the hit list for assassination by the Gestapo. At first André was shocked, but for him the problem quickly turned from a survival issue into a spiritual dilemma. He was troubled by the implications of going into hiding. He had never been confronted by such a threat, and he had only that report by the young maquisard to go on.[3] Furthermore, running for cover seemed more like a temptation than a solution. What should he do? Going into hiding might seem like cowardice, absolutely the wrong message to give his parishioners, especially after the way they had stuck by him during his month in the concentration camp at Saint-Paul d'Eyjeaux a mere six months earlier. And then there was the equally worrisome question: if he were to disappear, would his disappearance unravel the whole fabric of nonviolent resistance that he and his colleague, Pastor Edouard Theis, had worked so hard to create in Le Chambon?

He talked it through with Magda. As his intellectual partner and spiritual confidant, she understood why he might decide to risk staying in town, but as his wife and a mother, she simply couldn't say that he should take such a risk. She admired his courage but she needed his life. There was no question that she needed him there in the parsonage for all kinds of personal and public reasons, but even more she needed him alive when the madness of this war was finally over and their life together and as parents could return to something like normal.

Soon the word was out in the town that André was on the Germans' hit list. Now that this was public knowledge, the risk to André's life was higher, but he still could not resolve the spiritual and moral dilemma that faced him. Finally one of his clergy colleagues in the area notified the President of the French Reformed Church, Marc Boegner, about the

---

3. The question whether there actually was such a list was only settled when Vichy records for the Haute-Loire were made publicly available after the war. These records confirmed that such a "hit list" did exist and that Trocmé and Edouard Theis were both on it.

situation. Boegner dispatched the vice-president of the Church, Maurice Rohr, to talk with André and to dissuade him from staying in Le Chambon. The way André recalled it in his memoir, the conversation went something like this:

> Rohr: "The arrest of Daniel Trocmé and his students is enough. We have lived through many disasters. What would be the purpose of adding another martyr to a list that is already very long?"
> Trocmé: "But I want to give myself as an example because I have preached nonviolent resistance, and my duty is to go all the way."
> Rohr: "Your parish is in turmoil and has had enough. There is a price on your head. You know how these executions happen. You go for a ride in a car and your corpse is found at the edge of a forest. Or it could be a break-in at mealtime and your entire family is mowed down by machine gun fire. Are you willing, because of your stubborn attitude, to be killed and maybe also be responsible for your wife's and your children's wounds or deaths, and maybe even those of others who live under your roof?" (There were always refugees in residence at the parsonage.)
> Then Rohr asked the same question that had troubled Trocmé from the outset:
> "Do you believe for one minute that your parishioners would remain nonviolent after you have been murdered?" André admitted that they probably would not, and Rohr nailed down the argument with a serious admonition: "So, be reasonable and disappear for a while. The BBC has announced an allied landing this next summer. Your hiding will last only a few weeks. Exposing yourself to the worst would be insane. You are needed alive, not dead! The Church will pay your salary to your wife, and will pay for your expenses while you are in hiding." (A. Trocme 1953, 402)

All that had happened almost thirty years earlier. It seemed so long ago but now so immediate, now that he was thinking about the things that had shaped his life. Others called the war years "the heroic period" of life in Le Chambon, but for André those years were not heroic. They were sometimes agonizing, always intensely focused, and on occasion deeply gratifying. It was a period when his root convictions were most challenged and most sharpened. But heroism and heroics were not part of his vocabulary of assessment.

To be sure, he was an authoritative presence. One of his co-workers, Howard Schomer, characterized him this way: "Everything about André Trocmé was outsized. He towered above the average Frenchman, his big frame, head and hands radiating both physical strength and strength of will" (Schomer 1992, 1). But he had always dealt with an abundance of quite unheroic self-doubt.

Courage was another matter. Standing up to oppressive authority was a long tradition among French Protestants. It had been their lot repeatedly since the early Huguenots and their Camisards ("White Shirts") took their stand against King Louis XIV. Resistance to immoral authority was part of André's heritage, as it was for most of his parishioners. Many of them were members of one or another local family that had lived on the Plateau for generations.

Decades after the war, a young American film-maker who was born to refugee parents there on the Plateau would return to Chambon and try to understand what motivated the farmers of this remote country community to risk their lives by taking in refugees. When Pierre Sauvage addressed that question to the Heritiers, who had hidden his parents, Emma Heritier answered the question with a simple "I don't know. We were just used to it."[4] It didn't occur to those plainspoken evangelical farmers that there was any other real option. They understood the high risk of resisting the Vichy government and later the Gestapo, but they lived by their Bible, which said that the Jews were God's special people. So how could they not hide a Jew in flight from persecution?

For André, the question of whether to go into hiding was extraordinarily vexed. Should he take the rumor of the hit list seriously, heed the advice of Pasteur Rohr, and go into hiding, or should he stay in town and take his chances as a target for assassination?

---

4. " *J'sais pas; on y était habitué.* " Pierre Sauvage recorded Emma Héritier's comment in his documentary film *Weapons of the Spirit*.

Many years later, when writing down his recollections, he admitted to himself that he had never really resolved the dilemma at all, at least not rationally. He had allowed himself to be convinced that hiding was the best thing, but he was never really sure it was the right thing. For André, the greatest threat to his sense of integrity came with any departure from a moral commitment. It was both the strength and the price of his absolutism about moral essentials. He would have been even more deeply troubled about this decision if he had lived long enough to hear the claims that others would make later that the whole scheme had been invented to get him out of town and his teachings out of the way of the Maquis resisters and their plans for violent action (Bolle 1992, 252). In fact, he may have suspected something of the sort, because he wrote in the memoir, "To be sure, during my absence there were no arrests in Le Chambon, and the maquis took a direction that I wouldn't have wished for" (A. Trocmé 1953, 402).

In the end, he put his doubts aside enough to take Rohr's advice and get out of town. It was well that he did because there was, in fact, a hit list. Jacques Poujol reported in the first major colloquium concerning the war years in Le Chambon-sur-Lignon, "I saw in the Departmental Archives the telegrams received from Vichy and the orders to the prefect, which are very clear. The persons to be arrested or at least put out of the way are naturally Trocmé, Theis, Darsissac but also Guillion (a former mayor of Le Chambon); the four are on the same list" (Bolle 1992, 332).

When it came time to go, he and Magda took the children by bicycle for a picnic in the countryside a few kilometers down the road to Valence. There he was picked up by a hardware store owner from the town of Lamastre, M. Lespet, a man who had exercised his own sort of courage simply by undertaking the errand. Lespet drove André another twenty-five or thirty kilometers down the mountainous Ardèche road to Lamastre, where his friend Pastor Estoppey was filling in for the vacationing minister of the local Reformed Church. Estoppey had a room ready for him in the parsonage, a comfortable enough room but one that he was not permitted to leave. They were still close to Chambon, and the risk was high that he would be recognized. In fact, some factory workers in town had already recognized him when he stood at the window of his room, and one couldn't be sure that the villagers of Lamastre would be discreet coconspirators. When the regular minister returned from vacation, he was more than a little upset to find André in his house and immediately told Lespet to move him out. The local police had already searched Estoppey's own home in the nearby village of Intres, expecting to find André there. The time in the Lamastre parsonage had been put to good use. Estoppey had arranged for a food ration card, and André's fellow inmate in the concentration camp of Saint-Paul d'Eyjeaux, Roger Darcissac, had arranged for a false identification card.

Trocmé's next stop was a farm outside Lamastre, where he spent several weeks. M. Ranc was a prisoner of war in Germany, but the remaining family members welcomed André and provided him with a room next to the barn. The farm was on a hilltop, giving him a sweeping view of the valley and providing some protection against surprise. The weather was cold and unpleasant, and his room was about the same. But it was a safe place to be as he worked out the next steps in his odyssey.

Once again M. Lespet arrived to ferry him to another safe house further down the winding road from Lamastre toward Vernoux, this time at the farm of a well-to-do contractor and his wife. M. Pélissier the Frenchman was in the ambivalent position of being also M. Pélissier the contractor who worked for the Germans. He poured the concrete for the Atlantic Wall of bunkers that the German army was building along the Normandy coast in anticipation of an Allied invasion. The Germans provided his income, but the maquis provided his safety, as long, that is, as he continued to store weapons for the French underground in that part of the Ardèche. Trocmé couldn't help wondering whether the two roles of Pélissier were not meant to provide a major life and property insurance policy for himself and his family. Even now, years later, he wondered how anyone could live with himself under the conditions of moral compromise that Pélissier had accepted.

Then there was Mme. Pélissier, a bourgeois Parisian of great pride and little grace. André was a paying guest, but she treated him more like a hired hand, demanding that he tend the goats, milk them, and make the cheese, none of these being talents cultivated in the Faculty of Theology in Paris. He remembered the chores with a twinge of misery. He also remembered his vain effort to read a book while tending the goats, an effort that gave him a better appreciation of shepherds. The goats took full advantage of his inattention and wandered off at will. André finally tried to tether them in order to get back to his reading, but goats are hardheaded, and these beasts went on a noise and hunger strike when he tried to keep them in place. They bleated without ceasing and refused to graze. Reading would have to be left to the evenings.

Mme. Pélissier was about as hospitable as the goats, permitting but never inviting André to read in the living room in the evenings. In a long letter to Magda, he unburdened himself about the whole situation. Clearly, going into hiding was not a choice he had wanted to make, nor was there an ounce of romance and adventure about it. It was a bleak combination of isolation, boredom, and perpetual calculation.

Partly because he was intelligent, introspective, and analytical, and partly because he was a writer at home in his craft, his letters to Magda were remarkable for their ability to convey both circumstances and emotions. It was almost easier for him to put his doubts and anxieties on paper than to give them voice in a conversation. But writing letters without giving away your hiding place was a complicated endeavor at best. Ordinary mail was out of the question, but it was possible from time to time to persuade a sympathetic third party to place Magda's envelope inside another and mail it for him.

With the profound mutual understanding that had marked their relationship over two decades, Magda had shared his discomfort at being in hiding. She had also been working on a plan to get André to a safer house far from the gaze of the French police and far from the villages and towns where he might be recognized. When she finally got a letter, she knew it was time to see him in person and implement the plan. She rode her bicycle, taking the side roads, the forest lanes, and dried streambeds to avoid suspicious police on her long trip to the Pélissier farm, nearly fifty kilometers of steep and rough downhill travel. Once there she outlined the further escape she had worked out for him, to a remote village in the mountains on the far side of the Rhône river, a long way from any but a very few personal friends who might recognize him.

They set out together to put André in the hands of his first contact. Many years later he remembered their brief hours together as they traveled down to the Rhône valley and the west bank of the river. There they spent the night in a farmhouse and were met the next day by their underground contact person, M. Brunet, a garage owner in the city of Die, well east of the Rhône River. André gathered his things, said goodbye to Magda and set out with M. Brunet on the next leg of the trip: another 50 kilometers to the southeastern mountains of the Vercors. This was surely far enough to serve the needs of anonymity, especially since he was no longer André Trocmé, but André Béguet. He wore heavy framed spectacles and shaved his moustache.

At the end of his trip with M. Brunet, he was ushered into his new quarters in a handsome pension known as the Chateau de Perdyer, a country house in the Drôme valley south of Châtillon. Half of the property was owned by his old and trusted friend, Jacques Martin,[5] one of André's circle of close pacifist friends during his days at Theological Seminary. Although Martin was not living there at the time, he had paved the way among his friends, including a local chapter of the maquis, so that the French police would not discover André. The contrast with André's hiding places while en route was striking: a very large, light room with a high-beamed ceiling, a stove, and a galvanized metal bathtub. His hostess, Mme. Deloche, ran the half of the Chateau in which André lived and was somehow able to provide an abundance of deliciously prepared food, in spite of the shortages that plagued every part of France by that time. Finally, he had made it to a hiding place where he could read and write and live something approaching a normal life. A few of Jacques Martin's circle in the area knew who M. Béguet really was, but their lips were sealed and it was reasonably safe to wander outdoors. There were only two major deficits: the absence of Magda and the children and his own nagging questions about leaving his parishioners to seek his own safety.

That flight and those months in hiding posed other inner conflicts. Most would not have been nearly as agonizing for a more pragmatic soul,

---

5. Martin was denied ordination by the ÉRF because of his stance as a conscientious objector. During the war, he became active in the resistance in his home area. He later gave up hope for ordination, opened a bookstore, and worked for IFOR, the International Fellowship of Reconciliation. He died in the Château de Perdyer in 2003.

but André's soul was not very pragmatic. One of those morally conflicted moments was written unforgettably in his memory because it almost separated him from his son Jacques.

Lyon and the Encounter with Truth

A long time ago he had promised himself that he would never lie, no matter what the circumstances. This was not some abstract philosophical principle, but a very practical matter. He dealt with the question in a lecture he gave in the United States soon after the war, contrasting truth as an eternal reality with the common secular definition of truth as a social construct (A. Trocmé 1953, 32–41). He understood the meaning of truth not through its social construction, but through the person and actions of Jesus. For Jesus, truth was a gift from God that we receive and understand only when we act on it. And that is what distinguished Jesus above everything else: truth was his way of being and acting; it was not an abstract idea.

When Andre was writing his *Mémoires* he took a slightly nuanced view of truth, pointing to his differences with Absolutists. For them truth was an absolute proposition, self-evident on its face, and not susceptible to compromise. But, wrote André, "the practice of non-lying (like non-violence) can't be thought of as a blueprint whose lines and drawings have to be followed to the letter. . . . It presents itself as a series of small, unpredictable problems which have to be resolved one by one. . . . On the spot, one is not sure of anything" (A. Trocmé 1953, 275). Those two views of truth—in the lecture and in *Mémoires*—seem at odds, but as much as he tried to carve out certainties and live by them, André knew that life in time and history would never yield to such neat prescriptions. So he simply decided to take it on himself to tell the truth, whatever the circumstance, and be ready to accept the cost. That kind of vow admitted no compromise, but that was not a hindrance. André had a hard time with any sort of compromise anyway, especially if he thought a compromise would benefit him personally.

Then came the circumstance that could not have been anticipated, with a potential cost that could not be accepted. He had arranged for his son Jacques to come for an extended visit in Perdyer. They were to meet at the home of good friends in a residential section of Lyons. They would spend the night there and catch the southbound morning train to Valence, which would get them to Perdyer in the late afternoon. They left Jacot's suitcase in the baggage room at the Lyon-Perrache train station, planning to pick it up in the morning on their way to the train. That next morning, they got to Lyon-Perrache with very little time to spare, so André left the twelve-year-old Jacot at the top of the staircase while he ran downstairs to the baggage room to claim the suitcase. But running was a mistake. It gave the German police the impression that he might be trying to escape the dragnet they had set around the station that morning, expecting to catch members of the Résistance or Jews or both. André's recollection of the event is arresting:

> Just then, I heard a shout behind me, but I didn't pay attention since I didn't know it concerned me. I continued to run. Suddenly I found myself nose to nose with a German soldier, his face twisted in anger, his rifle pointed at my chest. Behind me there was another one, equally menacing. Terrified and ignorant of the reason for their brutish behavior, I surrendered to them. They screamed out guttural and inarticulate words and backed me up toward the wall. My heels hit an obstacle and I fell to the floor just in front of the rear gun port of the "salad bowl," that is, the police van. They picked me up and threw me into the vehicle, slamming the door and locking it from the outside. I was trapped like a rat.
>
> Regaining my spirits bit by bit, I sat on the van's wooden bench and slowly started taking stock of the situation:
>
> As irrational as it might seem, I had been arrested for an absurd reason: I had been running. It had nothing to do with being a suspect sought by the Gestapo; but I was caught. I was going to be interrogated, then taken to jail. My identification papers read that my name was Béguet and said I was born in a place I couldn't remember. I would have to lie to maintain my new identity. I had not foreseen the possibility of such a stupid arrest, and I had not memorized my details. These false papers were only intended to avoid having the French gendarmerie, which would recognize my name, turn me over to the Germans. It was also supposed to provide me with a ration card that would not give me away.
>
> I decided that I could not lie, because that would mean tempting God. Lying would also mean skidding toward compromises to which God hadn't called me. I should tell the whole truth. "My name is not

Béguet, I am Pastor André Trocmé." My decision calmed my conscience. After all if God had decided to catch up with me, the way he did with Jonah, if he intended my sacrifice, I would have a hard time revolting against Him. But, there was Jacot, waiting at the top of the stairs: poor Jacot who would not see me return. He would not be able to find his way alone back to the Paillots'. He would be bewildered, and I knew his sensitive temperament. I had to find a way of sending a message to him, along with his luggage tag so he could pick up his suitcase.

There was a small-screened window in the middle of the van's rear door and I signaled the German guard on duty in German. Thank God I spoke German: "Psst! Psst! *Hören Sie mal!*" He ignored my call and I insisted. He came closer and I said, "My son, a tall, blond twelve year old boy, is waiting for me to bring the luggage. He is at the top of the stairs in the railroad station. Could you please have someone get hold of him? I need to tell him where he should go because I have been *verhaftet* (arrested)." The guard was skeptical and he called a non-commissioned officer to whom I repeated my request. "I'll have to ask the Captain," he said.

I waited a long time for the Captain. Finally he arrived and I explained the situation in detail. "You are telling me stories," he said harshly. "Why were you running?"

"I was late and I ran to get the suitcase in a hurry so that we wouldn't miss the train. Here is the baggage check. You can verify it."

"You were not trying to flee from the police round-up?"

"What round-up?" I said naively.

"Haven't you noticed the station is surrounded by troops?"

"I didn't, I was in a hurry!"

"You have run across the police check point without noticing, I can't believe that."

"Nevertheless, I am telling you the truth."

"All right," he said, "we'll know the truth right away."

Then he said to the guard, "Escort this prisoner to the station. If his son is really waiting for him, bring them both back here. If not," he added, giving me a menacing look, "if you try to fool the German police, your number is up. And don't try to flee, or you'll be a dead man!"

I was allowed out of the van and the guard stuck the tip of his rifle between my shoulders. "*LOS!*" he said. I walked like a robot toward the front of the station, praying that Jacot would still be there. He was there and signaled to me with great relief.

"*Da ist er!*" I said to the guard.

"Jacot, the Germans have arrested me," I said to my son, who immediately saw the rifle pointing to my back. "Come along, we must see a German officer in front of whom I will explain what you should do and where you should go."

"Daddy, Daddy, what is going to become of us?"

Jacot was as upset and frightened as a child can be, and it was in that shape that we returned to the officer. The officer took a look at the child, who was tall, blond, and handsome, and crying in despair. He was very moved.

"You have told the truth. I understand," he said to me. Then he gave the order to the guard: "Take this man and his child to the *Kontroll* and stay with them until they have been checked out. Don't let them run away. Go on!" He saluted me! I said *"Danke schön"* to him, and didn't ask another thing.

The guard put us in a long line of travelers who were passing the control where their identity papers were looked over. At a distance, we saw an officer sitting at a small table. He examined each document for a long time, checking the names against his register of suspects and comparing their faces with a collection of photographs of wanted persons.

"This isn't over," I said to myself. "My papers are forged and I said Jacot was my son. The guard keeps close to us. Jacques's papers say his name is Trocmé; a name on the wanted list, while my documents say my name is Béguet. It will be difficult for me to lie. We have to get past this checkpoint, but how to do it?"

The line moved slowly and people complained about missing their train. The guard started chatting with his pals who stood in a group a little distance from us. Pretty soon, he fell behind as we moved forward a step at a time. I said to myself, "If only I can make it to that concrete pillar between me and the guard. Now I think there is an exit for travelers coming off the trains and headed for the city."

"Jacques," I murmured. "Do exactly what I do, and slowly, without running. Get ready." "OK Daddy," he said. Just for an instant, the guard stopped looking at us. I got out of line and walked only five steps, but it was enough to put me behind the pillar and out of the view of the guard.

Jacques followed me, and there was no reaction from the soldiers. I said to Jacques, "Let's go out of the station slowly with a group of travelers." And that is what we did, slowly, calmly, with the other people who got off the trains. Fortunately, the German control only concerned departing travelers.

We walked down a long and large stairway and climbed into a streetcar. It was on a Sunday and fifteen minutes later we were worshiping at the service in a church on the rue Fénelon. . . . I picked up a hymnal and I sang as I have never sung anytime in my life. . . . <u>I was free and there had been no need for me to lie.</u> I had been very close to death, I had even accepted death, but I was free. The only time, perhaps, in the history of the Gestapo that a prisoner, a *verhaftet* prisoner, already locked up in a police van, got out without being questioned once or ordered to produce his papers.

Saved! Saved by whom? My son, whose tears had moved the heart of a German police captain? By God? After a series of circumstances which started with our being late catching a train, my imprudent race to fetch a suitcase, which ended in this temple where I now sang? Didn't God want me to die NOW? . . . As we walked out of the church . . . Juliette Paillot was more than surprised to see us in church instead of riding on a train! She gave us shelter for a second night and the next morning her son went to the station to investigate and retrieve Jacot's suitcase. Nothing special was happening there and he came back saying we could go. We were in Perdyer that same evening. (A. Trocmé 1953, 406–10)

André's memory was legendary. Whatever errors were embedded in a re-told story, he managed to recall the narrative line, including the alarms and satisfactions that were threaded into the tale. The narratives of Perdyer and Lyon were still fresh in his mind, even though they had happened a quarter century earlier. His month-long confinement in the Cantonal Hospital gave him long periods of solitude, when remembering was one of the few things he could to do to fight the boredom.

2
Life after June 5

Magda had been looking forward to June and her own retirement. She had been as busy as André during these years in Geneva, teaching Italian in the Lycée d'Annemasse and as a second job teaching aspiring young linguists at the University of Geneva's Interpreters School. In Geneva's nest of international agencies and organizations a trilingual person like herself was much in demand. But now it was her retirement year, and she had plans for the garden and their house in Petit-Lancy, a quiet suburb on the high slopes southwest of downtown Geneva. Number 30 Avenue du Plateau was a modest place, comfortable in an old-shoe sort of way, with ample light and a side yard filled with flowers and trees. Now they would have time for enjoying it. Throughout their years together—it would be forty-five come November—they had focused their boundless energy on big issues and other people's needs. There had been little time to pay attention to their home surroundings. Now they could have that luxury.

André had promised Magda that in retirement they would have more time together, a less frantic schedule, and the option to savor life, perhaps even the chance to bring his memoir up to date. As he lay confined in the Cantonal Hospital, he recalled with regret the fact that he had not been very faithful about adding to his memoirs much about the years since they had left Versailles. Every decade of their lives had added the raw material of intensely interesting chapters that just waited to be written. The memoir was a document for the family, intended to illuminate a piece of history for the children and the grandchildren, who by now were widely scattered over Europe and America. But it would do only half the job he intended if he did not turn his attention to it again, and soon.

2. Jispa (Alice Reynier), 1950s. Unknown photographer.

André wasn't one to worry about his health, but now he did. So did Magda—and with good reason. It had all begun more than a month ago. On a Friday morning he got up with excruciating pain in his back and with his legs alarmingly numb. He was nearly paralyzed from the waist down, unable to walk. Magda was off teaching. Only Jispa was in the house—Jispa, the tiny woman they had dubbed their "Little Mother."

Jispa

Jispa had simply appeared in their lives back in 1943, during some of the darkest days of the war, just when they most needed support to meet the strains and obligations of family and community. She knew the area of Le Chambon-sur-Lignon from her days as a schoolteacher in the region and from occasional summer visits. She had joined a Protestant order of women in Pomeyrol who wanted to combine their religious life with various forms of social service. Their director had heard of the efforts in the Plateau Vivarais-Lignon to save refugees and of the work being done by the Trocmés to sustain that effort. It was she who suggested to

Jispa[1] (Mlle. Alice Reynier) that she go to Le Chambon-sur-Lignon and help Mme. Trocmé care for their house and their children. She did so, arriving on a snowy evening and walking from the train station to the Trocmé home in the church's presbytère. Magda recalled her arrival vividly:

> She walked in and said: "Bonsoir my friend," beaming with an affectionate smile. This greeting surprised me and I said to myself she was une personne originale. This unusual person soon became our friend and even my and André's "mother." Madame Marion had been a mother to me, to some extent, my wet nurses and teachers also. I had hoped Marguerite, my father's wife, would have shown some affection for me—but it never happened. A real mother arrived that day, a mother to me and to André, who had lost his own mother when he was ten years old.
>
> Jispa became our mother, his and mine. We had the same mother and therefore no mother-in-law, which was nice because there were no misunderstandings or disputes that are common when one or two mothers-in-law live under the same roof. Mademoiselle Reynier became an indispensable part of the family within a few days, a grandmother for the children and everybody's friend in the village. She became a great-grandmother later, when the children married and had their own children. Many people know her in Europe and in America and other places where we lived or traveled, Versailles and Geneva. . . . All of our friends became her friends. (M. Trocmé 1946, 239)

Jispa was not one to bother a teacher during a class, so when André got up in such pain, she called the local family doctor who prescribed (over the phone) bed rest and a painkiller. When Magda returned home from Annemasse, about four in the afternoon, she immediately sized up André's situation as an emergency and packed him off by ambulance to the local hospital.

---

1. Reynier's self-composed pseudonym was an acronym for *Joie de Servir dans le Paix avec Amour* (Joy of Service in Peace with Love).

Late Friday afternoon turned out to be a poor time to get expert medical attention at the Hôpital Cantonal de Genève. After the weekend, surgeons finally did an exploratory operation on his back, but found nothing. Days later they operated a second time, this time to deal with a massive duodenal ulcer. Then a week later they did the myelogram that should have been done the first time. This time they found and repaired the ruptured disk they had missed by a centimeter on that first round of surgery.

It had been a wearying and painful time. Now at last things were looking up a little. The last of the three surgeries was behind him. He was sitting up in a chair, receiving a few visitors, able to stay awake for good conversation, and enjoy rather than simply endure his life. Magda came in every day with an admonition: "André, you *must* live! We have so much still to do." He was beginning to believe that he would, and that it would be worth the effort. He had already drawn a design for a lift that would lower him from the porch level to the garden.

How One Dies

It was already June 5; André had now been in the hospital for a month, and it was still uncertain when he would be back home. Magda kept after him with her mandate: "You must live!" That was the way she dealt with problems, and she rarely took "No" for an answer.

Now, when André was so ill, her mandate was her medicine. André agreed that there was much still to do, and he wanted very much to do it. Yet he also recognized that the outcome was uncertain, no matter how much willpower and good spirit he mustered up, and he knew that there are worse things than dying: "I'm not afraid to die. The only problem is that I won't see the outcome of the Middle East situation." Little did he know that there would be no peaceful outcome.

This time, the answer to Magda's mandate would be "No," not from André's mind or spirit, but from his utterly exhausted body. It was then that Magda got the phone call from the Cantonal Hospital and rushed off, sensing that she would be too late to do anything but grieve and attend to the practicalities.

When she arrived at André's room, she found that he had been visiting with Nelly, his eldest child.² She was like her mother: a bundle of energy harnessed to a cluster of responsibilities. Also like her mother, when her sense of purpose was turned on full, there was no deflecting her. André had been in fine spirits, telling funny stories about family members when the nurses came in. They sat him up in a chair to bathe him while the bed was being made. Such a simple move, but one he absolutely could not make by himself.

The nurses asked Nelly to wait in the hall. She left, but reluctantly. Then there was a burst of activity in the room, with doctors and nurses coming in and out. Nelly read the atmosphere as an emergency and came back into the room. She found her father in the chair and asked him what was going on. André said, "I am fainting. Don't worry, they are putting me back in bed." Back in bed, he fainted and died. The cause was a massive pulmonary embolism.

Jispa would have to be told immediately, and Magda knew that she would be a solace as well as a level head. Still, here in the hospital, Magda had to deal with what was in front of her. She said to her daughter Nelly, "I have lost my husband, the father of my children and my best friend." That was her powerful summation of her adult life spent, so far, with André. It was a relationship that was never dull, never ordinary, never tranquil, but always deeply grounded. In spite of animated disagreements, always taken in stride, there was a peace underneath it all, a peace they cultivated in part by spending their Mondays together, by themselves whenever possible.

Before Magda left the hospital that day, the doctor in charge came to talk to her. Like many who took care of André, he regarded his patient as a friend, and admired both his pastoral attention to fellow patients and the range of his curiosity about the world and the people around him. Later he would put some of his observations in a letter to Magda, saying that André "even admired from his window the dexterity of the mason working on the second floor of the hospital."

---

2. This description of André's final moments was provided by Nelly, who was on the scene.

Later Magda would receive letters of a very personal sort from other doctors who had attended André. But there was one that she would remember best, for it described André as having become more than simply a patient. He had become a friend, a man who retained his calm and dignity even when the doctor himself was anxious.

As the weeks passed, all considerations paled against the mere and terrible fact that André was no longer with her. She felt incapable of carrying the burden of their common life alone. These two activists had lived life at a rapid and sometimes frantic pace. How could she possibly make up for André's absence by living at twice the speed of an already overextended life? The message staring at her was, "Carry on without me. Every decision is yours, no longer ours. And from now on you can only say 'we' about the past."

Carrying On

In spite of feeling alone at the barricades, Magda did carry on for a while. She met a few speaking engagements during the next three years. On one such trip, she spoke in a service at the chapel of Smith College in Massachusetts. When introduced, she bypassed the usual thanks for the invitation and compliments to the host and got right to business. Her opening words were, "There are no war crimes. The crime is war!" War crimes, she argued, are a subtext of war itself, not something separate. To be sure, the Holocaust was a terrible crime that happened both before and during World War II, but the Military Tribunal at Nuremberg classified that act of genocide as a "Crime Against Humanity." "War Crimes," by the Tribunal's measure, were such things as killing prisoners of war without cause, consigning civilians to slave labor, plundering public or private property, and the wanton destruction of cities, towns, and villages. The planners and perpetrators of those crimes were the persons on trial at Nuremberg.

By ironic contrast, no Allied leaders were held to account for the carpet-bombing of Dresden and Tokyo and the nuclear wasting of Hiroshima and Nagasaki, wanton acts of destruction of the sort the Tribunal defined as "war crimes." Were those unavoidable necessities, collateral damage, or unintended consequences, to use the cosmetic language of the victors?

Even in a "just" war, as World War II had been designated by Christian clergy on both the German and the Allied sides of the conflict, the tragedy of six million dead soldiers and civilians, plus six million victims of the Holocaust, was the consequence of undertaking war and then accepting the murderous solution of wiping out whole cities in pursuit of Unconditional Surrender, the Allies' agreed-upon goal.

In 1977 Magda and Jispa moved to Paris and a different kind of life. Now she accepted a few speaking invitations but no longer took an activist role in starting new peace projects. There were, however, occasions for her to be active in other ways as long as her waning energy permitted.

In 1981, she traveled to Philadelphia to attend graduation ceremonies at Haverford College and accept the honorary degree that was to be awarded posthumously to André. She had accepted the invitation on the condition she knew André would impose: that the degree be awarded to the people of Le Chambon-sur-Lignon.[3]

Another such award came in 1984, when she was invited to Washington, DC, to be part of a symposium titled "Faith in Humankind." The principal participants were interviewed on film, and the proceedings were published in 1985. One of the three chapters concerning Le Chambon-sur-Lignon consists of an interview with Magda Trocmé (Rittner and Myers 1986, 100). Other prominent figures were also on the agenda of the conference, including Holocaust historian Elie Wiesel and the widow of Martin Niemoeller, the German Navy officer who became a Christian opponent of Hitler, a survivor of Dachau, and later a major figure in the world peace movement. Niemoeller became a friend and colleague of André Trocmé, joining him, Howard Schomer, and a group of American clergy on a 1965 visit to Cambodia and Vietnam "to give support to the indigenous religious forces that were trying to stop the escalating Second Indochina War" (Schomer 1992, 7).

Other conference participants added to the awareness of the Le Chambon story. Theologian Robert MacAfee Brown, a member of the Council that put together the ideas that formed the U.S. Holocaust Memorial, was

---

3. See the Appendix for the full text of the degree citation.

another person who pointed to the Trocmé role as an instance of "Faith in Humankind." Pierre Sauvage's conference presentation, "Ten Questions," had the same effect, as did those who told their stories of rescue. Those personal interactions insured that Magda Trocmé would continue to be sought out as an oral historian.

Her opinions on public affairs remained as sharp-edged as ever during these years. The "protester" in her remained morally rooted, her indignation about injustice never softened, and her opinions were right up front for anyone who asked her. She accepted her role as resister willingly, but it was not a substitute for the projects in peace and social justice that André had hatched and both of them had nurtured.

During the late 1970s and into the 1980s, there was rising international interest in France's experience under German occupation, thanks in large part to the work of an American scholar, Robert O. Paxton. In his 1972 book on Vichy France, Paxton chronicled what Magda knew first hand: the willing involvement of the Vichy government under Pétain in furthering Nazi racist policies during the occupation.

One result of Paxton's work was a rising interest in the French experience during the war years, especially in the United States, a country that had pursued its role in the war at a great distance from its day-to-day realities.

Soon, thanks to another American author, Phillip Hallie, the story of Le Chambon-sur-Lignon during the war years caught the imagination of many. His 1979 work, *Lest Innocent Blood Be Shed*, was born out of his own preoccupation with the problem of evil. He made it his business to interview extensively in Le Chambon and to present the story of "how goodness happened there." As Hallie's book got wider and wider circulation, the story of Le Chambon became progressively better known, evidenced by the attention given to the villages on the Plateau for their refuge and rescue activities at the "Faith in Humankind" symposium.

When the story became more widely known in France and abroad, Magda tended to be called on often to tell it in person. But aging had slowed Magda's schedule. Her attention gradually moved from travel and speaking engagements to a more private but no less important undertaking. She was well into her seventies when she made it her project to put in order the papers she and André had accumulated over their forty-four years together. It was a major undertaking, since both were inveterate pack rats and both had written prolifically throughout these years. She also undertook the editing of André's informal memoir, a grand recollection of the stuff of a lifetime, which André had first written in longhand for the children and grandchildren.

When all those things were done, she finally acceded in her eighties to the urgings of her daughter to write her own *Souvenirs Autobiographiques*. Like André, she had an extraordinary capacity to recall pictures from the past and to embellish her stories with verbal illustrations: the color of the dress she wore when she met André, the names of the German nuns who were her childhood teachers in Florence, the color of her Aunt Olga's eyes, the shimmering color cast on the stairway wall in her childhood home by the sun shining through multicolored glass panes in the door, the names of innumerable people who had years ago sought her out for help of one sort or another.

While she was less a public figure in those years, she never lost her interest in the affairs that trouble the human community and impose suffering on its weakest members. So while public life quieted for her, she retained her ravenous appetite to know how things were going with individuals, their friends, their family members. Keeping her contacts alive continued to be a high priority, even when she was not as much the public figure as she had been. A longtime friend described one of the ways she kept all those relationships current:

> During her elder years, she and Jispa spent a month every summer in Le Chambon. To be sure that she didn't miss anything, she would take her folding chair to the weekly town market and take a seat near the entrance where she could greet and chat with the largest possible number of people.
>
> That worked so well that she decided one Sunday morning to do the same thing after morning service in the Temple. The new pastor stood in the doorway greeting the parishioners when he noticed that Magda had pulled out her folding chair and seated herself in a prominent spot where she too could greet everyone and have a little chat. It did not happen a second time, but that first and only appearance became part of the local legends about Magda.

She was a woman with an insatiable desire to know more. In her world, there were few national or cultural borders. Magda Elisa Larissa Grilli di Cortona Trocmé had already crossed at least as many thresholds as she had names. But her challenge after her husband's death was personal, not cultural or national, and it would both restrict and define her life. For example, she was never more at home than when she spent those summer weeks in Le Chambon. There she and André together had fashioned a ministry that lasted sixteen years, and both had said that those were the happiest years of their lives, as a team and as a family.

Their teamwork was more than a good, helping relationship between a husband and a wife. From his arrival in town in 1934, André had included Magda in everything. He saw to it that Magda was not relegated to the role of a pastor's wife who stood in her husband's shadow.

From the time they first met, Magda had remembered her feeling of being protected when she was with André. She recalled clearly riding on a streetcar with André and some other students: "He looked at me and, for an unknown reason, I felt protected. Why was it so?" (M. Trocmé, 1946, 117). Now she faced what would turn out to be a quarter century of life without him.

In a letter to her daughter Nelly a year after André's death, she described how it felt to be alone. "When I am happy, I hear André's voice that tells me: 'No matter what, you will still have a few beautiful days ahead of you!' . . . and then my joy, my feeling of being entertained flies away. The sea the mountains, the sun, the cypresses, all the smells of the vegetation akin to those of Italy acquire a bitter taste" (M. Trocmé letter, July 25, 1973).

3

Pacifism Discovered

André grew up near the Belgian border in St. Quentin, where the Franco-Prussian War of 1870–71 shadowed his early years: a disaster for France, for St. Quentin and for André's family. Then World War I dominated his teenage years, with the destruction and evacuation of St. Quentin, and with his experience as a refugee.

By the end of the Great War, his direction was set. Even though he was too young to have been conscripted, he had seen enough of war to understand its horrors, enough to question its rationale, and enough to know he would never accept it as just or inevitable.

First Confrontation with Death

André's discovery of pacifism was not sudden; it came through an accumulation of experiences. One was simply confronting death at close hand. The occasion was the loss of his mother, Paula Schwerdtmann Trocmé. Paula was the daughter of a German Lutheran pastor from the village of Petzen, a place André remembered visiting as a child. She was his father's second wife, the first having died several years earlier. He remembered his mother as rather stern. Typical of the households of the wealthy at the time, many of the ordinary maternal interactions with a growing child were delegated to the hired help. The two other women closely involved in his upbringing were the maids, Jeanne and Marie. They did the practical tasks of mothering—dressing, bathing, and putting him and his brother to bed. His mother read to him and taught him to read for himself. Not surprisingly, his memories of Jeanne and Marie, particularly Marie, were

3. Paula Schwerdtmann with André, 1901.
Photographer, D. Blanchara.

suffused with the warmth and affectionate presence that he wished for but found less often in his mother.

Whatever his differing feelings about his mother and the maids, it came as a painful and confusing shock when, at ten years of age, he witnessed his mother's fatal injury in an automobile accident.

The family had been at their summer home in the village of St. Gobain when father Paul Trocmé took them out for a ride in the country in his powerful new Panhard et Levasseur limousine (A. Trocmé 1953, 5). Then Paul made a fatal mistake. Getting caught up by the power of his machine, he pushed his car far too fast in order to catch up with a driver who had just passed him, leaving behind a trail of dust. The thrill of the chase turned into disaster when he ran his left wheels up on a pile of construction stones, throwing the whole family out on the road. André's mother was thrown the farthest and lay totally unconscious in the middle of the road. The ambulance took her back to their home, where she died just a few days later, in agonizing pain and audible distress. Ten-year-old André was in the room next to hers for some of this time and could not help absorbing her pain along with his own fears.

When she died, a family service was held in their home. Paul was in an agony of grief and cried out again and again, "I killed her, I killed her!" André took it all in. Killing was a numinous and awful experience, whether deliberate or accidental.

The Pale Hooligan

About a year after the trauma of losing his mother, another experience added to the pacifist outlook that was gathering within him. This one totally changed the way he thought about war and violence. It happened when he and his cousin Étienne were playing in the garden:

> Etienne and I often played "war." A rubber band tied between the two sides of a wooden crate was used as a catapult. We read about Julius Cesar in class and re-fought his battles. A tube between two wheels made a perfect cannon when we fought Napoleon's battles, and our inflated chests produced the necessary booms and explosions. Gravel gave us an inexhaustible supply of ammunition, and the glass lozenges on the kiosk were vulnerable targets. In 1912, we made paper airplanes and even constructed one with a propeller, which we motorized with a rubber band. Etienne's and my enthusiasm reached beyond the garden wall. Our victories were preceded by screams of "Charge!!" to which heavy artillery responded.
>
> Our garden was an area protected from the outside world, but one day we found the side gate open, where the gardener came to clean the place, trim the bushes and hedges, and plow the flowerbeds. He did not come through the house but through a small iron gate leading to the street. . . .

> One day the gardener forgot to close the gate and we did not know about it. The war game was in full swing and was so noisy that it was heard from the street. The gate opened slowly; the squeak made by the rusty hinges attracted our attention, and the face of a pale hooligan stared at us. He wore a flat cap, a short vest, elephant leg trousers. His face was pallid and a cigarette hung from the corner of his mouth. He examined us for a long time, without a word, with a bitter and sardonic expression, then inspected the garden and the house and nodded. Our screams had stopped and our excessive behavior froze inside our chests. We realized for the first time that the Trocmé world was not the only one to be considered as normal. The pale hooligan stared at us with pity, laughed mockingly, and said *tas d'cons* (bunch of assholes) before withdrawing and closing the gate.
>
> This experience . . . totally changed the course of my thoughts. From that time on, I could no longer enjoy my war games with a genuine conviction. I no longer felt I was the master of the world because the garden was under my control. I realized other persons could hear, look, and judge; and that during my entire lifetime I would be the subject of their scrutiny and that they would compare my ideas with theirs. (A. Trocmé 1953, 15–16)

In addition to sobering André's attitude about war, even playing at war, that encounter added something else to his thinking: there was a serious conflict of interest between the classes of people in his society. "Class struggle" became more than a political slogan wielded by socialist and communist thinkers and organizers. Workers and owners were, in fact, unequal citizens, unequal in what they had and in what they could hope for. André began to see himself as part of the wealthy class, his life both privileged and constrained by the buffers with which the wealthy tend to surround themselves, and by which they unwittingly become blind to the realities that dominate others' lives. The "pale hooligan" became a recurrent image in his thinking.

> The fact that the pale hooligan felt I was stupid and "a pile of shit" did me a lot of good.
>
> The face of the pale hooligan is still there and I will carry his image into my own grave. Etienne and I are the only ones who saw him. . . . My

pale hooligan survives in my mind and my children will never know him. He is my ever-present guest, just as if he were a member of my family. He is one of the mysterious inhabitants of my thoughts whom I can wake up or put to sleep as I please. "Go on, pale hooligan . . . Go and take a rest until I call you back. You are the one who revealed to me the struggle between social classes and I am thankful to you. You unknowingly did a good deed by insulting the world in which you lived. I had never heard these words before, you taught them to me and I often said them to myself quietly and pronounced them without saying a word when addressing the many ridiculous people who do not have consideration for people around them." (17)

War Is Not a Game

When André was only thirteen, the Great War had begun, a war in which wanton slaughter took place everywhere. By the end of the war, the armed forces of all the countries involved suffered nearly 30 million casualties, 8.5 million dead, and 21 million wounded. The largest casualty rates were on French soil. In the battles at the Somme River and in Verdun alone, dug-in and deadly trench warfare lasted for months on end. As the conflict wore on, its victims included not only the French, but also the British and American soldiers on the front lines. At the Battle of the Somme, the British forces alone sustained 57,000 casualties, a third of them killed.

Earlier in the war the casualty rate had been even worse. In 1916, the combined combatant armies suffered 700,000 casualties in the ten-month-long battle of Verdun. At least 180,000 of them died. That "Great War," as it is still known by the French, brought home to the whole population, including André Trocmé, the hideous toll of war.

Since his home city was so close to the border of Belgium, it was soon overrun by German troops. At first, he made a show of patriotism by flying the French flag from a high branch in a tree outside their home (A. Trocmé 1953, 50), but his father warned him to take it down or risk being shot on sight by the German troops. Lesson one of war? "Do not make brave gestures for the sake of the gesture." His next patriotic venture was to go about town with his brother Pierre, dodging the German patrols and tearing down German posters that warned of retaliations or announced executions. When they were chased by German military police, they felt courageous and maybe even a little heroic.

Their favorite patriotic gesture of all was a grand hoax that involved printing up message leaflets, supposedly signed by the Commander in Chief of the French army, Marshall Joseph Joffre, a name known to every French citizen. It was also inscribed on its back with the legend: "released from an altitude of 3,000 meters by Aviator Lieutenant Moreau" (57). The leaflets announced that St. Quentin was about to be liberated by the advancing French army. The boys took them around the city, dropping them at random to look as if they had floated down from an airplane.

They soon found that almost everyone in town took them seriously, even a family by the name of Moreau, who thought they recognized their son's handwriting on the leaflet. Only the boys' own father seemed to regard the leaflet as a farce, to their mixed embarrassment and pride. They were proud to have a father who could see through the hoax and embarrassed that their heroic gesture had been deflated.

But those gestures of the fierce young patriots soon paled against the very sobering things that were happening all around them. At one point, when French snipers seemed to be shooting from every rooftop in town, the German soldiers rounded up a group of civilians in the business district, including their father, and used them for hours as a human shield to prevent being shot at by the snipers.

Young André described his city as one vast hospital, smelling everywhere of carbolic phenol acid and the gangrenous flesh of wounded soldiers. During the night, whole trainloads full of corpses were carried from the Somme battlefield, only twenty miles northwest of St. Quentin, to the crematoria south of the city.

One day, André saw a file of wounded Germans whose miserable condition told him something of the reality of war. He wrote in his memoir of that incident:

> The horror of war struck me ... the day I saw a pitiful column of wounded German soldiers coming into town from the railroad station. . . . Three men walked slowly in front of the procession. The one in the middle had his head replaced by an enormous ball of bandages and he obviously

couldn't see. He stumbled and was sustained by the other two who were also covered by bloody dressings. As he came closer I saw that his lower jaw and chin had been blown off and in its place, a mess of rags from which hung strings of clotted blood. My heart stopped when I discovered that's what war was like. (94–95)

Perhaps because of the German relatives in his own extended family, André did not see these men first as enemies but as sufferers. He was, after all, as much at home in the German language as he was in the French, and in many ways both cultures were his own. His deceased mother had been German, as were the numerous uncles and aunts and cousins on that side of the family, people with whom he had spent memorable summers filled with music, games, and long walks in the countryside.

The other face of the family coin was a tradition of military service for France: three of his older half-brothers, Maurice, Eugène, and Robert, were officers in the French army. These were the children of his father's first wife, Marie Walbaum, and so were much older than he. He revered the youngest of them, Robert, who was badly wounded in the nearby battle of the Somme.

A painful question now surfaced: André, his father, his brother, and his half-brothers were French and his mother's family was German. Which of the Schwerdtmann family might now be in the German army shooting at which of his older half-brothers? A war like this one was a disruption of everything that family relationships should mean.

Two other incidents contributed to the making of his anti-war attitude even at that young age. One was a common experience of thirteen-year-old schoolboys. A leading bully in his class, Leroy, formed a gang that delighted in beating up the non-gang class members, André included. But when André saw them beating up a crippled classmate, he organized a counter gang to control the bullying, with the predictable outcome of many fistfights, many bloody noses, and a stern reprimand from the vice-principal. André remembered Leroy and wrote later on, "Leroy's dictatorship ended and he hated me with a passion. Thanks to him, I decided to hate anything military." It wasn't exactly pacifism yet, but it was a start.

There was also, about then, a spiritual experience of consequence that furthered the development of his pacifism. The spiritual is difficult to define, a notably slippery category of human experience. It has much to do with finding answers to the most human of all questions: Who is God? Or is there God? And who am I? Why am I here?

To understand the spiritual origins of André's pacifist convictions, the best place to start is with those questions of identity. As a child, he experienced so many confusions and uncertainties about himself, such lack of confidence in his own person, that the questions were never far from the surface: "Who am I really?—the awkward rich child, with his blonde curls, in the lace collar and the velvet suit? The frightened motherless child who lived in a garden apart from the world outside? The boy who was frightened at seeing his own anger boil over and scared by any loss of control over his own feelings? Or just a member of the Trocmé tribe, a separate race different from the rest of mankind." André lived under sanctions that were different and more confining than those of his contemporaries. The family watchword had always been *"tu es un Trocmé"* "You are a Trocmé," and all Trocmés shared a duty to live by the family's high standards of duty, honesty, and integrity.

At the conventional age of about sixteen, André attended the confirmation class that would prepare him for membership in the church. He was in the third of his six years in the lycée, the French combination of three levels of education, junior high school, high school, and early college. He attended Pastor Kaltenbach's catechism classes with his friends of roughly the same age. It was a threshold time in his life. The first hints of adult life were a catechism for the spirit and a lycée for the mind. Being confirmed in the church and reaching the midpoint of his lycée education were two signs that he had officially become a young man.

The Christian Union

One of his friends in catechism class was Albert Meunier, an amiable and earnest son of a working class family. He invited André to attend the Sunday afternoon YMCA meetings in the church. André was hesitant. He felt infinitely younger than the others. Class distinctions being what they were in the town, he also felt like a fish from another pond, not knowing exactly how to get on with youngsters whose life experience had been so markedly different from his own. So he said he would have to ask his father's permission, as he still did for almost everything at that age.

When permission was given, and he went to meetings of the Union, André found answers to questions he had not yet asked. He cites in his memoir such an instance of discovery. He had finished his catechism class with Pastor Kaltenbach, a man revered and respected by young and old. He had been the customary bright, diligent, and dutiful student who emerged from the series of classes knowing the answers to all the questions that would be put to him to determine whether he was fit to be inscribed on the church membership roll. But the Christian Union presented him with an experience he had not anticipated.

The meetings of the Christian Union seemed straightforward enough. They put on a play, they did some Bible study, and at the end of the meeting one member would lead a meditation, followed by prayers in which all joined. But there was something different about this group, and André kept a vivid memory of his experience with them. At the end of the first meeting he attended, he recalls,

> The boys then all knelt down. I never knew that people knelt down to pray, and I found myself standing as straight as a broomstick. . . . Their prayers were true prayers. They addressed God as if they were speaking to a living being who was present among us. . . . They spoke about all sorts of problems that bothered me also. One of them asked God to help him stop lying and another apologized for being violent. . . . They all spoke. I was the only one who kept silent, stunned but happy. . . . The experience was incredible! I discovered that the precautions I had multiplied since my childhood, hiding from other people's sight and controlling my words and my feelings, had all been wrong. My monotonous, disciplined, tamed and smothered life at home had wrongly muffled my aspirations and my enthusiasm. . . . I came home transfigured: light shining around me and a fire burning in my soul. Everything became possible and everything made sense. (78–88)

The Union was, however, about more than prayer that rang true and Bible study that was down to earth. It was also about developing a social conscience. At one point, its members decided to flout German military law and carry food and other supplies to the ragged, miserable Russian prisoners of war who were encamped nearby as slave labor for the German army. A sympathetic German guard cast a blind eye on their activities, but one of the Union members was discovered and jailed, and the German guard was replaced.

Encounter with a Pacifist Enemy

Soon after, another equally affecting but far different experience propelled André toward a more conscious and articulated pacifist position. It was a conversation with a German soldier who was bivouacked on the third floor of the Trocmé home. This young German telegrapher, Kindler, turned out to be a pacifist, even though he did not use that term to describe himself.

> I ran into a German in the stairs, at home. He stopped and looked at me with kindness. He reached over and touched my arm:
> "Bist du hungrig?" he said as he handed me a quarter of a large ball of black bread, the famous German Kommissbrot with the letter K stamped on it indicating it was a Kartoffelbrot, which we contemptuously referred to as KK bread, making a pun on *"caca,"* a French slang term for excrement.
> "No," I replied in German, "I am not hungry and, should I be hungry, I would not accept your bread because you are an enemy."
> "No, no, I am not your enemy."
> "Yes, you are my enemy because you wear this uniform and tomorrow you will perhaps kill my brother who is fighting against you trying to get rid of your presence. Why did you come here bringing war, suffering and calamity?"
> "I am not what you believe I am. . . . I am a Christian. . . . Do you believe in God?"
> My face lit up. This man was speaking the language that filled my entire life and I understood him.

"I met Jesus Christ in Breslau and I gave him my entire life. . . . I will not kill your brother. . . . I will not kill a single Frenchman. God has revealed to us that a Christian shall not kill . . . ever. My friends and I do not carry weapons!" "How can you do this," I replied, "since you are a soldier?"

"I explained my belief to my captain and he authorized me not to carry a weapon. Ordinarily a telegraph operator like me carries a revolver and a dagger. I don't carry anything. I often find myself in a dangerous situation on the front line and I sing a hymn and pray to God who decides whether He wants me to go on living . . . or else?" (96)

One Sunday afternoon, André invited Kindler to join him at a meeting of the Union. To his surprise, the invitation was accepted, and this unlikely pair of friends went off to a meeting of young people who did not know quite what to make of Kindler's uniform. As the meeting went on, Kindler's religious convictions became clearer and his acceptance by the young Frenchmen was total when they realized that their common experience with him transcended the difference between their languages (André was the only one who spoke both French and German) and the striking difference in their clothing.

A little later, Kindler's unit moved out into battle, but before leaving, he gave André some photos and a letter, with a request. Should he fail to return to St. Quentin with his regiment, André would know that he had been killed or injured. Would he please, then, send these things to his family? André never heard from him again and, about a month later, kept his promise to young Kindler. Whatever the history of pacifism in the decades before the Great War, this personal encounter had a more transforming effect on the young Trocmé than any history lesson could ever provide.

In the last spasms of the Great War, André came to another sort of discovery that influenced his ministry. It was a corollary to pacifism, an experience more akin to the "pale hooligan" than to Kindler the soldier-pacifist.

The most thoughtful advocates of pacifism at the time did not focus exclusively on war. They took economic violence equally seriously. Wealth concentrated in the hands of a few tended, then as now, to reduce the poorest people to dependent status. Decisions affecting their own well-being were too much in the hands of others who neither knew nor cared about them. The results were predictable: poorer health, shorter lives, a marginalized status in the culture, and unearned contempt, whether open or veiled, from those who used their wealth to control political and social power. Both religious and secular pacifists had understood the relationship between power and poverty throughout the latter years of the nineteenth century.

For André, his adolescent religious awakening had first persuaded him that true faith was a condition of the heart. He was just now awakening to the fact that faith was also a condition of the will that worked for justice. It was another kind of awakening, still religious, to understand that faith involves changes in both the sensibilities and the economic behaviors of the faithful. His awareness of the intertwined realities of faith and justice was sharpened when the Trocmé family became refugees.

Becoming a War Refugee

By late 1916, the city of St. Quentin was coming under heavy pressure from both armies, given the intensity of the fighting in Northern France. In order to have unfettered use of the city's resources, the German army decided to evacuate the entire civilian population. On a snowy day in February of 1917, the thousands of victims of this decision were packed into unlit cattle cars, each with a German sentry on duty, forbidden to look out the high vent openings, and carried off to Belgium. The winter weather and the protracted stops for military traffic along the way made a two- or three-hour railway trip into a twenty-four-hour passage, without food or water, with only the clothes on their backs, and without toilet facilities.

When late the next afternoon they were deposited in Belgium, it was in a small Flemish farming town well west of the Meuse River, the focus of the German army's attention. When the cattle car doors were pushed back, the occupants saw rows of clean brick houses. The farming areas of southwestern Belgium still did not bear the scars of war in the same measure as did St. Quentin. Although reasonably intact, the more westerly Belgian farm area was dirt poor. The families still had their clean brick houses, but the economic pillaging had affected them like everyone else. And here they were, faced with an immigration of thousands. They rallied, even though the immigrants were total strangers and appeared to be even poorer than they.

The refugee St. Quentin population was spread around the cities and towns of southern Belgium, from Charleroi west. The well-to-do Trocmé family arrived, like the others, with almost no money and with only the pitiful amount of baggage they could carry in their own hands. But unlike most others, the Trocmé party numbered nine: Paul, his daughter Louise, three children, two household staff, a cousin, and a helpless missionary they had taken in. They could not be accommodated together. In this new place of refuge there were no grand homes like theirs in St. Quentin.

André and Pierre were housed with the Demulder family, the poorest family in the area. The boys shared a small room with a rickety bed and a straw mattress in a run-down brick farmhouse whose only entrance was through the stable. They learned one very important lesson in their stay with the Demulders: the generosity of the poor. The couple moved their three-year-old son into their own room in order to provide space for the Trocmé sons. They also provided them with food by sharing whatever they had, nor did they ask anything in return. After the Demulders had gone to bed, the boys knew that they would always find a couple of bowls of warm sweetened sour milk waiting for them on the stove.

All of the refugees faced the problem of finding enough food to sustain them. The villagers in nearby Maroq teamed up to provide a thin vegetable soup for those who came, two at a time, to fetch their ration, one ladle per person, from the soup kitchen. It was the same soup three times a day, and cooked from the villagers' own meager food supply. Looking back, André's comment was:

> The poorest people in the area were the ones who fed us free of charge, without being asked. . . . Thinking back to the past I realize the extent to which these difficult months contributed to the scouring of my bourgeois attitude and habits. This experience was like a purifying bath, a dive into the working class world where I was just like everyone else because my silver lining had vanished. I have, since then, kept close to the real

world. . . . In Belgium, I felt the throbbing, multiple and laborious life of the blue collar working class and I felt like I was one of them. (106–9)

Here in Belgium, in his first experience of being uprooted and his first taste of poverty, was the turning point where Trocmé's evangelical enthusiasm became joined to the hardscrabble daily reality that is the lot of most human beings. It may also be the moment in his life when he became liberated, free to define his life by his own experience and convictions, whether or not they matched the conventions of the French Protestant church and its culture.

4

Fathers and Sons

The Burden of Being a Trocmé

André Trocmé had a father whose influence on him was great—sometimes for better, sometimes for worse, but always substantial and nearly always burdensome. The burden of being a Trocmé, however, was not Paul Trocmé's invention, for he had a father (Eugène) who in turn had a father (Jean-Pierre Eugène), and each one laid that burden of family reputation on the next. It seemed to them all that being a Trocmé involved a responsibility to history as well as to family. For hundreds of years, Trocmé fathers had been laying down expectations for their sons, and it was no different for Paul Trocmé and his sons, all seven of them. For Paul Trocmé that history was a constant reminder of a religious and intellectual inheritance that could not be brushed off.

Being the Littlest Brother

A large part of Paul Trocmé's responsibility as head of the family was to pass along to his seven sons and three daughters their religious heritage and all the social virtues and moral obligations that came with it. All but one of his surviving children gave their father what he could consider a fully satisfactory account of themselves. The one over whom he was most likely to wring his hands was André, his youngest.

The other sons undertook their responsibilities as Trocmés and Protestants with earnestness and success. One of them (Maurice) followed Paul as head of the family's cotton-weaving business; another (Francis) became a distinguished family physician; still another (Robert) served

4. Paul Trocmé. Unknown photographer.

[handwritten: Father to André]

France heroically as an infantry captain during the Great War, and ultimately joined the family business, becoming a major national figure in the industry: a member of the French Cabinet's Economic Council, president of the National Cotton Industry Association, and president of the Union of Textile Industries. A fourth son (Eugène) became a successful mining engineer, and a fifth (Albert) was ordained to the ministry in the French Reformed Church. These were the five older sons, children of Paul's first wife, Marie Walbaum. Her sixth son, Pierre, died in infancy. Paul's second wife would carry on his name. *[handwritten: What about 3 daughters?]*

Robert's influence multiplied when the family lived in Paris while waiting for their ruined family home in St. Quentin to be restored. Robert often took his younger half-brothers to the Louvre to see and study the fourteenth-century Italian artists, Fra Angelico, Giotto, and others. André remembered those visits as the time he truly awakened to beauty.

In some ways, the companionship with Robert filled the gap that André had always felt between himself and both his brother Pierre and his father. While Pierre was only two years older than André, André always saw him as "the child who could do nothing wrong" and himself as "the child who could do too little right." By contrast, Robert was warm, candid, creative, and solicitous of André's experiences and questions.

André knew in his head that his father loved him, but hard as he listened, he never seemed to hear that kind of direct emotional expression from his father. Paul Trocmé, while not a severe or uncaring person, nonetheless fit the description provided by Antoine Jaulmes, the writer of the family history:

> He was certainly a little authoritarian, but that was the style of management in vogue at the time. . . . He was a demon for work. Methodical and ambitious, he committed himself to the business with as much conviction as efficiency, and to the St. Quentin church with great energy. (Jaulmes 1990, 24)

Paul Trocmé was clearly the patriarch of his extended family, a family whose gatherings were treated as conventions, according to Nelly Trocmé Hewett. She described the 1984 gathering, recalling that about 250 attended from various branches of the family, disparate enough that name tags were used, color coded to indicate which branch of the family the wearer belonged to. She also remembered the large exhibition of photos, books, and examples of lace produced by the family factories.

It was at the 1984 convention that Paul's number three son and now senior person, Francis, gave a talk in which he described his parents and grandparents this way:

> They were of the bourgeoisie, the businessmen of the cities. They had all the exterior characteristics: the costume was frock coat and top hat, and they dressed that way to go to church and to take a Sunday afternoon walk with the family, children in front and parents behind, arm in arm.
> They lived in upper middle class houses with formal drawing rooms and great larders filled with canned goods and sweets. Their wives, with the help of the maids, directed the housekeeping and supervised the education and instruction of the children by tutors, secondary schools, and lycées. And they never went out without their hats and gloves!

> If we don't blush about our peasant ancestry, [then] we should be proud of our bourgeois ancestors. They were reserved, masters of themselves, balanced in their thinking, holding their feelings in check, reading little (other than the Bible), always sincere, respectful of themselves and others, very confident in social relations and very direct in their family relations. . . . They put the demands of conscience above their own interests. They did what they thought was their social and religious obligation, because their faith dominated their lives. For example, these bourgeois ancestors founded the first housing for the needy, the first retirement funds and retirement societies, remarkable works of social aid (the Red Cross, orphanages, foundations for the handicapped), and evangelizing works that theologians and intellectuals are wrong to underestimate. (27)

Francis's comments at this Trocmé family convention make it clear that the Trocmé burden was not an altogether negative influence on the lives of André and his siblings. It was simply the inescapable and comprehensive sense of social responsibility that was part of the family's heritage.

How did André himself view his father? He had a lot to say about him, but it was cast in the language of someone looking back analytically on his own early childhood experience. He understood his father very well. The words of his brother Francis painted a portrait he could recognize. He chafed at much of what he dealt with and experienced in that relationship, yet there was also a large element of respect, respect more than affection. Later in life he would speak both poignantly and directly about the hunger for love that he felt as a youngster:

> Duty was the key that controlled everybody's attitude and conduct at home on Boulevard Gambetta. This duty curtailed the free expression of all sentiments, dreams, and impulses. I had dreams, impulses, and still do today; but at home, they were carried by a wave, which died on the polished stones of an austere beach. The polished surfaces of Père, Mère, brothers, and sisters were such that my dreams and impulses ran down my little arms like water. There was not a single little cavity, even a small one, where some love and tenderness could find shelter. (A. Trocmé 1953, 3)

The root of his need for hunger and tenderness was in the experience of seeing his mother die. He describes a "torrent of love" that went out to his mother as she was being carried away from that fatal auto accident in the ambulance. Looking back, he said, "I had discovered my mother the day I lost her and I was growing up carrying in my chest a huge quantity of love and tenderness, which I hadn't expressed when she was alive; an unquenched desire for a love which had shattered before I could share it, a love which, later in my life, I was able to exteriorize very slowly under the form of deep, sad and religious impulses" (8).

The relation of father and son in André's family did little to satisfy that craving. It was realized only when he married Magda. Theirs would be a warm and sharing relationship, tempestuous at times, but a relationship in which he was totally secure.

For all its defects, his relationship with Paul had a profound effect on the way André came to interiorize his religious, social, and moral inheritance. To be sure, he was a renegade, choosing to break with many of the external characteristics of his French Protestant upbringing, but he was intellectually rigorous, morally tough, and thoroughly earnest.

He refused, for instance, to play the game of ecclesiastical politics at the cost of demands on his conscience. But his appreciation of beauty, his sense of humor, his artistic cartoons, and his rich, engaging children's stories: these he owed more to his German cousins, his brother Robert, and later to his relationship with Magda and the children.

Duties, Taboos, and Regimens

The result was a Trocmé both like and unlike his father. In his sense of duty he was like Paul, but in family relationships he did more than establish the rules. He and Magda communicated the meaning of duty to the children, both in conversations around the table and in examples of behavior. There were rules, to be sure. There was no smoking in his house and drinking was out of the question. He had grown up in a nineteenth-century industrial town, where alcohol exacted a terrible price on many laborers and their families. He had been Croix Bleue since his twenties. The Blue Cross organization came into being in the worst days of the urban industrial revolution, with the sole purpose of fighting what would be a determined but losing battle with French culture on the question of alcohol use and abuse.

In Andre's family there was no dancing either, which only meant that daughter Nelly went off to dance at her friends' houses. When André was growing up, dancing was regarded as a threat to the restrained and controlled heritage of a Protestant youngster; it was a sensuous indulgence, fraught with peril for the inquisitive adolescent. Further, it was not acceptable behavior for decent, God-fearing, and dignified people, for whom sex was generally kept under wraps.

For André, the maladroit manner in which his father addressed sexual matters with his youngest sons did more harm than good. Duty could simply be accepted, but sex had to be figured out, and Paul did little to unveil its mysteries to the boys. When Paul noticed that André and his brother Pierre were coming into adolescence, writes André, he "silently put into our hands a terrible red brochure which described the horrors of immorality. Everything was described vividly" (89). There was no heart-to-heart talk as a follow up to the horrible red brochure, but again, that was more normal than abnormal for the arbiters of morality at the time. One could bet that much more straight talk about sex went on in the homes of the factory workers in St. Quentin than in the homes of their employers.

For many Protestant families, the cinema was another on the list of things that were out of bounds. When one recalls the seductive screen heroes and heroines, the free-wheeling jazz music, the dancing girls and feather boas that were all part of the early days of movie-making, it is not hard to understand the feeling of many Huguenot families that sending the children off to the movies would be risky at best.

Interestingly, André and his colleagues took exception to this in Le Chambon, for the simple reason that the lack of any public amusement available to young people presented them with another sort of potential for risky behavior. An evening at the movies, particularly when the church leaders were picking the films, was clearly less risky than cavorting in the haystacks, with unwanted pregnancies as the outcome. So André and his associate, Pastor Edouard Theis, set about establishing a movie theater in an abandoned blacksmith workshop in the center of town. That was an expression of a pastor's duty to his congregation. In André's vocabulary, duty had a face as well as a name, and in this case, the face was that of the town's younger generation.

Whatever temperamental differences there might have been, André had bought in to his father's taste for good order and disciplined learning in daily life. When he was still in elementary grades, his daily regimen was rigid and demanding:

1. 7:00: Arise
2. 7:10: Breakfast bell
3. 8:00 to noon: Home schooling classes
4. Noon: Second bell: Wash up for lunch
5. 12:15: Lunch
6. 12:50: Walk in the garden
7. 2:00: More classes until 4:00
8. 4:15: Snack of bread, chocolate, and milk
9. 5:00: Homework until 7:00
10. Two bells for dinner, followed by fifteen minutes visiting with the grownups in the living room
11. 8:00 until 9:00: More homework
12. 9:00 Lights out (9–10)

Thursday rather than Saturday was the traditional day off for school children, so it was scheduled differently but hardly less firmly. Sunday was the only day that included a two-hour period for the children to do as they pleased.

However productive that kind of regimen was supposed to be, André was never able to establish a similar one for his own children. For all his stolid resolve to teach his children intellectual discipline, André was also inclined to be very playful with them. The children were expected to do their homework thoroughly and on time, and sometimes they actually did. Their hours were to be spent but not wasted. There were other richer dimensions to life in the presbytère, especially the dinner table conversations, as often as not two or three of them going on simultaneously, with parents, children, and the inevitable guests all taking part. And then there were the June vacations afforded to all ministers, when the children usually had their parents all to themselves. That was very different from the busy and very public life the family lived during the rest of the year.

A Storytelling Enthusiast

Unlike his father, André understood the power of storytelling. Even when he spoke and wrote about war, it was most often through telling stories of specific people whose lives were shaped by the conflict. And in his preaching, he showed an aptitude for carrying his message in the vessel of a story.

He also had both a fancy and a talent for making up children's stories. It was a talent that showed up in his church in Le Chambon especially on Christmas afternoons, when he gathered the parish children around a great balsam Christmas tree festooned with candles and tinsel. There he paraphrased or created spin-offs of the Nativity story in a series of tales only recently published in English by his daughter, Nelly Hewett, under the title *Angels and Donkeys*. They are stories designed to give children a way to understand and adults a way to teach the call to love and justice, the core of the Christian message, and to do so while living every day, even when living under the shadow of an occupying army.

That same creative love for storytelling infected the content of his sermons. In one, for example, he tells side by side the legendary stories of Moses the Jew, who exacted from Pharaoh Ramses II the liberty of his people, and Daedalus the Greek, who sought freedom for himself from captivity in the labyrinth he had constructed for the king. André draws their contrasting portraits in a rich story form to help his hearers understand that liberation for ourselves is best achieved by seeking freedom for those others who are captive to poverty, hunger, and enslavement (Boismorand 2008, 331).

One of his favorite story-telling venues, however, was the dinner table in the presbytère after supper with the children. There were often tales of the family: the parents' adventures in America, the children's escapades when they were younger, and the odd things that some of their relatives did. The most fun were the stories he made up on the spot, tales spun out of threads of pure imagination and designed to capture the interest of his small children. One such series of spontaneous tales was the story of "The Little Beast" (La Petite Bête). The Little Beast was the Superman of the animal world, endowed with a flawless sense of what was right and just, and with magical powers to make it all happen. The flea-sized Petite Bête could become as tiny as a grain of sand or as huge as a mountain, as light as a fly or as heavy as a hippo. And as any chapter of the story began, no one knew where it would lead (including André, who made it up as he went along), except that some catastrophe would be avoided, some innocent child rescued from danger, or some great crime foiled.

That creative and playful streak also showed up in many other ways. When the spirit moved him, he might take out his small concertina after supper and lead the children in a rousing folk song or two before sending them back to their homework. Then there were the letters he sometimes wrote to his children when he was away. One was designed to encourage his six-year old son, Jean Pierre, to learn to swim. He drew a cartoon of Jean Pierre taking the four simple steps necessary to swim: (1) stand on the beach and dip your toes in the water to see if it is cold; (2) let a wave break over your body; (3) walk out (carefully) to where you can no longer touch bottom; and (4) then swim the breast stroke, which is "easy and elegant." The other half of the page, addressed to a younger son, Jacot, showed a satirical cartoon of Papa, with a wet moustache and wearing his trademark round glasses as he bobbed around in the water in an old inner tube.

While André earned his living by words, he also enjoyed hugely his own relationship to them. They were things to be toyed with, arranged in unexpected combinations, things to be released to do their mischief or deliver their satire, their real intent often concealed behind a façade of slant rhymes designed to catch the reader off guard. He once described two ladies with odd gaits, the elderly Mme. Marcel and her daughter Mme. Deloche, by the rhyming names *Mme.* Deloche *qui cloche* and Mme. Marcel *qui chancelle* (Madame Deloche who limps and Madame Marcel who wobbles). He did not regard himself as a poet and that was just as well, but he was a versifier who sometimes could not restrain himself from stretching and bending the rhyming words until they were pure whimsy.

5. The storyteller (image of a letter).

One of the ways he did this was by writing verse messages for his family members, none of them intended for publication, most of them designed to provoke a smile or a laugh, and one of the best ways he could articulate his affection for those around him. On Christmas Eve of 1951, the twenty-fourth year of his marriage, André prepared a poem entitled "If I were to begin again," a poem which provided the whole family with a hall of mirrors. Addressing the first stanza to Magda, he wrote,

> If I were to begin again, I would write at the top of my agenda
> to choose a wife who is calm and sweet,
> who would accompany me so smoothly
> all the way to the end of my adventure
> without a word, without combat, without a murmur;
> but it would be necessary for that woman
> to be you, Magda.[1]

The verse was sure to have drawn a chuckle from the rest of the family. They all knew that their volatile, vocal Italian executive of a wife and mother was no such person. At another moment, when André was in a less golden mood, he described Magda walking along the street full tilt, head down and errand bound, saying "I think I married a volcano!"

Like Father, Like Son?

Paul Trocmé was a stalwart churchman and the major lay leader to preside, in 1938, over the merger of the Evangelical Reformed Churches of the North and the rest of the Reformed churches of France. It was an effort that had been under way since 1929, when a council of Reformed Churches met in Marseilles and founded the French Protestant Federation, headed by Pastor Marc Boegner until the merger came about. From 1848 until 1938, churches of the Reformed tradition had been organized in regional

---

1. Appears in the private family papers and letters as part of a Christmas composition prepared "for Magda and my children, after twenty-five years of marriage: November 12, 1926 to December 24, 1951."

clusters, the more liberal in the center and south of France, and the more conservative in the north. In 1879 the conservatives established themselves in a formal union as L'Église Réformée Évangélique, known informally as L'Église du Nord.

Along with his lay church leadership, Paul Trocmé was also a major leader in the business community in St. Quentin and the surrounding region of Picardy, an intelligent and purposeful man who contributed a great deal to his community. He insisted that his household, including his children, be cared for in orderly fashion, for that was the key to the success he had in rebuilding the family cotton-weaving factory and providing amply for the family's needs. But being already well into his fifties when his two youngest children were born, he left to the women the tasks of nurture and expressions of affection that these two youngsters required. Mothering and fathering were distinctly different roles that had little in common. If one had to describe his temperament in a single word, it might well be "Director."

Paul's youngest son, André, was different: an enthusiast with a sense of humor, a man whose religious experience had included moments of spiritual illumination and elevation, an instinctive organizer and teacher who enjoyed his moments of playfulness, where the fun was purpose enough. He loved puns and drew cartoons. He took his faith seriously, but if it came to a choice between theological certainty and spiritual inspiration, he was likely to choose the latter. The heart of the matter was following the claims of his Christian faith, wherever they might lead. From the outset, he was destined to become a radical and prophetic voice in the Reformed Church, even when he knew his voice was not always welcome in the councils of the Église Réformée de France. He was a man of principle and a person of consistent, sometimes relentless moral character who could nonetheless say to me in a conversation in our kitchen, "Watch out for men of principle. They're the worst kind."

Like father, like son? Yes and no, but more no than yes.

5

Out of Siberia

A Revolutionary Ancestry: The Decembrists

Magda Trocmé's independent spirit and her habit of practical response to human needs came straight out of her Siberian heritage. Her ancestors on both the Italian and the Russian side were aristocratic people born to wealth and privilege, but the Russians in her family tree were notable for not allowing privilege to blind them to the human misery at the bottom of society, a misery endured by the moujiks (slaves) to serve the interests of the rich. Not so her Italian ancestors. They were much more inclined to assume that privilege was their birthright and poverty was other people's fate. In her family tree, Magda had two important revolutionary figures, Cesare Bettini the Italian and Alexei (or Allesandro) Poggio the Russian. Even her name was wired into both sides of her ancestry. She was Magda Elisa Larissa Grilli di Cortona, Elisa for Bettini's wife and her Italian great-grandmother, and Larissa for Poggio's wife and her Russian great-grandmother.

As any youngster might, Magda took her strongest cues for her own life from her closest elder relative. That was clearly her Russian grandmother, Poggio's daughter Varia Alexandrovna Poggio Wissotsky, born in Siberia in 1854.[1] Varia's parents had been exiled to Siberia because of her father's participation in the Decembrist revolt of 1815, a conspiracy to unseat the Tsar and inaugurate a democratic regime in Russia. Poggio became a member of that conspiracy of officers in the Tsar's Royal Guard. They refused to take the oath of loyalty to Tsar Alexander's eldest son Nicholas, a prince

---

1. Following Russian custom, she had a given name (Varia) followed by her father's given name (adjusted to her gender), her family name, and her own married name.

6. Varia Poggio Wissotsky, ca. 1915. Unknown photographer.

known for his harsh treatment of commoners. They demanded instead the accession of his younger brother Constantine, but their rebellion was poorly organized and quickly suppressed, leaving 289 Decembrists arrested, five executed, thirty-one imprisoned, and the rest banished to Siberia, among them Poggio and his friend Prince Sergei Volkonsky. Their years in exile gave Poggio and the Prince a close and personal experience of poverty and serfdom. It was Grand-Maman Varia who shared with Magda the story of her revolutionary parents, what they stood for, and why they were exiled to Siberia. An amnesty finally allowed Poggio and his daughter to leave Siberia and travel to Florence, and later to Switzerland.[2]

With such remarkable people as these Decembrists in the lore of her family, it is no wonder that Magda shaped her life around serving the needs of simple folk in factories and on farms, and others whose share

---

2. See the Appendix for a more detailed outline of the Poggio heritage.

7. Allesandro Poggio and daughter Varia, 1864.
Photographer, L. Ferini in Venezia.

of the bounty of society was limited; nor is it surprising that she and her cousin Lalli formed their own secret charitable society in Florence when they were eight years old. It all came out of Siberia.

The Bettini Revolutionaries

Grandmother Grilli was not at all the same sort of "personage" as Grandmother Varia, nor did she leave the imprint of values and purpose on Magda's life that Varia did.

The Italian ancestry was important nonetheless, because Magda could find there another tributary to the revolutionary stream that flowed across Europe in the wake of the American and French revolutions. The Italian revolutionary in her past was her great-grandfather, Cesare Bettini, a member of a group of young revolutionaries organized by Giuseppe Mazzini in the early 1830s. Mazzini and his followers, like the Russian "Decembrist" group, were much affected by the French Revolution and its purposes. They thought the time was ripe throughout Europe to raise the goal of republican government, democratic ideals, and the liberation of oppressed peoples.

On the road to Italian national unity, Bettini, like Mazzini and his other companions, was sentenced to prison more than once for his activities in the Young Italy movement, La Giovine Italia.

From childhood, Magda was keenly aware of her Italian revolutionary roots, but when speaking and writing of her own background, she was more likely to turn to the Russian story as having the principal impact on her. Varia was a presence, but her father, Oscar Grilli, was more a figurehead than a presence.

As with the Russian ancestral stories, there were rich stories of the revolutionary figures in her Italian family tree, but there were two larger differences. The Russians were stateless immigrants with only marginal influence in their new country. By contrast, the Italian revolutionaries had not been refugees, nor had they any occasion to see themselves as outsiders in the Italian establishment. The difference in style and activities that Magda ascribes to the two grandmothers tells the story succinctly: "Grandmother Grilli had her special reception days for her friends, Grand-Maman Wissotzky had her specific days for her poor" (M. Trocmé 1946, 29).

The Same but Different

Magda's lineage was like André's in some respects and different in others. French and Russian aristocrats were both jealous to protect their wealth and their social status, but given the French Revolution, the criteria for aristocrats were different in the two countries. While Russian nobles still had an inherited place, French aristocrats gradually lost their place to a democratic meritocracy, one reason why the Protestant haute bourgeoisie moved into the upper echelons of business and, in some cases, of government. The French had more than a century to develop their form of democracy before the Russian nation finally ventured down a similar path after the Tsar abdicated his throne in 1917.

Magda's linguistic skills showed the imprint of aristocracy. She grew up speaking Italian to the servants, the vendors, and the children in the streets, and French or sometimes German or English at home. Her French, with its markedly Italian accent, was very good because it came to her from both sides of her family. The Grilli family spoke it well and often. French was also the preferred language of the Russian court throughout the nineteenth and early twentieth centuries and therefore the language of her mother's Wissotsky family. They spoke some Russian as well, of course, but mostly while back in Russia, where Russian was the language of the peasants and therefore reserved for communicating with servants, vendors, and priests. All this left Magda feeling very much the outsider at school and in the playgrounds of the park.

André's linguistic skills were also broad ranging, but with the exception of German, his languages were learned during his student days and beyond. German was a gift of the German cousins with whom he spent many visits during his childhood. He became proficient in German at a very early age. He acquired English in the upper years of his schooling and steadily improved his command of the language by much use over the years of his career. Later he would develop a workable level of Italian, thanks to having Magda as his tutor.

Magda's religious history was both similar to and different from André's. It was similar in the fact that both grew up under the influence of religious establishments of a sort, André's being Protestant and bourgeois, Magda's being a hodgepodge of Russian Orthodoxy, Catholic, and Protestant strains. It was similar in one other more important way: both defined themselves in vigorous opposition to the ecclesiastical forms of religion handed down in their families. For both, that opposition was motivated in large part by a passion for social justice. They each had little patience with the conservative conventions that came in the religious packages delivered by their parents. But they came to their similar ends by very different routes, André by intensified religious commitment and Magda by equally intense religious skepticism.

Magda's personal religion was neither Russian Orthodox like her mother's family, nor Protestant and Catholic like her father's. The Catholicism of her years in the convent school, the Anglicanism of her father's parents, the Orthodoxy of her maternal ancestors were all traditions far too liturgical for her restless, inquiring mind and her very non-mystical reading of Christian faith.

Grand-Maman Varia had added to the mix by creating her own religious montage. She retained her Russian orthodox cultural connections while supporting and attending the ancient Waldensian Protestant church when she came to Florence.

So Magda amassed a most confused and unusual religious history. Her parents were married in the Russian Orthodox Church, then married a second time in the Waldensian Protestant church. Later, when her widowed father married again, it was to a Catholic Italian in a Catholic church. What was the young child Magda then? Protestant, Orthodox, Catholic, a religious hybrid, or none of the above?

Her mother, Nelly Wissotsky Grilli di Cortona, had died of childbed fever just twenty-seven days after giving birth to Magda. In her childhood, Magda was painfully aware of being motherless and wondered often why that beautiful person in the picture on the wall was not left to bring her up. But she accepted the fact that Grand-Maman Varia was her loving substitute for a mother.

So it was normal that her marginally Orthodox grandmother had seen to it that Magda was baptized in the Swiss Church in Florence. Magda later discovered her baptismal certificate and found that the Swiss church was really part of the French Reformed Church. That was a new fact: she was a Protestant by her baptism in a branch of the same church as André's! Now there were four religious traditions in her direct line of heritage.

When she went to church (irregularly) it was either to the Swiss Church, where the sermons were long and boring, or to the Francophone (and pre-Reformation) Waldensian church, where the atmosphere was as dour as the simple black clothing of its adherents. After the Reformation,

8. Nelly Wissotsky, 1899. Photographer, Studio G. Brogi; Prager and Lowda, Berlin.

nelly's grandma

many Huguenots in flight from a repressive French Catholicism had joined the Waldensians. Nonetheless, they remained conscious of their origins in the twelfth century, when they were called "The Poor of Lyon." Keeping faith with their past, they were very attentive to the needs of the poor there in Florence. It was no accident that Varia gravitated to the Waldensian more than to the Russian community, nor was it a surprise that Magda gravitated to this church more than any other.

Attending to the needs of the poor, that brighter side of the Decembrist inheritance, was something that Magda could relate to very positively. It squared with her temperament, her practical disposition, and her growing commitment, even in childhood, to issues of social justice. Magda had already made that cause her own when she and her cousin Lalli formed their own charitable organization. They were enthusiastic enough to try anything once and young enough to be undeterred by their lack of experience. Magda's description of the well intentioned debacle is touching and amusing:

> When we were 7 or 8 years old, Lalli and I exhibited our qualifications as apostles. We had our own secret charitable society; a religious and humanitarian calling which later became a mystical obsession for Lalli and a social duty for me. We had to find a way to help our fellow-creatures like Grand-Maman did at the Salvation Army or at home, on predetermined days when the homeless and the poor would knock on her door.... Among them was ... Signora Bronconi whose job was to weave straw around the Chianti bottles for a few cents each. She also would accompany us to school and she revealed to us the misery of the lower classes.
>
> We had little wicker baskets with food for lunch at school and each day we gave half of what we had to a little old man who was waiting for us on Piazza Indipendenza. The number of our "protégés" increased rapidly and they waited for us in places other than Piazza Indipendenza. They were of all ages and we made appointments with young children to whom we gave all sorts of things as they climbed on the wrought iron gate of our garden at Viale Margherita. Our enthusiasm led us into giving objects that belonged to George and Dudy (Lalli's older brother and sister) and our charity ended in tragedy.
>
> Grand-Maman unintentionally aroused our first conscious remorse. Our charitable activities were increasing and we needed money. We organized a "professional" fund raising campaign at school and some of our friends gave us a few coins. Seeing this money, Grand-Maman, forgetting to inquire about its origin, made us buy *Panini di ramerino* for our afternoon snack. We didn't want to reveal our fundraising and charitable activities which were our secret and we spent the money to buy something for ourselves instead of using it for our poor protégés.
>
> It was a tragic situation for us, a dramatic, intimate, religious, humanitarian secret. To recover the loss we started selling pieces of cloth by weight to the rag-and-bone man and I do suspect that there were good quality rags among the things we sold, who knows? One day, since we were more than disappointed with the proceeds of our sale, which only represented a few pennies, we decided to moisten the clothes to make them heavier. The result is that we didn't get paid and lost everything

and we decided that God had decided to punish us for being swindlers. We decided we had to find other ways to run our charitable organization but they weren't very successful. (42–43)

Siberia's Darker Side

For all the positive impact it had on her moral and intellectual disposition, the Siberian heritage left another and less favorable impact with Magda. During her earliest years, her family lived in an apartment in center-city Rome. The Russian Orthodox Church had established its headquarters on the ground floor of the same building, and its priests went in and out its dark hallways frequently. They too were garbed in black, but in their case, black left a darker hue in her memory. There was something frightening about these priests, especially about their dress. The archimandrite priest wore a large black cylindrical hat and floor-length robes, also in unrelieved black. Add to this the requisite long black beard and it is easy to imagine the feelings of fright Magda describes in her memoir.

The Orthodox priests she saw daily spoke a language totally unfamiliar; their faces were as somber as their garb, and they were not in the habit of jollying children. Furthermore, given her mother's affiliation with Russian Orthodoxy, her whole impression of their form of Christianity was overlaid with the mystery of her mother's death.

The chatter of the maids, who spoke of her mother Nelly's death after childbirth as if her child had caused it, compounded that impression. When, as a small child, Magda overheard one of the maids say that she was "the child who killed her mother," she was very upset and harbored that distress in her memory for years. Until the end of her life, she retained an extraordinary fear of death. As a child, that also translated into a fear of the dark and a fear of falling asleep. While many children experience fears that lapsing into sleep will really turn into dying, their fear subsides when they wake up morning after morning still alive. But for Magda, there remained an anxious foreboding whenever she contemplated death.

To Rome and Back

By the time Magda was ten years old, she had already traversed a course of religiously sponsored education more complex than most. First it was elementary years in the Deaconesses Institute in Florence, an educational hodge-podge of German Lutheran habits of mind and Swiss Reformed theological traditions. For Magda the child, it seemed a prison as often as a school, although she later had fond and appreciative recollections of some of the Sisters. She was a boarder at the Institute because she had no real home in the city. She had been brought up by a mostly absent father, who depended on wet nurses and later governesses, some of them more nurturing than others.

It was her grandmother whom she remembered as her principal source of imaginative and intellectual development during those years. Her multilingual grandmother taught her languages, so she always wrote to Magda in French and expected her to reply in French. She then returned Magda's letters, their French errors all carefully corrected. The fact that

9. Oscar Grilli di Cortona, 1900. Unknown photographer.

she lived nearby meant that she could take Magda for walks in the park, give her a little pocket money on the side, and be her refuge during school recesses.

After a year in a public school, it was time to get on with secondary education, and for that it was back to the religious orders. By now Magda's father had remarried, this time to an observant Italian Roman Catholic, who was determined that her stepdaughter should live and be educated in a Catholic convent school. A few years in a convent of the Mantellate nuns would be a more promising avenue to confirmation in the Catholic Church, after all.

Her father was a pragmatist who deferred to his second wife's decision. Life would be smoother for Magda in Italy if she were Catholic. Certainly it would be easier to find an appropriate marriage partner for her if she were a member of the real Italian church and a graduate of the Mantellate nunnery's school.

Magda was ten, so she was obedient in spite of the distaste she had developed for Catholic belief and ritual. For her, the strength of the Catholic tradition was in the rich and colorful heritage of art that surrounded her in Florence. She loved the stained glass, the murals, the sculpture that Catholicism had inspired over the centuries, an inspiration as much present in the public squares as in the churches and monasteries. But creeds and rituals were another thing. Nonetheless, she obediently tried to sort things out.

> The Catholic religious teachings were contrary to the Protestant faith I was raised in without really understanding its true meaning. I tried to understand and in my room I copied long Catholic prayers that I recited with more boredom and fear than joy. It was impossible for me to . . . recite the bizarre words I was mumbling without thinking about something else.
>
> Going from "heresy" to "truth," Protestantism to Catholicism, is not a simple matter and I didn't know whom to ask for guidance. . . . [My baptism] was registered in the so-called Swiss Church on Lungarno Guicciardini but my family had stopped going there years ago. We sought advice from Pastor Giovanni Rostagno of the Waldesian church. . . . I

was not a member of his church either, but he decided I should talk with his friend Padre Magri, a highly respected Catholic priest. Padre Magri felt I should be instructed by a high-ranking Prelate, a renowned theologian [who] . . . never understood that I was a child seeking security, not answers to Theological questions . . . with a capital T. The beautiful d'Or San Michele church (where we met) is one of the splendors of Florence but is a place of terror for me. On the left hand side of the church there was a sacristy, the odor of which was acrid. . . . The room was damp and smelled like incense. I was suffocating and frightened to death. (53–54)

Her parents continued making arrangements for her Catholic confirmation, but she bristled when she discovered that she had to be baptized again, this time "conditionally." For many generations, Catholic priests had been instructed to be on guard against invalid baptisms among those receiving the sacraments. Conditional baptism was the hedge: if a first baptism had been invalid for any reason, this conditional baptism would be the one that counted. Magda also resented being told that part of her conversion to Catholicism was the requirement that she renounce the Protestant faith. How does a ten-year-old do that, and to whom would she address her renunciation? There was a further problem: she had never formally affirmed her faith in any Protestant theology. Theology was precisely the game she did not play.

Then came the first communion. It was scheduled to take place in the private chapel of the Cardinal Archbishop of Florence. That would be a suitable place for an aristocratic stranger: out of the public view and therefore out of reach of public criticism. It was set to include two of her young cousins, Marcello and Fiorenza. It was an event she looked forward to with a terror equal in its strength to the delight felt by her two cousins about that ceremonial point of passage.

As soon as it was over, Magda realized that she was not a real Catholic; she was just a convert who had never carried much theological baggage and probably never would. Now she had to learn more rules of being a Catholic, one of which was keeping a list of thoughts and deeds that would be considered sins. After all, she had to have something to confess on Fridays. Sins were necessary if penitence was to be real. Keeping account of the venial and mortal sins she had committed seemed a strange sort of moral bookkeeping, which further offended her. She found it more calculating than inspiring. Why, she asked, is the theft of ten lira a mortal sin, but the theft of only five lira is a less onerous venial sin?

While still a student in the convent, she went into the confessional booth one day and said, "Father, I have decided not to confess, because I don't believe in confessions." She also said she would not leave the church, would go to confession only once a year, and never take communion because she didn't understand it and it didn't do anything for her. At her first communion, she recalled, "I swallowed and didn't feel anything, nothing special at all. The sky didn't open up, my body was not jolted, and my mind remained, as it was before, concerned and disappointed. So what? Precisely nothing!" (56–60). She found her consolations of religion in Grandmother Varia's tiny Waldensian Protestant church, where people made clothing and prepared food for the poor. Their concern for people in need and their free-spirited denial of Catholic authority was refreshing. For her, no religion, Protestant or Catholic or Orthodox, had muted her fear of death, that dark Nothing beyond. Her religious consolation came by being useful in this life.

Magda and André were the same age when the Great War began, but their experiences of that momentous tragedy were altogether different. André saw the war in his front yard, with German soldiers patrolling the streets outside his garden gate and German officers bivouacked in his home. The flood of wounded and dead from the nearby battlefield of the Somme flowed through his city, leaving the hospital smells of carbolic acid and gangrenous flesh. The war was a vivid reality that left its brand on his memory and his thinking for the rest of his life.

By contrast, Magda's experience of the world outside the convent was confined to what she could glimpse occasionally through a small peephole in the garden wall. The war was elsewhere, some place where her father was on duty with his soldiers. Even that was hardly a change from life before the war. In the Mantellate Convent school, students were allowed to receive visits from their parents three days a year and her father, having moved to Verona, was rarely one of her visitors.

The five years she passed with the Mantellate Sisters were an academic success, a religious disaster, and a nurturing period. However unimaginative it might have been, the regime was firm and demanding. It was often the sheer boredom of her curriculum, focused as it was on domestic skills such as embroidery, that led Magda to spend her time studying, reading Dante over and over again by the light of candle stubs purloined from the chapel. Magda did her best to come to grips with Catholicism, but she never got past her fierce independence, so the contest was a draw at best. She and the Catholic Church went their separate ways. Mother Church would never replace her own lost mother.

Abandonment led her to self-reliance, and boredom to study. The result was the rare award of a National Honor Diploma earned through a frightening oral examination before the State Examination Committee. She had opened the door to higher education. As in most European countries at the time, breaking into higher education was a trial by many exams. She wanted to be admitted to the Istituto Superiore di Magistero, a top-level institution of higher education, but that would involve a special admissions examination in addition to her National Honor Diploma.

Why this ambition? Young women of establishment families were ordinarily content to be educated well enough to manage their social and family roles with an acceptable level of Italian grace. Of her graduating class in the Mantellate convent, only nine students were selected for a special stream of preparation for higher education, and Magda turned out to be the only one of the nine who qualified for the National Honor Diploma.

She had made up her mind to qualify for a professional role in social work, an ambition thoroughly consistent with her childhood dreams and the defunct charitable foundation that she and Lalli had organized when they were very young.

6

A Renegade Gentleman

From Refugee to Guest

When on that snowy day in February of 1917 André and his family were deposited in the Flemish countryside of southwest Belgium, they qualified as refugees. They had been uprooted and thrown out of their home and country. Now they had to scratch out a living by some combination of their own wit and the kindness of others, others who owed them nothing beyond a shared humanity.

André realized that among the forms of wealth he enjoyed as a child was a broader network of connections than most, a network he took for granted. It was his father's task to find a new social fabric that would protect and support his family. Fortunately, the Gallic Trocmés had left footprints almost everywhere in Picardy and in southern Belgium. Ancient as those footprints might be, the Trocmés were more likely than many to find a cousin almost anywhere, someone to whom they could appeal for help in coping with all those perils of the dispossessed.

It wasn't long before Paul discovered such a cousin. Other networking followed: a St. Quentin neighbor, a former customer of his cotton business, and a member of the Royal Court. These four helped him put life back together again. Having arrived in exile in February, he had a place for his family to live in a Brussels suburb by August, and there they would relocate before the new school term began.

The former customer loaned him the money; the cousin and the former neighbor introduced him to their socially well-placed Brussels friends and got the boys enrolled in the best lycée. The member of the Belgian Royal Court found them a suitable house in a suitable neighborhood, one that had been temporarily vacated by a Brussels banker and his family who had fled to Paris when Belgium was invaded, then stayed there for the duration of the war.

André would have his difficulties adjusting to all of this. To be a refugee is a statement of condition, but not of character. André's condition had changed from wealthy child to penniless refugee sheltered by a poor farmer, then back to wealthy child in a matter of months. His character had not changed as radically except in giving him a heightened sensitivity to the meaning of poverty. He was still the sheltered child of an haute bourgeoisie family, a late-blooming adolescent carrying a great deal of social and emotional baggage not of his own making, especially his profound need for affection and his restless, obsessive, intellectual curiosity.

Then there was the enthusiastic embrace of his religious awakening and his determination to live a pure life, a purity defined largely by the merger of his relentless logic, his self-doubt, and his sexual awakening. Whatever their origin, these were his own burdens, things only he could resolve. So far, it wasn't going all that well.

His friends in the St. Quentin Christian Union had made it clear to him that it is never enough to claim the right creed. A statement of faith only makes sense when it is matched by the web of loyalties and responsibilities the creed implies. Even so, he would soon confront situations that would raise practical challenges to his moral commitments.

Once in Brussels, it was possible to reestablish the St. Quentin routine of daily life: read a book, go to class, do homework and, on Sunday afternoon, take a walk or go to a museum. While the return to a normal regimen of student life was cause for gratitude, it was certainly not permission to forget the help of the Demulder family, who had taught André and Pierre the generosity of the poor.

Recollections of that family cropped up sometimes without warning. While visiting the Brussels museum with Pierre one day, André's attention was caught by a densely populated painting, *The Massacre of the Innocents* by the sixteenth-century Flemish master Pieter Brueghel the Elder. Breughel frequently used New Testament themes and set them in Flemish surroundings. This one recalled Herod's angry order to kill the firstborn of every Jewish family rather than let the infant Jesus escape. The setting could have been Maroq, the village near the Demulder farm, and one of those Innocents could have been Clement, the Demulders' little son. It was a stark reminder of the misery that armed authorities can visit on innocent people while "just obeying orders."

It was in Brussels that André discovered he was really a renegade gentleman student. He was a gentleman in the class-bound sense of the term. At the intellectual level, he could not escape his upbringing and experience. He loved to analyze, formulate, and postulate theories about the human drama he saw around him. Socially, he was quite at home with the wealthy bourgeois cousins in Brussels, even when they annoyed him with narrow views on important human issues.

One thing about the Brussels society he saw made him very uncomfortable, the gay and frivolous lifestyle of the Brussels country club set: lots of tennis, just the right wine with each course at dinner, a more or less blind eye for the conditions under which most of the city lived, conversations that were most often confined to social chatter.

A case in point was the day Paul's cousin, Mrs. Hilgenstock, wanted to do a favor to the family by inviting them for a day at an exclusive club where she was a member. Because the boys had left their whole wardrobe behind when they fled, she borrowed some clothes from her son and offered Pierre and André the obligatory white flannel suits, tennis rackets, and tennis shoes. Looking back, André wrote about this:

> We finally shied away, and decided it would be ridiculous for us to behave like dandies among the Brussels bourgeoisie. I sometimes think about what would have happened to me had I accepted: I was 16 years old, I would have learned how to speak to young ladies, I would probably have more or less fallen in love, and I would have learned how to dance. [But] I was a member of the Christian Union and considered such frivolity as sin. (A. Trocmé 1953, 115)

The fabric of life in the St. Quentin church still held him in too tight a grip to let him revel in the unfamiliar clothes and the gay abandon of teenage flirtations in a Brussels country club. He simply could not allow himself that taste of minor bacchanalia. He would never feel completely at home among the established business class of his own society. He would have to find his fulfillment elsewhere.

He had long since talked with his father about going into the ministry, but now he began to understand that a ministry defined by upper middle class values and aspirations would never do. In the next decade, all he had absorbed of the Trocmé sense of duty would take an unconventional turn, one that left him calling for justice when no one seemed to be listening, calling for sacrifice when no one was giving up self-interest, calling for Christians to be peacemakers when even his own Église Réformée de France would not take up the theme. He was becoming a renegade young gentleman who would become a renegade minister. It was only when he married Magda that he began to shed some of his spiritual body armor.

Throughout his nearly two years in Brussels, another Trocmé-esque quality would not let go of him. He became a compulsively good student. His curiosity seemed as bottomless as his drive to excel. From here on he was rarely without a book to read, an idea to develop, or a thought to write down.

Once established in the Lycée Athénée in Brussels, André put his mind to the upcoming first of two decisive baccalaureate examinations that determined the track of future education and, therefore, future career options for a French or a Belgian student. He would have taken the baccalaureate in Brussels except for the Armistice. The war ended in November and he knew he would do better with the exams in his native culture. Paul decided that the family would return to France as soon as possible and take up residence in Paris, at least until both Pierre and André were well established in their university careers.

The Armistice itself was an eye-opener for André in more ways than one. He saw soldiers of the occupying German army strip off their epaulets, their medals, and any other military decorations and trade them for red badges, or for one of the thousands of red flowers showering the city's center point, the Grand-Place. They did this not because they were afraid of Belgians seeking retribution but because the time had come to renounce war as a form of profiteering by kings and their industrial supporters. The ordinary soldiers on both sides had much more in common with each other than they did with their own aristocratic officer corps.

As French and American soldiers flooded into Brussels looking for liquor and women and finding plenty of both, André also saw how war stripped men of their dignity. It was one thing to see German soldiers dancing in the streets with Belgian women. It was another to see soldiers of every uniform streaming in and out of the brothels in an alcohol-drenched haze. Dancing with the enemy was just politically bewildering, but for a sixteen-year-old well-brought-up French Protestant boy, obvious debauchery was morally bewildering.

One would have thought that revenge and retribution would have been at the top of the agenda for the victorious military and the newly liberated civilians. But something deeper brought the soldiers of both armies together in an attempt to change the face of their governments. The steadily growing Industrial Workers of the World (IWW) had, since its foundation in 1905, preached class struggle to huge and receptive audiences of laborers, enlisted military men, and government employees throughout Europe. Now that the Kaiser had run to Holland for refuge, the IWW and its sympathizers exploded on the scene with cries of "Fire the bosses" and "Abolish the wage system" and "Down with the capitalists."

November 11, 1918, became the threshold moment of great and sudden changes. When Kaiser Wilhelm II abdicated the German throne, other royal persons and families throughout Western and Eastern Europe fell from power as well. It was the beginning of the end for government by royalty. The socialist movements in many countries were quick to vie for power and assert their claims for social justice on a broad scale. The IWW was only one of dozens of socialist movements, most of which united under a red flag that represented no one nation but the common interests of workers in all nations.

Now André saw their adherents marching by the thousands, including soldiers who had been firing at each other the day before. At the head of the columns were three flag bearers: at the center a red flag and on either side a French and a Belgian flag. Among the marchers were hundreds of German soldiers singing the Marseillaise, and singing it in German! They were marching into Brussels to declare the foundation of the Blue Collar Workers and Soldiers Republic (BCWSR).

10. Bombed home church in St. Quentin. Photograph of photo in the church archive. Courtesy of Richard Unsworth.

André was not a Socialist, and he did not know quite what to make of them. Their issues were not necessarily his. He was a student bound for a theological education, and Paris was the next stop. As exciting and dizzying as was the Armistice Day outburst in Brussels and elsewhere, republics were not simply declared and then established by aggrieved workers and soldiers. The Socialist parties that blossomed in Europe, like the one whose president succeeded Kaiser Wilhelm, were middle class organizations with strong liberal convictions about social justice, but the Socialists were not calling for class war between workers and employers. Nor were they totally internationalist in their aspirations, as were groups like supporters of the BCWSR. In fact, as much as these revolutionary groups wished they could erase national borders in favor of common society with justice at its core, the structure of the nation state remained firmly in place across Europe.

In the jubilant atmosphere of that day, no one would have guessed that movements like the BCWSR would inadvertently plant the seeds of the next equally horrible war. Less than a year later in Munich, Hitler would begin his rise to power by marshaling the frustrations of those workers and ex-soldiers and then turning their anger toward Jews into aspirations for a Thousand-Year Reich.

Adolescence in the Diaspora

A lot happened in André Trocmé's development during the long months of refuge in Belgium. His whole home network of friends and school and church had been uprooted and dispersed. German officers who made it their bivouac had plundered the house on the Boulevard Gambetta. It would be five years before it could be rebuilt, and when it was, much of it was no longer recognizable.

Another assault on the network of friendships and faculties happened at the church, which had been so much a part of André's life. It was nearly leveled by a combination of Allied bombing and German occupation during the two waning years of the war. To this day, the rebuilt church's meeting rooms hold photographs of the crumbled shell that was left when the congregation regrouped in 1918. The main sanctuary had been commandeered by the Germans and used as a barn for their horses, and the adjacent parish building had been left in ruins. One photo portrays the handful of families who had found their way home from the Diaspora and gathered together outside the partially restored building on the occasion of the first post-war service of communion.

The rebuilding project was immense. Eighty percent of the city of St. Quentin had been destroyed during those two years. Rebuilding efforts were going on everywhere, stretching the resources of money, labor, and building supplies beyond their limits. Fortunately, funds came in from other, less-injured, French cities and churches, and from church groups in England and America.

During their exile, only a few church leaders were able to keep in touch with each other and gather news of the scattered families. Even before the Armistice, however, church leaders were able to renew publication of the church's newspaper, the *Bulletin de l'Église Réformée*, for its constituents. One of the most important sections of each issue was called "The Diaspora," in which news of the dispersed families was printed as quickly as it was gathered. The issue of August 1918 even carried a dispatch from Brussels noting André's bout with diphtheria and the treatment that restored him to health. The *Bulletin* was used to reconstitute, as much as possible from the community's memory, the records that had been lost or destroyed. So, André Trocmé's reconstituted baptismal certificate takes a best guess at which of the two assistant pastors had actually baptized him. It was probably, but not certainly, Pastor de St-Affrique, who had become a good friend of the Trocmé family. In fact, two of his daughters married two of Paul Trocmé's sons.

André's growing up continued through the Diaspora and beyond, while he pursued his education as a gentleman who was becoming a minister and a renegade in the process. Growing up always involves separations, but for André some separations had been difficult to accomplish. His father carried most of the emotional burden of raising his youngest boys. His second wife, Paula, had borne them, but parenting did not seem to be her strongest talent. In any case, at the age of twenty-nine, she had married into a family that was already large: five older sons and two older daughters.

The eldest, Maurice, was only three years younger than she. He and two other stepchildren were already either launched in their careers or well along in their university preparations, but four of her stepchildren from nine to sixteen were still at home. There was also the task of managing a large house and all the social obligations that attended being the wife of a man who was a major church leader in Northern France and a major force in the city's business community. According to the mores of the wealthy French in that era, it was right and proper to turn over most of the infant care to wet nurses, maids, and governesses. In fact, the nineteenth-century French employed more wet nurses than any other European country.

No surprise, then, that André grew up feeling motherless. He did not see a great deal of Paula in the daily routine of his young life, and then she was killed in the auto accident when he was only ten. Unlike Magda, he did not have a grandmother who would fill the gap. Only his half-sister Louise would step into the role after his mother died, and she did not provide mothering, only instructions. She was simply not a warm and motherly person. André described her as "cold, intelligent, firm and lucid ... [and] very close to Father, whom she resembled." She also brought into the family her own two young children, Yvonne and Étienne, both close in age to André, and both absorbing the lion's share of the attention she could spare for any young child. Etienne became André's best friend and playmate.

It was partly the missing mother who left André feeling so extraordinarily timid, even frightened, in his relationship with girls his own age. When he went to public school for the first time at the age of twelve, he was disturbed by the older boys and their story-swapping about sexual adventures—peccadilloes, most of them, but they provided grist for the mill of adolescence that requires young boys to convince themselves they are men by convincing their friends of their conquests, real or fictional.

One way he managed his growing sexual uncertainties during those years was by encasing himself in the protective armor of the social formalities that went with being a Trocmé, a member of that proud and successful tribe.

Stepping out of that armor was a thing that came in fits and starts, sometimes by accident, sometimes in an adventure, sometimes by intent. It was an accident of history that he found himself standing at the edge of the Grand-Place in Brussels one day, watching the soldiers, liberated at last from the hellish trenches, flock into the city to find release in a grand-scale bout of drinking and sex.

As he watched the spectacle, he felt both revulsion and fascination: revulsion at the sight of those troops, who once paraded off to war with uniforms pressed and heads held high as the crowds cheered them on, only to return in moral collapse, with ragged uniforms and famished emotions. But fascination is the other side of revulsion, and after dinner that Armistice night, he went back to the Grand-Place to see more of the behaviors that he had been told would lead a person to downfall and condemnation.

The first view of Armistice antics was accidental, but his return to the site was deliberate, perhaps just because it left him with questions about his own moral armor. Surely he did not want to follow the debauched example he saw playing out in the Grand-Place; but equally surely, his overwhelming timidity with girls was not "normal" and he knew it. He understood that he needed to move beyond the sexually confused place where he was stuck.

In the next six years of his education there would be other moments of maturing, most of them less rattling than the mob celebration of Armistice in the Grand-Place. Some of them would help him step out of his increasingly ill-fitting moral armor and allow him greater trust in his own inner resources of self-confidence and moral maturity. Others would send him back into a bulletproof morality where he could be safe, consistent, and secure.

Paris and Its Universities

In the midst of the postwar confusion, the Trocmé family established a temporary life in Paris while their decimated home in St. Quentin was being restored. It had taken a month for train service between Brussels and Paris to be reestablished. So it was only on December 11, 1918, that they boarded the first train out. It took fifteen hours to make the trip (now an hour and forty minutes) with stops at one devastated town or city after another.

By the time they arrived in Paris, the date for administering the baccalaureate exams had passed. Pierre had already taken his *bachot* in Brussels, but André was aiming to sit the exam in Paris. Missing the date meant another entire round of preparation to take the first *bachot* in the spring. He would still have to take the second *bachot* at the end of June in 1920.

André was one of a large group of students who came to Paris at that time from the so-called "liberated areas," all of them hoping to sit their second examinations as soon as possible in order not to be overly delayed in getting on to university. The students from liberated areas were almost all older than the students who had kept on schedule with their education. The latter were not only younger, they were quite unblemished by the realities of war. Paris had not been bombarded and the Germans had not laid it waste as they departed. So these younger students thought of war primarily in terms of rationing and other inconveniences. André found that the returnees often had little to talk about with their younger classmates. He would also learn that older students from the liberated areas would find themselves under higher expectations from their faculty.

He knew that he was capable of a prodigious amount of study, thanks to years of the St. Quentin daily regime. So he determined to finish the first baccalaureate with honors right away and then plunge ahead to do the final year of lycée and his first year at the Faculty of Theology simultaneously. It was a good enough plan, but it almost did not work. This first *bachot* presented no threat because, the war having broken into his progress twice, this was the third time he would prepare for that examination. It was smooth sailing until the end. Then he met with the professor who was to examine him in English, first in conversation and then in reading. His first question was "You have mingled and conversed with British and American soldiers. They have told you about their experiences in the trenches. Please describe these conversations to me in English."

André was still dealing with timidity and inadequacy, but this question threw him off stride. In fact he had not mingled and conversed with American and English soldiers. His English was learned from a textbook, and the only soldier with whom he had spent any time was Corporal Kindler, the German soldier assigned to live at his house in St. Quentin. He mumbled a few words and then burst out crying.

It was a humiliating disaster. He tried to explain to his instructor that he was from one of the liberated zones, but the examiner was not impressed. He asked, "If you can't speak English, what the hell are you doing here?" Reluctantly, he handed André a book and told him to read the selection he pointed out. That was better by far. His translation was accurate and his vocabulary was rich and accessible, and the instructor passed him.

That restored a measure of self-confidence, to which his school friend, Jacques Diény, added more. He invited André to join the Christian Student

Federation in the student-saturated Left Bank and then asked him to give a welcoming talk at their meeting. He got so excited about André's ideas and his facility as a speaker that he asked him to turn the talk into an article for the Federation's monthly magazine. André said later, "To me, the magazine represented the Holy of Holies which only published articles written by VIPs" (127).

Crowding two years' work for two different faculties at two different institutions into the next academic year was daunting but not defeating. He studied Hebrew, Greek, and Church History at the Sorbonne, then commuted by bicycle uphill to the Montparnasse and the Alsatian Lycée on the Boulevard Arago to do his philosophy, then home to Rue Jacob to keep up on the German, English, geography, and literature which would also be required for that second *bachot*. The only relaxed moment came during the downhill bike ride from the Montparnasse to the apartment on Rue Jacob.

Following the two courses of study simultaneously required a blinding amount of reading. Most of it was done under a single lightbulb above the small table that he and Pierre and cousin Etienne daily shared as their work place. Between the distractions of a small apartment and the endless blandishments of Paris, André managed to keep a tight focus on his work and finish this double-stacked year with distinction at both the lycée and the Faculty of Theology. It did not leave much time for exploring Paris, but that was just as well. He was still at the point of thinking of the city as a nest of bookstores surrounded by a tangle of temptations, most of them designed to undermine the moral character of the urbanites. Later he would look back on that period with a certain chagrin.

> I remember walking back home late on Sunday evenings, along Boulevard Pasteur when the county fair was in full swing under the elevated subway. There were merry-go-rounds, swings, sharp-shooting stands, live monsters, lottery wheels, and candy stores. Boys my age hugged young girls who burst into laughter, sounding like waterfalls. Girls walked toward me as I accelerated my pace and stiffened my neck. Things were mixed up in my mind because I was unable to see the difference between sin and innocent amusement. Father had told us he

knew he could have confidence in us and he obviously was so right. He had branded us for life! Life was white in church, at the Christian Union meetings, when we strolled through the Meudon forest . . . and black at the movie theater, the circus, and brothels. The great Babylon never stained me. (125)

The comment sounds almost as if he wished it had, but just a little. Later in life, he was less likely to draw such distinctions in black and white terms. He was absolutist about a few things: not using alcohol, refraining from premarital or extramarital sex, not smoking, and telling the truth at all times and at all costs. But even those were less things to be feared than they were practices that kept together the threads of integrity in his and others' lives.

Refraining from the use of alcohol was important because its effect on the lives of poor families was often so tragic. Sex confined to marriage had important social consequences. The pregnant teenager suffered greatly in a Protestant Christian society, and families could be torn apart by extramarital engagements. Not smoking was more about decorum than it was about social threat or even health threat. And truth telling was a practice he was forced to compromise a few times during World War II.

In spite of his confining study disciplines, that second year at the Faculty of Theology provided this late maturer with some further experiences that relieved him of his excessive timidity with girls and his disquieting shyness in so many social situations.

One of the most important was the marriage of his half-brother Robert, who had come to live in Paris. When Robert prepared to marry Germaine Pacquement, he asked André to serve as his best man. André was delighted and honored, even though he felt clumsy and awkward when the time came.

The wedding took place in Protestantism's most prestigious church, the Oratoire du Louvre. Maybe it was the public character of the wedding, or the presence of so many distinguished Protestant families in the congregation (M. Pacquement was a very wealthy cotton merchant whose social standing in Paris was like Paul Trocmé's in St. Quentin), or maybe it was just André's persistent timidity. Whatever the cause, he felt clumsy again, and blushed mightily when he took Germaine's younger sister Suzanne down the aisle on his arm. He was twenty years old and here he was, for the very first time, escorting a woman on his arm.

Robert had made another gesture intended to get André out of his moral and psychological cage. He established something he called the Mind Widening Bank, designed to fund the purchase of novels (no theology allowed) and attendance at theaters and concerts. Pierre and Étienne would make more use of it than André, who was the victim of his own sincerity about becoming a minister. He thought he should not spare the time for such frivolities. Whatever psychological constraints might have arisen from some external influence or another, they were now thoroughly his own and only by his own self-discoveries would they lose their grip.

A Circle of Pacifists

Until Charles de Gaulle made it possible for conscientious objectors to do alternative civil service, every young man of eligible age was required to do a term of military service in the forces of the French Republic. A similar requirement existed in all the nations of Europe at the time. World War I still loomed very recently, and the vast majority of the French people backed that requirement.

Still, there were conscientious objectors in the Église Réformée and in the ranks of those preparing for its ministry. Their pacifist commitments had been stirred by the experience of that war, as were the anti-war sentiments of so many soldiers who had seen its horrors at close range.

To be sure, pacifism was a political lightning rod, and the general opinion in the culture was that pacifism was a form of treason. The equation was simple enough. If all age-eligible Frenchmen had taken this position at the outset of the war, the armies of the Kaiser would have overrun France and French honor would have suffered a mortal blow.

André met and heard some of the principal pacifist figures in the church during his first and second years of Theology, 1919–21. He listened to André Phillip, an impressive person who would, many years later, become a strong supporter of André's work in Le Chambon and the Minister of Finance when the Fourth Republic was put together in 1945.

By the second year, André had made several good friends, among them Jacques Diény and Arnold Brémond. Diény had already been a help in bolstering André's self-confidence, and he would do so again before the year was over. Brémond was the one whom Paul Trocmé would later assume was responsible for André and Magda planning to go to India to visit Gandhi.

In that second year he also developed friendships with three other students with whom his path would cross often during the 1940s. They were Henri Roser, Jacques Martin, and Philippe Vernier, all committed pacifists who had taken very public stands on the matter. Roser, in fact, had simply returned his conscription papers without filling them out, a decision that would land him in prison for the first time but not the last. It also cost him his standing as a reserve officer in the army and the loss of his intended career when the church took him off their list of prospective parish ministers and refused to ordain him.

These three also earned a loud protest from the majority of their fellow students for their pacifist stand. Inevitably, as the criticism got stronger so did the convictions of the pacifists.

The Adventure at Clamart

André admired these men for their principled stand on war but he was not yet ready to make such a commitment himself. He did not find it easy to identify closely with the workers and the poor, and political affiliation with the radical left was not even a question. In any case, he and his friend Diény were busy evangelizing the whole world, beginning with the working class, a tall order even for such devout and devoted men.

They focused their attention on Clamart, a small working class suburb of Paris. They organized the four boys and four girls in its tiny congregation into a young people's group, and then started going from door to door to talk to workers and their wives about the Gospel. They were disappointed to find that no one seemed at all interested to hear what they were saying. When their first strategy failed, they turned to another more practical one: they set about a building project. The church was so small that it had only one small room, the sanctuary, and no meeting rooms at all. The young people's group started meeting in a room above one of the local bars, a messy room that smelled more of smoke than of sanctity.

Diény set about finding a piece of vacant land that they could use to build a meeting place for the young people's program. A good lady of the church gave them a vacant lot near the church building.

They could not afford building supplies but they could afford the give-away price that the government would charge them for an abandoned barracks that had been built for refugees during the war. All they had to do was dismantle it, move it to the vacant lot, and rebuild it, without benefit of an engineer or a contractor, of course.

At this point, Jacques Diény, the inspiration for the whole project, decided to give up his student deferment and go ahead with his two years of required military service. What became of his enthusiastic pacifism was hard to figure out. All we know is that he ultimately renounced it, and André was left with a woodpile stacked on a vacant lot, the raw material of a dream, but a long way from the finished product.

The other members of the Clamart Team pitched in and built the building by working a couple of afternoons a week over several months. Then came the great day when it was finished, except for a few details.

The students invited all the townspeople to come to a dedication ceremony in the finished building, and they turned out in numbers enough to fill the room. The young theologians of the Clamart Team were convinced that, indeed, this *was* the way to begin evangelizing the population of Clamart, just as Diény had predicted.

André was appointed to give the welcoming talk and describes the experience in his memoir:

> My discourse was inspired by the "vision" and, after a few minutes, worrisome cracking sounds were heard. The audience calmed down when they heard my reassuring words. I went on, worried, and was interrupted by a terrifying noise. The barrack started breaking apart and the floor broke into two sections under the weight of the screaming crowd.
>
> "Don't worry," I shouted. "There is no danger and the building won't collapse." My inexperienced affirmation was fortunately correct

because the walls and the roof resisted. The beams under the floor were the only part of the structure that had given way.

The end of the celebration was somewhat strange as I looked and spoke to the audience, half of which was leaning to the right while the other half leaned to the left. In fact, the two halves of the floor leaned toward the center and this prevented them from falling.

Diény's "vision" never came to be. But, thanks to a few young adventurers who had believed in God, a few Protestant families re-created a little church which this time had a minister. (137–38)

7

The Military Misadventure

A Gathering Disquiet

André knew he was a renegade, but it wasn't a status he aspired to. He was at home as a member of the haute bourgeoisie Protestante. While the Protestant upper class was bourgeois and not noble, it was a sort of non-royal aristocracy, exemplifying the meaning of the original Greek term: the morally and intellectually best who act in the interest of all. At the same time he was deeply conflicted about many things that came with upper class standing. His issue was straightforward: could he continue to enjoy his social status without running afoul of the religious and ethical aspirations he was still unfolding? It was a tug of war between a social heritage and a religious calling.

From childhood, he had learned that privilege exacts a price in duty and social conformity. He was more than willing to adapt his life to his religious calling, but his own inner turmoil told him that the social conformity part of church membership often required the wrong sort of compromises. Furthermore, he was awkward, angered by hypocrisy of any sort, and maladapted to the role of a Trocmé, at least as he saw that role defined by his father and his father's friends. The internal logic of the moral life made him intolerant of any self-serving display of privilege. His own privileged position was becoming more and more of a challenge, sometimes even a moral embarrassment.

Like most young men of his age, he saw family values that deserved to be carried on in his own life and other values that he could not imagine becoming his own. For one thing, his experience with his peers in the Christian Union taught him that discovering a new and different relationship with God was an experience full of excitement, joy, and elevated spirits. Those were not the first impressions that came to mind as he observed the dour face of the religion he saw in the generation of his seniors.

After two years of theological study and disquieting encounters with the direction the scholars of religion were taking, he still could not forget his feelings when he left that transformational meeting of the Christian Union back in St. Quentin: "Light was now shining around me and a fire burning in my soul. Everything became possible and everything made sense" (A. Trocmé, 88). He had become a Christian enthusiast who recognized the beckoning presence of a God whose face was inviting but still unfamiliar.

He still did not feel free of the social constraints he had inherited. He kept trying to figure out which ones to embrace, which to reject, and which to let die on the vine. A few of the restraints had weakened, thanks to those moments of self-discovery in Brussels and Paris, and thanks also to the encouragement he had gotten from friends like Diény and the Clamart group, and from the affectionate way his brother Robert had taken him by the hand to lead him toward maturity. Still, many very fundamental decisions about how to define himself, how to set his own course, were floating loose, untethered to any anchor in his own life.

Trying to understand all this thirty or forty years later, André saw three clusters in his crisis, one theological, another personal, and the third a replay of old uncertainties.

He was getting his theological education at a time when the waters were roiled in Christian scholarship. The tension between religion and science was running high. Scholars of major stature were raising discomfiting questions about religious certainties that had defined the ministry since the time of the Protestant Reformation.

Maurice Goguel, his professor of New Testament, was insisting that the Bible needed to be read critically and analytically, just as you might read any important historical document. One of his most influential books, *Jesus the Nazarene: Myth or History*, was just out in Trocmé's final year. Goguel's book dared to challenge the myth of Jesus in the name of history.[1]

---

1. Payot, Paris, published the original French edition in 1925.

Emile Durkheim, a professor at the Sorbonne, was looking at religion as a sociological phenomenon that needed the same sort of scrutiny as any other question about what drives communities to act as they do. His study of religion, *The Elementary Forms of Religious Life*, published in 1912, was one of the foundations of sociology and had become essential reading for theological students of André Trocmé's generation.

The Swiss theologian Karl Barth was writing his eight volumes of Church Dogmatics. They were weighty tomes, awash in footnotes, whose effect on the preachers who read them, André thought, was to make their sermons desiccated and boring, void of enthusiasm and unable to convey the real vitality of Christian faith.

Ultimately, pacifism would become the major anchor for knowing himself and deciding how he must live his life, but that had not yet happened. He admired the self-evident integrity of fellow students like Henri Roser and Pierre Vernier. For them, refusing military service was more than a conviction; it was an axiom. As much as he was drawn by their commitments, this still class-bound Trocmé was not ready to make their convictions his own.

Like it or not, it was a matter of class, not with Roser and Vernier, of course, but with the laborers and military veterans who were the backbone of the IWW. Having seen the Armistice Day demonstrations in Brussels, he knew he was not one of them. He could not imagine himself parading across the Grand-Place wearing a red paper flower in his coat and singing La Marseillaise under a red flag.

He looked back on that period and called it a major turning point in his life. Gaining self-confidence, acknowledging his own sexual drives, dealing with the moral conflict of killing another person just because some absent general gave the order, these and similar issues were creating more inner turmoil than he could abide. At the same time, the issues were making it urgent that he find just where he could take his stand.

A Pacifist in the Making and in the Military?

Right now was the moment to address the personal part of his growth crisis. Until now, he had enjoyed automatic deferment of his term of military service because he was a student in the Faculty of Theology. Was that right and fair? Probably not. He decided to take time off from his studies to fill his military obligation, to sort out the issue of pacifism, and to consort with "real-world people."

The military obligation cut across all class lines, and it would provide one thing he knew he needed: a firsthand knowledge of the kind of people who would make up a parish if he did finally go on into the ministry. If he enlisted right away, he would be a soldier just before his twenty-first birthday, and he could at least take ethical comfort in knowing that he had not used the privilege of military deferment. He moved ahead to enlist, against the strenuous objections of his father and all the advice he got from his professors.

Even though his decision was a way for him to learn more about himself by learning more about the "real people" and their ways of life, he did not want to be totally immersed in that learning. So he applied for a post near the family's summer home in St Gobain. That way, he could get away from the army over weekends and enjoy the life he might ultimately decide to leave behind.

His army career took a number of bizarre turns. Since he was sure he could not violate the Ten Commandments by killing another person, he decided he would have to be a soldier without a gun, like his German friend Kindler. He was first posted to a disciplinary platoon in the First Company of the Fifty-fourth Infantry Regiment. It was a platoon that included university students who had enlisted or whose deferments had run out. They quickly became the butt of harassment and abuse by the ordinary soldiers who resented their upper-class status. The job of the captain in command and his non-commissioned officers was to toughen up these fellows. They were all slated to become officers, so the toughening up would have to come now. The captain in charge of his company put up with the bourgeois Trocmé even though he was an outsider in every way. He was not interested in the brothels, he drank only coffee in the bars, he did not smoke, and his language was bereft of all those crude expressions an army depends on for ventilating its frustrations.

With his fellow soldiers, it was another matter. Even though he had been promoted to corporal over his own objections, most of them still ragged him about his puritanical take on life and did their best to get him into compromising positions of one sort or another. Among them were a few who ultimately became friends. There was Potel, a hapless young man largely untroubled by intellectual or moral conflicts. He had been an underling clown in a circus, and clowning was about the only thing he did well. He did whatever it took to get a laugh, including being a pest, and that he was, especially when André was trying to read a book.

André liked Potel well enough, but when he was in mid-paragraph of some serious reading one day, Potel started tossing things at him to get attention: first a sock full of pine cones, then a boot, then a shoe. André lost his composure. He got up, dumped Potel from his bunk, and ordered him to put on his uniform and come outside the barracks to settle things. Potel was frightened; André, trying to act like a corporal, sounded stern. He marched Potel off to a nearby snack shack, pushed him inside, and then ordered a big steak and French fries for each of them. Potel was awed, speechless, and confused. André ordered him to pick up his knife and fork and his napkin, an amenity strange to Potel, and commanded him to eat. Not a word passed between them, either as they ate or on their way back to the barracks. It worked. Potel quit his practical jokes and the two became silent friends.

Another friendship became his avenue to service without a gun. Crépin was a resourceful private who worked in the captain's office. He routinely opened the captain's mail, where one day he saw an inquiry from the colonel, asking whether the captain had anyone he could recommend for a slot just opened in the Geodesic Brigade, a unit about to undertake major mapping assignments in northern France and Morocco. Crépin inserted André's name in the appropriate slot and tucked the reply form into a pile of routine papers requiring the captain's signature. Then he waited.

The opportunity came when he saw the captain going out for drinks with his friends. Knowing he would be at least three sheets to the wind by the time he got back, Crépin waited up for the captain and, when he stumbled in, handed him the whole sheaf of papers to sign, apologizing that they were due back to the colonel first thing in the morning. The captain signed everything without reading, and off the papers went to the colonel. Fortunately, the colonel remembered André as the fellow who

11. Geodesic Brigade, 1921–22. Unknown photographer.

had drawn a first-rate map while the company was on field maneuvers. When his company assembled in the drill yard a couple of days later, they heard several announcements from the colonel being read out by the ill-prepared captain. One of them caught everyone off guard, including both André and his captain. The captain announced that Corporal Trocmé had been reassigned to the Geodesic Brigade and would leave in three days. Captain Queyroi was outraged by his own surprise and went off to the colonel's office to protest the assignment. He returned chastened a little while later, and André went off to what he hoped would be a thoroughly unmilitary military duty. When he discovered how this had all come about, he went to thank Crépin, whom he never saw again.

Disarmed in Morocco

While André's soldiering was idiosyncratic throughout his military career, it became especially so in Morocco. There he became serious about being the unarmed soldier. When he entered the Geodesic Brigade, he was issued a rifle and 250 rounds of ammunition. None of his armament had ever been readied for use. It went along with him to Morocco, however, because the Geodesic Brigade's assignment involved working in a potentially dangerous area, protected only by their own rifles and a handful of policemen from French-controlled cities.

To make sure they were in good shape to defend themselves should the need arise, their commanding officer one day called for a full inspection of their weapons and equipment before their departure for the Bled, as the desert area was called. Now André had to make a major decision. Having a rifle in France was not a problem, because the need to use it was virtually certain not to arise, but in the Bled, who knew? There were rebellious tribal groups out there, some of them already preparing for a military confrontation with French forces.

The morning for inspection came and went, and André decided he had only one recourse. Regulations called for soldiers to deposit any unused weapons in the armory and to take a receipt for use when they wanted to retrieve them. So he greased and oiled his rifle, wrapped it up in cloths bound with surgical tape, and took it to the sergeant in charge of the armory. Since no one asked his reasons for making the deposit, he did not offer any. He just returned to his barracks, gathered up his belongings, and set off with his mapping team into the Bled.

All went well for a few weeks, but eventually the brigade was about to cross an invisible border between an area secured by French forces and an area that still belonged to the Berber tribesmen. Lieutenant Tardy warned his men that they might meet an ambush here. He needed them to be ready, and he needed them to bring out their rifles for inspection. When he got to the end of the file, there was Corporal Trocmé, empty-handed. An incredulous officer quizzed his inscrutable corporal:

> "Weren't you issued a rifle when you left France?"
> "Yes sir, I was."
> "Was it stolen from you?"
> "No sir. I left it in the armory in Rabat and here is my receipt."
> "You are completely nuts!"

"Yes sir, ... but I just can't envisage killing anyone. I am a Protestant theology student and I try to behave as a Christian. How do you expect me to preach God's and Christ's law to my future parishioners if my own hands are stained with blood?"

"Trocmé, I simply don't understand. Weren't you a volunteer for this mission in Morocco?"

"Yes I was, Lieutenant."

"Your scruples are honorable and demand respect [but] should we be attacked tomorrow, the absence of a single rifle could make a big difference in the end result of the battle. If every one of us reasoned the way you do, we would be massacred in no time at all."

"I understand, Lieutenant."

"A refusal of obedience in front of the enemy means an instantaneous court martial and an immediate execution by a firing squad ... do you understand this?"

"Yes sir, I do."

"I should condemn you to a long jail sentence and send you back to Rabat in handcuffs [but] I can't do that because I need all of my men, ... I tell you what. I will ignore your case for the time being. I don't give a damn whether you have a rifle or not as long as we are not attacked but, should we be ambushed, and should I order my men to fire their weapons in self defense, and should you not execute my orders for any kind of reason, you will be court-martialed and only God knows what will happen to you after that. Is this understood?"

"Yes sir." (86–87)

André thought to himself that his commanding officer was right, of course, so he forthwith made two vows to himself, one that next time he was drafted he would refuse induction, and the other that he would now pray especially earnestly that they would not meet an ambush.

Fortunately, or providentially, they were only attacked once, but it was during the night and they were able to take cover behind a stone wall until the firing stopped. They completed their assignment, returned to the coast and caught the boat for France.

A final bizarre episode happened after they arrived back in Paris. André's home unit, the Fifty-fourth Regiment, had been dissolved and their barracks taken over by a battalion of Air Force balloonists. André spent several days trying to find someone who would discharge him from the army, but the more they searched for his records, the clearer it was that he had simply disappeared from bureaucratic view.

Finally, after weeks of fruitless searching for his former commanding officer, or anyone else who could discharge him, he wandered into an office in the balloonists' quarters and found a sergeant asleep at his desk. He told his story to the sergeant who, like everyone else, said there wasn't a thing he could do, but he finally relented and put the battalion's rubber stamp on a paper that said Trocmé was discharged from an arm of the military he had never been in! So completely had he disappeared that he never heard again from the army, not even for the periodic requirement that discharged soldiers received to report for summer training.

The Tortuous Twenties

France took special pride in being an armed nation, always at the ready to respond to a threat from Germany, but the Great War had seriously eroded this pride. The special horror of the killing fields at Verdun and the Somme River had cost the combatant armies over two million lives. By the end of the war a generation had been utterly decimated. When the hostilities were over, the surge of patriotism, which at the outset had energized both the career military and the civilian conscripts, gave way to a disgust and cynicism that sapped war of its glory. The nations honored their dead and mutilated, but few of the survivors could any longer honor the deadly dance of war itself.

In the decade of the twenties, France's pride in being an armed nation was still being reinforced in the language and initiatives of its government, but it was being rendered suspect by many of its most literate citizens. The defeat of Germany had been decisive and total, but both the German and the French economies were now in shreds and their political structures under heavy stress. By the time Trocmé finished his tour of duty, it was already clear that the Treaty of Versailles had not simply harvested the fruits of victory; it had also cast the seed of the next world war.

The summer of Trocmé's demobilization, 1923, was the summer when a lonely, ambitious Adolf Hitler used his political power as the leader of the National Socialist German Workers Party to attempt a seizure of national power. He succeeded quickly, and in his new role cultivated the passion for war as a source of heroic virtues.

In Germany as well as France, the impact of the war experience was everywhere. It transformed the works of the artists and the lyrics of the poets and gave rise to a new literature about war. It also gave an enduring voice to the struggle for a lasting peace.

A new generation of French writers had direct experience of the Great War and its grinding erosion of a generation of the French population. They took the human debacle of 1914–18 as a central theme. Of the 8.9 million Frenchmen mobilized, sixty percent had been killed or wounded, a rate of destruction far larger than in any other of the nations involved in the hostilities. Their consuming theme was no longer patriotism, glory, and national honor, but the absolute horror of war's devastation (Rasson 1990, 11–15).

Like any other French intellectual, Trocmé could not avoid this torrent of vivid writings that turned to the battlefields and trenches for a raw new look at the human experience in general. The novelist Romain Rolland had published his *Above the Fray* (Rolland 1915), and later his *Journal of the War Years: 1914–1918*. Both got wide attention in France and throughout Europe. Henri Barbusse published his novel *Under Fire* in 1915. It brought the foot soldiers' experience to life in graphic imagery. The composer Camille Saint-Saëns asked, "After the massacres of women and children, how can one find French people who will listen to Wagner?" (Rasson 1997, 62).

For Trocmé, the issues of his post-military life were narrower and more personal than the grander scale of new international conflict in the making, but the question of pacifism was still a central agenda. Because his outlook and expectations had changed, André was now less committed to flawless performance in his studies than he had been during his days as the dutiful and brilliant lycée student. Now he and a number of his fellow theological students were more committed than ever to searching actively for alternatives to violence as a means of resolving social conflicts. Their public witness to the Christian life could only be one that moved beyond theological systems and critical analysis of the Bible to address the claim of pacifism on their vocations.

A Christian Face of Pacifism

All these young theologians were teenagers during the Great War, although not all of them were eyewitnesses to its horrors in the same degree as André Trocmé. They were also sorting out their own vocations against a complex backdrop of religious and secular understandings of pacifism and conscientious objection. While they might share a hope for peace and justice with the Communist and Socialist party members, their definitions of the issues were overlapping in some places and contrary in others. One of their greatest challenges, therefore, was to give a distinctly Christian profile to their pacifism.

The earliest Christians had been an aberrant cluster of religious people who routinely refused, as a tenet of their faith, to give their ultimate loyalty to the Roman emperor and their bodies to his armies. But now pacifism had as many voices as it had political and social centers of loyalty. In the French mode of classifying and analyzing, the term "integral (i.e., whole or pure) pacifism" was coined to describe those forms that arose from the roots of personal and religious conscience (Faruggia 1992, 286). "Instrumental pacifism" was the term applied to convictions that were political in origin and intent and subject to amendment depending on the strategic circumstance. It might still be regarded as pacifism, but the latter term recognized that when pacifism was bent to political purpose, it was susceptible to compromise and corruption.

The official position of the Communist Party, for example, was antiwar, but the platform on which it was erected was a political one. The Party was against wars mounted by the Right against the Left, but favored revolutions of the Left against the Right. The Spanish Civil War would make that abundantly clear. The Party's stand against killing was not rooted in irrevocable principle. It was strategic: thou shalt not kill when required to do so by a morally illicit government, but thou shalt kill when it is the clear avenue to justice.

If he were to thread his way through these fundamental issues, André needed more than ever to be fully independent from his father and the family network. Fortunately, that independence came as a side effect of postwar reconstruction in his home city. The summer he was discharged from the army his father gave up the apartment in Paris and moved back to St. Quentin to put his life together. His only asset was the now-restored house on the Boulevard Gambetta. The family's lace factory had been sacked by the German military, which took all its weaving machinery with them when they fled to Germany. It was Robert's job to go to Germany, find the machinery, and bring it back to the factory.

For André, however, it was not a matter of reconstructing a past life. The question now was how to piece together his future life. The army experience had taught him something he wanted to know but was very uncomfortable knowing. He had left his theological studies to find out more about the population he felt increasingly drawn to serve. Now, on his return to civilian life, he understood some of the answers.

For one thing, his family background was still in charge of a lot of his perceptions. He was still not able to view his fellow soldiers outside the grid of his experience growing up in the upper social ranks of Protestantism. In his memoir he made this particularly revealing observation: "My fellow-soldiers were not necessarily bad. They simply were coarse, gross and vulgar" (A. Trocmé 1953, 159). It was a sentiment felt like a renegade, but spoken like a patrician. A class war was still going on inside his head and his heart. He continued to look at his own family in action as an observer with an axe to grind. Why were these people so intransigently self-satisfied? Why did they consume their conscious life with petty gossip, with attachments to style and comfort, all the while making their church the arbiter and the guarantor of their privilege? Nothing quite squared with his experience as a religious enthusiast, the one who only a few years before had felt light shining around him and a fire burning in his soul. He put the dilemma plainly: "I could not reconcile the experience I had of the world at large, the army, and the street with that of the church of Christ, the Christian Union in Clamart, and the Theological Seminary" (170).

This inability to reconcile his experiences of the church and the world would remain throughout his life, and would create a severe rift between him and the inner councils of the Église Réformée de France (ÉRF).

Pacifism Becomes Inescapable

With no more rue Jacob apartment, he had to move into the dormitory at the university. It turned out to be a better move than he imagined. That was where the late-night discussions and the testing of one's self against peers took place. It was also the place where he made friends who would have a great impact on his career in the ministry. In their separate ways, each one drove him increasingly toward identifying himself as a pacifist with politically radical leanings.

Four of those friends stood out, each one representing one of the several faces of pacifism at that stage in French history. Jacques Martin was a brilliant member of the ÉRF and was the co-founder with Henri Roser of *Cahiers de la Réconciliation,* the journal of the MIR. Martin was an outspoken proponent of pacifism and had refused conscription for military service, and so was never ordained until very late in his life.

Martin's refusal to serve in the army brought him at least three arrests and three jail terms. The first two convictions, in the early thirties, carried one-year jail terms. The third became the stuff of legend. He was arrested by the Vichy regime's police force in 1944, presumably because of his participation in the Résistance. In fact, he had withdrawn from active involvement in the Résistance by that time, having concluded that there was no place for nonviolent action in its mission. Instead, he had turned his attention to work with refugees.

When he was arrested, it was his friends and former colleagues in the Résistance who came to his rescue and negotiated with the police for his release. They offered 1,000 sheep for his release, and the deal was accepted (Faruggia 1992, 281).

A second friendship grew up with Henri Roser, a person who later led André to a more formal and explicit role in the International Fellowship of Reconciliation (IFOR). Roser was two years André's senior and had finished his term in the army just as André began his. When Roser was discharged, he returned to his theological studies, swearing that he would never again take up arms. It made an impact on André's thinking about pacifism when, in the winter of 1922–23, Roser sent back all his military papers, including his discharge, together with a letter explaining his reasons for doing so. He was under the care of the Missionary Society of the church, and it had responsibility for oversight of his theological education. His action caused the Society such embarrassment that they excluded him from their company, which meant he could not continue his studies. He remained in Paris to run the French office of the IFOR until he was finally allowed to continue his studies at another theological faculty in faraway Montpellier (Faruggia 1992, 286).

The face of pacifism that showed in Roser's life was that of absolute refusal to participate in or cooperate with the military requirements of his government in any manner. If there were a separate category for absolute or "integral" pacifists, Roser would have been a prime member. He had already drawn significant attention for his pacifist activities when he joined in a gathering of fifty pacifists from ten nations at Bilthoven in Holland. That meeting in 1919 gave rise to the formation of the IFOR, and Roser became its French representative.

A third classmate was one Trocmé knew less well, although he was another committed and active pacifist. He was Edouard Theis, a man who, like Roser, was two years older than Trocmé, and whom Trocmé describes as "a day student who kept silent, who was huge and who, from time to time briskly exploded with indignation. We were all paralyzed. He excelled in his studies and we all, to some extent, feared him" (A. Trocmé 1953, 203).

Theis had also served in the army, but in a role that did not require him to bear arms. Like Trocmé, he had enlisted for service ahead of the date he would be drafted, and was attached to a health unit posted to the Dardanelles Strait area of Turkey. Theis would play a very large role in Trocmé's life during the thirties and forties, when they were co-pastors of the church in Le Chambon-sur-Lignon. He also became co-founder and first director of the school that Magda and André put together. The face of pacifism represented by Theis was that of a conscience-driven individual whose conscientious objection derived directly from his faith and admitted of no compromise.

The fourth of this foursome was Arnold Brémond, a young Swiss idealist who presented yet another face of pacifism: the idealist who linked his convictions about violence to his concern for the workers and the poor. During his final year of theological study he got a job in a factory in Ivry, lived there among the workers' families, and became the first blue-collar parson to give impetus to the "worker-priest movement" that brought Catholic and Protestant clergy into a rare instance of ecumenical ministry.

Brémond had sent word to his father in Switzerland asking that he cease sending funds for his studies since he was now supporting himself by his factory job. He was also able to set aside something from his meager factory wages for a 1926 trip to India to spend time studying the work of Mohandas Gandhi and Rabinandrath Tagore, the men chiefly responsible for the nonviolent resistance that brought an end to British imperial rule of the sub-continent. He invited André to join him on the trip, and that became André's plan for the year following his studies at New York's Union Theological Seminary.

Sorting out just what it meant to be a pacifist was not easy. The word "pacifist" had not entered the common language until the period running up to the Great War. The term made its first appearance in the *Dictionnaire de la langue français* in 1845, but the first major publication about pacifism did not appear on French bookshelves until 1908. It was Emile Faguet's *Le Pacifisme,* written for the purpose of excoriating the movement. By then it was a term widely used to condemn those who took the position, chiefly the social idealists of the international labor movements who were so bitterly opposed to capitalism and capitalists.

André's church leaders tended, officially at least, to classify Christian pacifists with all other pacifists, whether religious or secular, and to regard them all as defeatists, or worse as traitors. He had no real option but to accept the label.

It was only a question of which manner for resisting war would be his model, Martin's nonviolent public service, Roser's absolutism, Brémond's identification with the industrial poor, or Theis's and his own attempt to accept an unarmed responsibility in the military. Theis's option was already ruled out, both by Trocmé and Theis himself, and in both cases by their personal experience in the military. For both, it had cemented their hatred of the inescapable military values that blessed and glorified violence.

In the end, Trocmé incorporated all four models into his ministry and into his characteristic responses to events. Martin's nonviolent forms of resistance to war and injustice appeared again and again, as did Roser's absolutist mentality. Trocmé brought such absolutism to his own temptations to compromise any core moral commitments. Like Brémond, he took the situation of the industrial worker very seriously, although the real formation of Trocmé's ministry took place in Le Chambon, where the bulk of his parishioners were rural rather than industrial workers. Like Theis, he remained a conscientious objector, although both men were spared conscription during World War II because of the number of their children, Theis's eight and Trocmé's four.

There were a few other university classmates in this circle of pacifist friends, including the two Vernier brothers, Philo (Philippe) and Piot (Pierre), both of whom would serve years of imprisonment for their pacifist convictions.

A Badge of Honor

Prison terms became a kind of badge of honor among the leading Christian pacifists of the era, a badge that neither Theis nor Trocmé would wear, since neither had been jailed for their beliefs. But Jacques Martin, the Vernier brothers, and Henri Roser—all had served time in jail.

When the German invasion of France began, the Vernier brothers were both in jail. As the German troops approached Paris, confusion was everywhere, not least in the jail system. The guards feared what would happen to them under a German occupation, and in their panic, simply opened the lockups and fled, leaving the prisoners to fend for themselves. Philo and Piot fled their jail and headed south, hoping to gain shelter in Le Chambon until they could design their next move. Nelly Trocmé recalls Piot's arrival at the presbytère mounted on a junior-sized bicycle he had found. It had no handlebar, so Piot fashioned a substitute out of a broom handle, and on this rude vehicle he had made the longest and most uncomfortable bike ride of his life.

Trocmé saw in the arrival of his friends the promise of putting them to work in Le Chambon, providing him with support in the effort to create the City of Refuge. That was not to be, however. They were both utterly exhausted and both still at risk of being jailed, this time by the Pétain government. They needed to keep a very low profile.

A particularly ironic sidelight to the imprisoned pacifists' story came to light later, when they discovered that a clause in the Armistice agreement with the Germans required the French to release any French prisoners who had supported Hitler's cause. In the foolish consistency of the German military bureaucracy, their authorities listed conscientious objectors among the groups supporting Hitler's regime! It seemed not to matter whether those pacifists were members of Communist, Socialist, or Christian communities or whether they had openly opposed all that Hitler represented. It was enough that they refused to serve in the French army. When André discovered that fact after the war, he despaired that neither their friends nor their enemies really understood what pacifists were about.

As close as these pacifist classmates were in seminary and in the decade leading up to the Second World War, that badge of imprisonment became more of an issue among them after the war years. Ultimately, it was imprisonment for being a pacifist that distinguished Martin, Roser, and the Vernier brothers from their friend and colleague, an increasingly sore point as Trocmé became the more publicly celebrated personality. In one case at least, it led to a particularly puzzling and painful rupture of an enduring friendship with the Rosers.

One of the ironies of social radicalism is the tendency for its adherents to judge themselves and each other by absolute standards. Every point where their behavior falls short of perfect adherence to those standards tends to become an occasion of guilt or judgment, guilt when the radical makes a compromise and judgment when a fellow radical fails to meet the standard. It is only one of the reasons that radical communities so often fall apart and lose their capacity to bring about the social change they espouse.

It was hard for his pacifist friends to forget that Trocmé had enlisted in the army voluntarily, that he had been promoted to corporal and had been assigned the role of instructor. "I hated being an instructor in the army," he wrote, "especially when recruits were taught how to fight hand to hand with bayonets, how to trip the adversary down to the ground and pierce him with the blade and, finally how to press on his chest with a foot to pull the bayonet out of his corpse. I was shocked by the excited gleam in the recruits' eyes when they imagined they were in combat, drawing real blood" (173).

Whatever others might think, it was clear that there was no one right way to be a pacifist. Since Trocmé would never become a single-issue person, he might always be a renegade, but he would never quite fit the conventional image of a political radical.

8
The Turnaround Year

In 1925 both Magda and André left for New York, Magda in August and André in September. Both were searching and escaping: searching for wider dimensions to their intended careers and escaping from the family and the cultural constraints that constricted their future. Neither one was ready to comply with conventional expectations.

Two People on the Run

André was on his way to New York because he had won a scholarship to Union Theological Seminary. He took it, but without great enthusiasm. It was actually a third choice. His first was archeological study in the Near East, but he lost out on that scholarship when a classmate with astounding linguistic skills got the award. His description of the winner suggests that he had observed him very closely: "André Parrot was a young man with a stern face, angular cheek bones and pursed lips. He seldom left his room where he spent days bending over little slips of paper no larger than playing cards. . . . He was an ace in Hebrew, Syriac, Greek and in everything else. It was therefore impossible for me to disagree with his having been chosen" (A. Trocmé 1953, 207).

André knew almost nothing about America and had a Parisian's view of American education (a little sloppy around the edges compared to the Sorbonne). He would rather have gone to Edinburgh to study with eminent Scots, but he had lost out on that competition as well. Nonetheless, he found that Union had a strong faculty, including a few men of international reputation, and he thought New York might be an interesting

12. André Trocmé, 1925.
Unknown photographer.

place to explore. Little did he know that New York would provide a benefit much more important than another degree.

If he seemed a little diffident about choosing where he would go, escape was about as important as the search. More study was fine, but study abroad was a way of breaking the chrysalis and learning to fly on his own. It was all part of being late to mature.

He began to understand the stages of his own maturing. He was somewhat less focused on his studies than he had been during his lycée years in Paris. He had enlisted in the military to see how the other half lived and found what he thought he would: that life has to be about more than academic success and social standing. It was clear to him that everything bourgeois irritated him. That did not endear him to his sisters-in-law, of course. They were upper echelon bourgeois and treasured being there.

Perhaps most important, he had accepted the scholarship at Union Seminary in spite of the fact that his father did not approve of his decision.

For the first time, Paul Trocmé showed a side of himself that was unfamiliar: in spite of his emotionally cramped relation to André, he was very much invested in his "Benjamin,"[1] his promising youngest son. André realized now that this was the reason Paul could not share his son's enthusiasm about the catalogues of these foreign universities.

Paul wanted André to move directly into the ministry, take a parish, settle down in northern France, and begin climbing the ecclesiastical ladder. Paul was still the lay president of the Église Réformée Évangélique. Why would he not expect André to work up to a distinguished post in a prestigious church? Why would his son want to study a continent away?

Magda's reasons for wanting to leave Italy had been accumulating steadily as she matured. Lots of things contributed to her restiveness: her conflicted relationship with Italian Catholicism, her dysfunctional family, her effort to establish an independent professional life in a country not accustomed to extending professional independence to women. And then there was her relationship with an eligible young bachelor who wanted very much to marry her, even though he could not understand why she would never become an active and observant Catholic. All those things were strands of the noose she felt tightening around her future.

Without planning it, she stumbled into her opportunity. Her friend Aimée Jalla worked for the YMCA in Florence and drew Magda into some of its social work projects, an opportunity that fit with Magda's experience and career plans. It was Aimée who mentioned the New York School of Social Work as an excellent place to train, one that would also get Magda some of the international experience she hoped for.

Then came Miss Wilcox, an American woman studying and traveling in Florence for the year. Miss Wilcox needed to find a language tutor who would also be an acceptable travel companion as she drove to the museums and to her mountain-climbing expeditions. It was a pleasant

---

1. The reference is to the Israelite Benjamin, youngest son of Jacob and Rachel, whose tribe were forerunners of the Jewish people. Paul Trocmé was fond of using this reference in his letters to André, whom he spoke of as "my Benjamin."

13. Magda Trocmé, 1925. Unknown photographer.

assignment for Magda and provided her with income she very much needed as she worked to finish her degree at the *Magistero*, one of the two most competitive universities in Italy at the time.

The assignment brought her another benefit she had not anticipated. When Miss Wilcox learned of Magda's intention to do graduate study in social work, she invited her to continue her tutoring on shipboard as she returned to America at the end of the year. By this time, Magda had already been accepted into the New York School of Social Work, but she had no idea how she would get there. This whole adventure was typical of Magda. She was as good at creating opportunities as she was at seizing them when they appeared.

Magda was also in flight from the limitations she saw threatening her own aspirations. She needed to get away, at least for a year or so, from her persistent suitor who could not seem to understand why she should have a mind of her own and be unwilling to bring up children in the Catholic Church. John Falkenberg was a handsome young bachelor with a promising career in the American Express firm in Florence. He came from a distinguished Belgian Catholic family, had a good university education, spoke five languages, and, more to the point, was totally bewitched by Magda.

She was flattered by his attention and appreciative of his kindness, but she foresaw a birdcage life as wife and mother if she were to marry him. A busy life committed to helping the poorest and neediest of her fellow human beings was infinitely more appealing.

Both André and Magda were looking for freedom to make their own decisions about their life's work and to do so on their own terms. Magda was clearer about those terms than André, in fact. Since Grand-Maman Wissotsky's death, she had become increasingly resentful of the restraints that bounded her life. She had no rich emotional sharing with her father. He found shows of emotion irritating, even when he found Magda crying at her grandmother's funeral. Her stepmother, Marguerite, was resentful and jealous of any attention that Oscar Grilli showed her, and of the social work training that brought Magda into conflict with the family's cultural attitudes.

When she worked in a program for unwed mothers, she was disillusioned by the attitudes of those who staffed the program. Their clients were regarded as sexual miscreants, wayward women reaping the shameful consequence of their own decadence. Everywhere, it seemed, she felt surrounded by the moralistic darker side of Catholicism. It was not her way of thinking about people in emotional and social need. She needed to be unburdened of all that and its reputation as an open society made America sound like much the better place to learn to practice her trade.

André's search had more to do with choosing his identity. He had tried to shape himself by moral absolutes, but they were not enough. They only told him what he must not do, not who he must become. Since his return from the military, it had become much more important to know what he would embrace than to be clear about what he must avoid.

He had long admired Mohandas Gandhi, and he still had the invitation from his friend Arnold Brémond to accompany him to India that next summer. Was he going to follow Gandhi and become a penniless spiritual leader? Better to be penniless than bourgeois, after all. Or was he going to become a stalwart witness to pacifism, a leader with nonviolent reform as his craft? Poverty or peace? It was hard to imagine living for both. Gandhi, after all, was a very particular combination of moral resolve and historical accident, a combination not possible to re-create by a simple act of will. This was a dilemma André carried around but could not resolve—not yet, at least.

A Taste of Gentility

Once settled in his new academic environment, André's dilemma was compounded when he received a surprise phone call from a man with a world-famous name. "I am Mr. John D. Rockefeller Jr., 10 West 54th Street, and I need a French tutor for my sons. I was impressed with the young Frenchmen who lived with us before, so should you be interested, would you please come and meet Mrs. Rockefeller?" (217–47).

One of those young Frenchmen was his Paris classmate, Edouard Theis, the man who later was his companion and colleague for many years in Le Chambon. Yes, he would be interested, so he made an appointment. The following paragraphs are excerpts from a longer narrative about his year with the Rockefeller family. They are remarkable in many ways, not least in their detailed accounts of elements of family life, details that square with those recounted by David Rockefeller in the first four chapters of his *Memoirs* (Rockefeller 2003, 26–44).

> I entered a little reception room on the ground floor where I was asked and answered a few questions before a butler came and led me to the elevator. . . . I was in the home of John D. Rockefeller Jr., the only son of the founder of the Standard Oil Company, John D. Rockefeller Sr., who was said to be the wealthiest man on the planet. . . . He lived half-hidden from the outside world while his son managed to make people forget about the origin of the family fortune by creating foundations and making several generous donations. . . .
>
> Mrs. Rockefeller, a descendant of the old Aldrich family of Boston, was approximately fifty years old. Her gentle and kind smile was spoiled

by a pointed nose, which was out of proportion with the rest of her face, but she was much more intelligent and cultured than her husband. [For André, beauty began with symmetry. He noticed when it was lacking.]

Mrs. Rockefeller described what our obligations would be. I was to fetch her two youngest sons, Winthrop and David, each day, at 4:00 PM, at the Lincoln School, north of Central Park and bring them back home by bus. I would then share their afternoon tea and their dinner if I wanted to, but I could also choose to be on my own from 6:30 PM on.

On Friday nights I was to ride the train along the Hudson River to Tarrytown, where the family's country estate was located. I was to spend the night there as well as the entire day on Saturday before coming back to New York City in the evening, by car, with the family. I was to be free on Sundays.

She hired me for 175 dollars a month. This meant wealth to me and I immediately opened a savings account. A marvelous project was born in my mind: after eight months, I could travel around the world with the 1,400 dollars I would save, and visit with Tagore and Gandhi in India and thus find the answers to the many questions which still preoccupied my mind.

The Rockefeller parents tried to hide from their sons the amount of the immense fortune they would inherit someday, just like the parents of Gautama Buddha tried to hide illness, old age, and death from their son. They each received each week a limited amount of money with which they had to buy their books, school supplies, Kodak film and the other things they might be tempted by. My pupils enjoyed intensely their privileged situation in spite of all of their parents' precautions. They knew that someday all the pleasures would be within their reach: cars, luxurious homes, estates, ranches, boats, art works, paintings, and exotic trips.

Such excess of wealth did create, in my pupils' minds, a particular attitude. They knew that everything was . . . or would someday be at their disposal and the result was that they didn't have any strong desires (except perhaps David's desire for a leather briefcase). In fact, they were totally blasé before they reached their twentieth birthday. I felt they were bored and that they didn't work hard because they already knew they would never have to work hard. It isn't good, at age 15, to already possess, as Laurence did, the most sophisticated professional photographic equipment available.

Mr. and Mrs. Rockefeller were right to teach their children that they didn't come from genes that were different from the genes of the rest of humanity. This was true when one knew that their great grandfather was a village quack and that their wealthy grandfather, John D. Sr., had started his career sweeping the floor in an office building. . . .

Old John D. Sr., the founder of the dynasty, was very old but still very much alive. . . . As he always did with newcomers he inquired about my name, my age, my profession, and my nationality. "So you are from France," he said. "You Frenchmen don't pay your debts. I always paid off my debts. Young man, if you want to get rich, you must learn to pay off your debts. I am going to do something for you. Here is a dime." He searched for a ten-cent coin in a little velvet purse he had in his pocket and showed it to me. "Promise you will invest this money as soon as you are back home." I promised and he gave me the dime. "It is the way I started in life, and I became rich," he added.

He then inquired about my parents. "My father is still alive," I said. He searched in his purse again and gave me a dime for my father. "Do you have brothers and sisters?"

"Seven," I replied, full of pride.

"That's too much," he declared, "you would make me bankrupt."

Later, to my great surprise, I was asked to accompany Laurence to Florida during Christmas vacation . . . I remember Christmas Eve in Ormond Beach. John D. Sr. wore a golden cardboard crown on his head and he nervously unpacked his many presents with trembling hands, like a child would. After dinner, the governess sat at the grand piano and played while the billionaire, standing next to her, sang Baptist carols in his goat-like voice. He had tears in his eyes because he was very pious and moved.

It is in this strange and surrealistic atmosphere that I lived the last days of 1925. I pinched myself, from time to time, to make sure that I truly was André Trocmé, a theology student from France, who, not long before, slept under a tent in primitive Morocco, shared the life of nomads and was now living with millionaires. (A. Trocmé 1953, 222–27)

Sentimental Stirrings

During the Christmas recess of 1925, André found emotions stirring in him, feelings he had always dismissed as obstacles to his goal of living in poverty and taking on Gandhi's way of life. Sunday was his own. He was free from the Rockefeller regime, and it was during that time alone that he sensed something happening not of his own choice.

> On Sundays, I sometimes gave myself the time to go to the movies alone. The films were silent, sometimes funny with Harold Lloyd or sentimental with a happy end. The moving expressions, in the actresses' eyes, did, however, become engraved in my mind and I slowly started dreaming about the happiness a man can find and feel by being in love with a woman, provided she was beautiful, intelligent and good hearted.
>
> Father, I said to myself, wants her to be warm-hearted, pious and accessorily pretty and intelligent. He claimed that beauty was not important. I, André, like beauty and I can only fall in love with beauty.
>
> My equilibrium was not only disturbed for sentimental reasons. My future was also at stake and the Rockefellers were inquiring about my plans for 1926–27. They had suggested they would appreciate it if I stayed one more year with them. I would easily be granted another scholarship and work toward a PhD (230–31).

It was a very tempting proposal, but one that put him again at cross-purposes with his father. Paul wanted him back home, serving a church in one of the mining towns of northern France. That was clearly more in keeping with his self-understanding than another year with the Rockefellers.

His sense of himself was closely tied to finding a non-bourgeois path for his career. His internal compass needle quivered away from New York and toward the east, where he knew he had to find some accommodation between Paul Trocmé's plan and his own desire to explore the lifestyle of Mohandas Gandhi. As much as he liked the Rockefeller boys and as much as it would have been a comfortable and convenient way to support a PhD program, it was no way to find out how he could serve a God whose claims were more demanding than his father's.

Ironically, his life would be fundamentally changed during the next few months, and so would his plans for the academic year 1926–27. Those sentimental awakenings that he experienced during that Christmas season had caused some ripples. He still thought that he must remain sexually pure, but just what that meant was a lot less clear by the spring of 1926. His other moral obsessions had followed him to New York. The questions of poverty and peace and alcohol abuse and sexual purity all had different dynamics and made different demands, but they had one common thread: each one served as a counterfoil to things he feared most about his own life out in the world.

As a youngster in Brussels and later as a soldier he had seen people turned brutal by lust, made slaves to alcohol, corrupted by money, and destroyed by their own violence. He wanted no part of any of it, and he was just short enough of self-confidence to fear that a life lived in the swirling eddies of the Rockefellers might open one of those destructive possibilities for him. What he lacked in self-confidence he was again trying to make up by sure-footed piety and severe self-discipline.

As he set out to return to France at the end of the summer of 1926, he acknowledged feeling great regret that he had not accepted the Rockefellers' request that he spend one more year as the boys' tutor while pursuing a doctoral program at Union Seminary. Nonetheless, the Rockefeller appeal was no match for the force of his underlying convictions and his discovery of Magda.

An Easter to Remember

Because he was born on Pâques (Easter Sunday), André's middle name was Pascal. Now he had come to the turning point of his life at Easter. A few days before Easter, he just happened to sit at a table with Magda in the International House cafeteria. The happenstance had been carefully orchestrated by a friend who thought those two should get acquainted. In their separate memoirs, written many years apart, both André and Magda remember the maneuver, but differ about who was the victim of the setup. Maybe they both were. No matter; the meeting took place and the conversation was confined to the minimum amenities of two people accidentally seated at the same cafeteria table. André did come away from that lunch table with a very clear impression, however. Three or four decades later, he wrote, "I don't remember whether she was pretty but I found her to be understanding, straight, simple, and intelligent. . . . Things were quite different, a few days later. There was a party at International House and I sat in the theater. My eyes were attracted by an animated group of young ladies who were chatting on the second floor balcony, on the left side of the stage. One of them stood in the center of the group. She was more beautiful than the others. Her face was harmonious, her forehead luminous and her eyes were dark and magnificent. She laughed and the sound of her laughter rang marvelously in my ears" (233). Whatever the elixir that had been served him in the cafeteria, it had an effect on his memory. Decades later he could recall every detail.

Their conversation continued on an Easter weekend trip to Washington, organized by the Cosmopolitan Club for students from the International House. On the train, he again noticed "the Italian," as he referred to her. He became very aware of this stunning woman, but would never have considered approaching her to launch any kind of relationship. His celibate thinking was still in place.

André recalled one conversation with particular clarity. It took place that Saturday evening, when they sat with a group of friends who were having a picnic in a shelter next to Potomac Falls. Magda spoke about her Decembrist revolutionary heritage and her unease with organized religion in general. But André was listening with only one ear. With the other he heard his own mind saying, "She is the one! She is the one who will understand me. She longs for freedom and for truth, she is courageous and she abhors anything conventional" (236).

Magda remembered the conversation, but with a flash of embarrassment. As their exchanges on the Big Issues grew more animated, she realized that the group of friends had abandoned their own conversations and fallen silent, listening to theirs.

Easter morning, April 4, 1926, Magda discovered from a friend that "the Frenchman" had taken an early train back to New York. What she could not have known was that he was in full flight from his own feelings. The Pascal lamb had succumbed. Any thought ever entertained about a life of pious celibacy had vanished.

They did meet, awkwardly, two more times back in New York. Then the second Sunday after Easter he proposed that they take a picnic over to the Palisades across the Hudson River from Manhattan. Once into the picnic, his inimitably blunt style took over and he went to the heart of the matter: he proposed that she marry him. It was also his style to present the logic of his proposal, which he did—a little like the opening arguments in a debating society. He had thought the matter through very carefully and was convinced that they were made for each other. But Magda did not quite see why. She talked about the obstacles: her health, the chaotic history of marriage in her family background, and her lack of interest in theology. While she was an Italian Protestant, a rare species at the time, she carried the label uneasily. "I am indeed a Protestant because I was protesting more than the true Protestants. My religion was an expression of indignation" (M. Trocmé 1946, 106). She regarded herself as a most unlikely candidate for the role of the conventional minister's wife. But then, she was going to marry a most unconventional minister and would find in their marriage what she most wanted: "an open life, real work, some kind of revolution, a fight against the traditional and the sterile" (123).

André had an answer for every doubt, and his reasons were stronger than her doubts. When they took the ferry back to Manhattan, they were engaged. Now that they had discovered each other, they would have to figure out how it was all going to actually work.

They both wrote to their parents about their decision. Oscar Grilli responded by warning his daughter to be careful of Protestant ministers, and Paul Trocmé warned André to be careful of Italians. But it wasn't about ministers and Italians; it was about two people who recognized in each other their best hope of making sense of their lives.

Among their plans for the future was André's idea that they would meet Arnold Brémond in India and visit with Gandhi and Tagore. They wanted to learn how these remarkable men were using their nonviolent resistance to lead their nation away from war and the politics of brutality. Father Paul Trocmé put a stop to that idea, however, when he insisted that his son's ministry was needed in Northern France and that he must begin that work immediately after his return from the year in New York, especially now that he and Magda were to be married. He persuaded André to abandon the plan by giving him a guilty conscience, and did so with colorful imagery in a letter to André, written on July 3, 1926, and received just as André and Magda were preparing to leave New York for their wedding in St. Quentin. He wrote, "Brémond can give himself over to all these eccentricities . . . [because] he is a bachelor . . . but you, who are going to get married, who in 15 or 18 months will have a family to raise, you must not immerse your wife in that kind of bohemian life style. In doing so, you would . . . put your poor wife in a garret full of bedbugs and your children in a nasty and unhealthy place."

The letter had its intended effect. It put a crimp in André's aspiration to school himself further in nonviolence by traveling around the world and visiting with Gandhi en route. He opted, somewhat reluctantly, to begin his career in the ministry among the urban poor in the industrial cities of northern France. After all, Brémond's example had also included a ministry with factory workers in Ivry.

During the weeks these letters passed back and forth, André continued his duties with the Rockefeller boys and, when the occasion permitted, shared with Mrs. Rockefeller the good news of his engagement. She promptly got in touch with Miss Forsythe, the nurse at the International House, and inquired about this Italian girl, Magda Grilli. It was a carefully measured reference call. Miss Forsythe was forthcoming and gave Magda high marks on all scores except her health. Her long-standing problem of an elevated temperature persisted and was not being helped by Magda's incessant attention to studies and fieldwork assignments at the expense of eating and sleeping properly.

Mrs. Rockefeller took it from there. She invited Magda to join the family celebration of David's eleventh birthday and during the visit made a suggestion and an offer. She suggested that Magda should pay serious attention to entering married life in the best of health, and she offered to send her to an excellent spa in upstate Clifton Springs, New York, for several weeks of total rest. Magda accepted the offer and was very grateful to be given a legitimate reason for taking a leave from her studies.

Clifton Springs, it turned out, was a healing place but a boring one. She did not know what to do with a regimen of total rest. André's weekly visits were the only real bright spots of her stay. They had a chance to discuss their wedding plans, for one thing. They had wanted their own simple sort of wedding. In fact, they had already made arrangements to be married by a retired Methodist bishop under a tree near the Clifton

Springs Sanitarium. They had even gotten their license from the Town Clerk. But their little idyll was not to be. When Paul Trocmé's inopportune letter arrived, they learned he had made all the arrangements for the wedding, even extending an invitation to Oscar Grilli di Cortona to be his houseguest for the occasion. André was a Trocmé, and he simply could not marry a foreigner in a country foreign to them both. It was just too bizarre.

Magda's stay in the sanitarium turned out to be even longer than originally planned. The Rockefellers asked André if he would stay on through the summer and join the family retinue for an extended trip around the western United States. It would give Magda an even longer opportunity to gain weight and strength before they set out for France.

After the summer's travels with the Rockefeller family, André's duties as a French tutor-companion to young Laurence and David were finished. He and Magda prepared for the trip to Paris and the wedding in St. Quentin.

All the way across the Atlantic, André did his best to prepare Magda for the nest of Trocmés she was about to meet.

9

Real Church, Actual Church

Freedom and Obedience

Some days it felt very confining for André to be returning to the bosom of a family whose bourgeois values were the bars that had caged his freedom. He had not defined freedom as liberty from duty or anything of the sort. Alexandre Vinet, the man on whom his thesis was focused, had written a mandate that expressed André's vision: "I want a man to be a complete, spontaneous individual, in order that he may submit, as a man, to the general interest" (A. Vinet 1837, 178; see also A. Trocmé 1926, 42). It was André's dream to fulfill his calling by a life of voluntary poverty and service to the poor. By choosing the career of a minister in the Evangelical Reformed Church of the North, he had taken the first step.

All he wanted was a place where the "real" church would be visible in some actual church where he could be the minister. It seemed much more likely that he would find that combination in a blue-collar church than in a prosperous bourgeois church.

The salaries of Protestant ministers in those years were deliberately set very low, not because a bourgeois congregation could not afford more, but for fear that too much prosperity would breed spiritual corruption. An abstemious style of life was the only way to insure that it was obedience, not worldly ambition, that characterized the minister's life. Even if modesty could not be measured in money, immodesty could at least be tamed by the lack of money. It was a theory that sought to make marginal poverty into a virtue.

Another virtue was expected of ministers as they went about their work, the virtue of obedience to ecclesiastical authority. That expectation grew, in part, out of the understanding that a church body needs to present a full measure of unity in the claims it makes on society, especially when it represents only three percent of the national population. One of the church's functions was to serve as the conscience of society, a function that would be amply displayed and tested during the Second World War, just a few years ahead.

If conscience is the inborn will to do the right thing, then a church's mission must be to will the right thing when confronted with the ethical failures of the society. It is that need to bear witness together that gave rise to the expectation of obedience to church authority.

For the Église Réformée de France, church authority rests not on the single voice of a bishop but on a consensus of conscience among its ministers and lay leaders. For André's church, there was a strong expectation that its ministers would obey that consensus once it had been arrived at. Proper obedience and submission had long been enshrined as characteristic of the Christian life. There was not much room for non-conformity.

All this had special meaning for André. Obedience and submission were traits he found reinforced while writing his Union Seminary thesis on Alexandre Vinet. But obedience did not stand alone in Vinet's thinking. He linked it to liberty, saying, "For the Christian, submission is born of liberty. . . . Liberated from human fears, he makes freely all the sacrifices that are necessary to love. For the Christian, liberty is born from submission because, being submitted to God, he is the slave of no man, and even when he obeys a human order, he obeys God" (Vinet 1841, 308; quoted in A. Trocmé 1926, 32).

Having just affirmed Vinet's thinking in his thesis, how could he do anything but respond to his father's wedding plan with obedience? Maybe Paul Trocmé was right in worrying so much about his son's "enthusiasms." Maybe he was thinking that their plan to marry under a tree would lead to a rumor that André and Magda had to have a shotgun wedding, an inauspicious start to a career in the ministry. In any case, André was determined to get on with his life as now prescribed, setting aside any lingering hunger for what might have been.

By November of 1926, the question of freedom and obedience would show itself in the person of André's first supervisor in his first ministerial assignment: Pastor Jean Perret, the administrative supervisor of the little church in the parish of Maubeuge known as Sous-le-Bois.

Finding a Functional Family

Magda, too, had come to accept the Trocmé family's expectation that their marriage must take place on André's home ground, but her acceptance rested on very different and non-theological grounds. She had always described her family to André as dysfunctional. She longed for the vigor and energy and complexity of a real family with a shared history, and the Trocmé tribe was all of those things. She was apprehensive about meeting them, about the very strong role of her future father-in-law as head of the house. That was understandable. But being the strong and resilient person she was, her apprehension was hardly fear, just uncertainty about how she would be received.

When they arrived in Paris, Magda was a stranger to France, but one steeped in the French language. She was also a stranger to French Protestant culture, including its penchant for unflinching critiques of ideas and persons, an intellectual virtue long touted by French philosophers as the proper expression of reason. So she was taken aback when André's eldest brother, "Uncle" Francis, looked down through his trademark pince-nez and greeted her with, "You are not as plain as you are in the photographs."

14. Homes in St. Gobain and St. Quentin. Unknown photographer.

Later, when they arrived in St. Quentin, her new father-in-law was equally direct. As she got off the train, he looked at the modest design of her dark garnet dress, bought especially for this occasion, and said, "That's good! You wear long sleeves and you have long hair!" (M. Trocmé 1946, 134).

There followed a drive to the family's summer home in St. Gobain, where dinner was served, but only to Magda and André. The others had eaten promptly at 7:00 p.m., following the firm schedule of the household. Now they came back in and stood around the dining room, sizing up this new member of the tribe. It was all very bewildering.

Here is Magda's account of that first meal with the family:

> I was being stared at and I didn't know what to do or say. . . . I (also) didn't know what to say when huge artichokes were brought to the table. In Italy we only eat young artichokes and we eat nearly everything. This one was colossal and I didn't know how to tackle it. I watched André and saw he was tearing the leaves off with his fingers, dipping them in some sort of seasoning and I imitated him. I was truly shocked to see that people could eat like that, using their fingers. When I reached the [artichoke's] heart I saw a forest, a huge jungle of hairy stuff that I had never seen in Italy. Again I watched André and was relieved to see that he carefully removed this hair, which was obviously not edible, and left it on the plate. This was the vegetable course and, for the life of me, I can't remember what else I ate (135).

Several weeks would pass between that awkward dinner and the wedding. The French and the Italian bureaucracies had created a veritable jungle of documentary requirements that had to be met and their approvals awaited. But those weeks gave Magda a chance to become a true member of the family and to earn the affection and respect of her new father-in-law. As they became closer, Paul felt free to pass along his paternal advice to Magda, as he would have to one of his own children. The day came that he could say to her as he had said many times to André, "You know that I love you very much, but be careful, because you are both overly enthusiastic and this can become dangerous." She took it as it was meant, an expression of loving concern.

Once the wedding had finally taken place, André and Magda set off for a honeymoon trip to Italy, where Magda could introduce him to the glories of Florence and give him some sense of the cultural context in which she had grown up. Sadly, part of that context was her stepmother's enduring hostility to the daughter of the hauntingly beautiful Nelly Wissotsky Grilli. But a wise priest and confessor to Marguerite insisted that it was long past time to deal with these feelings properly and put them behind her. She did so and invited Magda to bring André to tea in the Grilli home. A measure of civility had finally colored her relationship with Magda.

Except for that difficult transition, the month in Italy was restorative and happy. For that month, they put aside all Paul Trocmé's cautions about being overly enthusiastic and did whatever their whimsy suggested on a given day. But this unencumbered freedom came to an end. Early in 1927 it was time to show up in northern France to begin their first year as minister and wife in an industrial town.

Sous-le-Bois and the Kitchen Meetings

When Magda first heard the name of their initial post, she wrote to an old friend in Florence to give her the new address: Number 1, rue de l'Hermitage, Sous-le-Bois. A note came back saying: "I can imagine your nice manse on Hermitage street, under the trees." The town's original name, "Under the trees," antedated the industrial revolution in France and was now a nostalgic malapropism. There were no longer any woods to be under. They had been replaced by the large, loud, ugly steel mills that spewed coal smoke over the region. Under-the-Trees had become Under-the-Smoke.

Sous-le-Bois was one of the several communities strung out on either side of the sixteen miles of steel mills, row houses, all in blackened brick, and uniformly depressed health conditions. The whole area was now under the smoke. To add to the disenchantment, the "nice manse" turned out to be what a friend and fellow minister, Christian Mazel, described as "pathetic."[1] The building was an abandoned tavern that had been slightly

---

1. Mazel's comment in an interview, May 2001.

converted to serve as a manse. There were no running water or bathing or toilet facilities in the house. Water was pumped by hand from a pump in the so-called garden, and the toilet consisted of a cramped little outhouse at the end of the back yard.

They found their new home filthy and in poor repair, so poor, in fact, that the back legs of André's desk chair went right through the worm-eaten flooring when he sat down in his study. They had opted for a simple life ministering to the working class, and here it was.

Although their housing was shockingly run-down, their congregation was rewarding. André had hoped, following the example of his Paris friend Arnold Brémond, to make his link with the factory worker community by taking a manual labor job in one of the steel mills, but no manager was interested. One of them said he would hire the head of the Communist Party rather than a Protestant minister.

They had cordial relationships among the steel mill workers anyway, in large part because their own simple life style enabled the workers to get past the rigid class divide that separated most laborers from most of the bourgeoisie. Education was the hallmark of that divide, most laborers having only an elementary education and most bourgeois having at least a lycée education. Their vocabulary was different, their slang was different, even their accents were different.

Three things enabled them to bridge the divide. One was the Croix Bleue, the early Temperance Union, another was what André called kitchen meetings, and the third was the local Socialist Party.

The Croix Bleue was a given in this district. Even the most conservative pastors recognized its usefulness. Alcohol had become, here as in other industrialized cities, a major problem, both because of the havoc it wrought with family budgets and because of the violence it unleashed in homes and neighborhoods. The fact that André had such a strong interest in, and was a member of, the Croix Bleue was taken by his pastoral colleagues as a strength he would bring to the ministry in these alcohol-impacted towns.

His parishioners also knew of his commitment to the Croix Bleue, and they went to him for help with family members who were being destroyed by alcohol. He had some success with helping workers' families shed the pain and the economic strain of alcohol addiction. The result was a large

15. Pastors of the Église du Nord. Unknown photographer.

measure of gratitude and admiration that linked him tightly to parts of the worker society.

The church at Sous-le-Bois was part of the Maubeuge parish, whose minister was Jean Perret. He was responsible for the character and mission of all the churches in his charge. From the reports of both André and Magda in their separate memoirs, he could be a compassionate friend and a severe, conventional, and demanding supervisor, all at the same time. The compassionate friend emerged when he and his wife talked to the Trocmés as fellow professionals and fellow members of the bourgeoisie. The severity surfaced whenever André proposed or explored new approaches for the ministry in his little satellite church community. It was as if Perret assumed that the minister's role with parishioners was to instruct and discipline the flock, to impose order on the natural chaos of his working class sheep.

André had other ideas on the matter. It was the summer of 1927; Pastor Perret was a Swiss and so had taken his two-month holiday in

Switzerland. This might be the time to nudge the restraints, poke around a bit, and find out what his flock needed and wanted from their minister.

His aim was to build a sense of community that rested on the hope and promise of the Gospel. But people who hope too much can begin to expect too much as well, and their expectations can upset the tranquility of the church. André did not see why that should keep him from exploring a new possibility. "The peace of the Church" was all too often invoked as a rebuke to new ideas and new initiatives. So André began what became known around Sous-le-Bois as the kitchen meetings.

He had a small meeting room in the presbytère, but he quickly found that the men parishioners always doffed their hats and acted submissive when in the presence of the minister in his own house. He also found that very few of his parishioners would ever come to share a meal with him and Magda. They were uncomfortable at table with those they considered their betters. By contrast, the little spontaneous neighborhood gatherings that happened in people's kitchens had an altogether different atmosphere. They were the place for relaxed conversations, some good humor, a little gossip, and a lot of friendship. And they were already happening.

André asked himself, "Why not have some conversations in the kitchen about the practical meaning of the promise and hope of the Gospel?" He made some visits to people's kitchen gatherings and found himself welcome. The atmosphere was quite different from those he called together in the presbytère. These little informal gatherings with the pastor gathered momentum. They moved from one home to another and the numbers in the room grew steadily. When the weather was right, some of them moved outside, where men passed by on their way home from the factories. Some of the men paused to see what the chatter was about and a few considered the idea of becoming Protestants. It seemed to them that Protestant talk was more down to earth, less shrouded in mystery.

Then Perret returned from his holiday to find something new going on, something that was not on his approved list of ministerial functions. He decided to attend one of the kitchen meetings and, of course, took over the conversation from André. The atmosphere quickly changed. The agenda went from listening to telling, from hopes of the spirit to sins of the flesh. As the atmosphere changed, so did the group in the room. Some were restive, others grumbled out loud, and an exodus began. After a few minutes, the only ones left in the room were the two ministers and a handful of the old faithful.

Perret felt vindicated. It just showed that initiatives like this never lasted, because these people were not serious about putting their lives together in a more respectable fashion. The kitchen meetings had been assassinated.

André's mind went back to Vinet: "I want a man to be a complete, spontaneous individual, in order that he may submit, as a man, to the general interest." Granted, he was not yet complete, but he was certainly spontaneous, and he was trying, at least, to submit to the general interest of his parishioners. What was he to make of Perrot's clumsy wrecking ball?

He heard again from Perret on one of the other explorations he made while his boss was on holiday. He had obeyed the church authority's injunction not to preach conscientious objection from the pulpit, but word had gotten around town that he was, in fact, an anti-war person. Nobody had told him that he couldn't discuss his convictions in other venues than the sanctuary.

The local Socialist Party had organized a meeting to discuss peace issues and asked André to be one of the speakers. He gladly accepted and gave an impassioned talk about the incompatibility of war with the Gospel. The applause was vigorous, so vigorous that the local newspaper took note and published an article about this unusual occurrence. The officials at the Evangelical Reformed Church reacted immediately with a strongly worded letter of admonition.

The score was now one win (the Croix Bleue) and two losses in his relations with the official church, but it was three and zero with the workers.

The best thing that happened to Magda and André during this period was the day their first-born, Nelly, joined the family. The delivery was an inept and painful one that made Magda all the more sure that she, like her mother, was going to die while giving birth to her first child. "Uncle" Francis, a skillful physician, was near enough to come immediately and get the situation under control. The highly functional Trocmé family was functioning, and new warmth grew between Magda and the man who had greeted her in Paris with "You are not as plain as the photographs."

Another warm memory from Nelly's birth was the pastoral visit from Pastor Perret. Here his best attributes came out. He was thoughtful, concerned, and supportive, and brought both the new parents the reassurance they badly needed. His only gaffe occurred when he wanted to share some reading from the Bible and used Magda's still swollen belly as his reading stand. Magda clarified the situation immediately, telling her husband's superior to "Get that fat book off my belly, if you please. It hurts!" (165).

All in all, the apprenticeship in Sous-le-Bois had its good and bad moments. But it had become clear that Perret treated his supervisory role as if he were guardian angel to these young, irrepressible people, checking everything from the syntax in the sermon to the pot on the stove.

It was time to move on. In the fall of 1928, André accepted a new assignment and moved to another of the Maubeuge satellite churches, this one in Sin-le-Noble. It was another industrial population, but this time the product was the coal that fueled the steel mills.

Sin-le-Noble's Test of Conscience

When André and Magda moved to their new parish, they found that a solidly built three-story brick house would be their presbytère. It too was filthy and messy on their arrival, and its infrastructure had seen better days. The Germans had looted the furnace as they retreated toward the border in 1918, and it had never been replaced. Because there was no indoor water supply, the water for use in the second and third floor bathrooms had to be pumped in the neighboring courtyard and hauled up the stairs by hand. With no central furnace, the upper rooms could only be heated by small coal stoves, fueled by coal buckets that came one at a time up the same stairs.

Three sons, Jean-Pierre, Jacques, and Daniel, were born during the years in Sin-le-Noble. To meet the duties of motherhood and the obligations of the parish, Magda relied on the help of *jeune-fille au pair* girls, some of whom were Germans who came for a year to live in France and learn the language.

Alexandre Vinet had called for the separation of church and state more than a century earlier, and the French government had acknowledged the principle long since. But the message seemed not to have arrived yet on the desk of the coal mining company's CEO. Sin-le-Noble was a company town and the company's religion was Catholic. Miners and their families were expected to show up for mass on Sunday, and when they became too lax, there would be a visit from one of the nuns to caution the family that unless they mended their ways they might lose their subsidized housing.

Religious coercion never quite works, however. There were many miners whose faith was solidly planted in the communist or the socialist party, whether or not they showed up for mass. Then there were the few who chose to become Protestants rather than communists. André had only a handful of members who, like himself, had deep roots in the Protestant tradition. Most of his small congregation were lapsed Catholics.

The Catholic establishment in Sin-le-Noble was sometimes an obstacle to his Protestant ministry, but in one case it posed a serious and costly test of conscience. André was concerned about the children of the miners. They had no place to go or any activity designed for them during the school holidays. The Waziers housing project seemed a good place to start. Since boredom is a seedbed for mischief with most children, he and Magda decided that they would mount a vacation program for as many of the Waziers children as wanted to come. Problem number one was finding a location. The church had no meeting rooms nor any useful outside space.

He discovered a small tract of empty land owned by the mining company and so far unused for any company purpose. Why not ask permission to use the land as a play area for these vacation periods? He wrote to the chief executive officer of the mining company, asking for his help, and was pleased that a letter came back inviting him to the Director's office to discuss the matter. Here is his recollection of that interview:

> I was well received by the director (who) very kindly told me three things:
>
> "We have several Protestants among our stockholders. They are very influential. But, in order to maintain peace in this area, the Board of Directors has decided to ask the Catholic Church to handle both the education and the social work the working population requires. The

population, you must agree, is mostly Catholic. It is not at all in our interest to see a sect (sic!) organize any kind of project in Waziers and we won't, therefore, rent anything to you. However . . . we recognize that your project is deserving because it contributes to the morale of the workers who need it so much. We therefore offer to your organization, as we do for the Catholics, the use of our stadium, our sport installations and equipment, as well as team uniforms, free of charge. We will also give you an annual subsidy."

He opened his desk drawer and handed me 2,000 francs to finance the project.

I was embarrassed, very young, and just about to accept this money, our parish being extremely poor, when the director added:

"There is one condition, however. . . . We are anticipating a period of unrest and social agitation which, we feel, will be extremely tough. You will have, as the Catholic clergy have already agreed, to give good advice to your parishioners when you preach. Your sermon will have to explain clearly to them that it is in their best interest to cooperate with their employer."

"Does that mean you want me, as a pastor, to tell my parishioners to split away from their companions and disregard instructions from their labor union?"

I stood up, as red as a tomato:

"I am sorry sir, my duty is to preach the Gospel and I can't subscribe to your request."

"It's up to you," he replied with a mean smile.

The drawer slammed shut on the 2,000 francs. (A. Trocmé 1953, 266)

When it came to compromising an issue of conscience, André had nearly zero tolerance, little interest in negotiation, and a short temper to boot. It would not be the last time he would have to choose between the power of money and fidelity to conscience.

At those moments, an unconscious moral tape would start running: "Resist any compromise of the conscience." It was a moral tape that ran through his decision to decline the Rockefeller family's invitation to stay on in New York for another year or two, and it was all of a piece with his stance on conscientious objection to war.

An Encounter with Hitler's Brown Shirts

One of the things that provided the Trocmés with a counter to some of the more stifling moments in Sin-le-Noble was André's continued participation in the work of the IFOR. He had been elected to its International Governing Committee, which brought him together with long-time pacifist colleagues from time to time. In 1932, the IFOR organized a March Through Europe to bear witness to the essentials of peace and reconciliation if Europe were to avoid another conflagration.

Since André was fluent in German, he was assigned to speak to many of the groups that were brought together in Germany. These meetings drew a great deal of public attention, but much of it was confrontational or downright hostile. In Heidelberg, the hall was filled with two groups of young men who were looking for a fight. One group was Nazi and the other was Communist. The only thing they had in common was their contempt for the pacifists on the stage, since each group saw pacifism as favoring the other. André recalled that he was nearly lynched after the meeting by Hitler's Brown Shirts, who accused the IFOR team of "soaping us up so that later England and France can shave us better." One of them threatened him with a handgun, which of course brought André's defiant streak to the surface. "I suggested to him in German that he should kill me right there in front of everybody. My proposal seemed to have calmed him down because he disappeared into the crowd" (290).

Another meeting was scheduled for Reutlingen, in southern Germany. This time the IFOR team was warned that the hall was packed with Brown Shirts who had sworn none of the visitors would get to speak. André was selected to speak first because of his fluent German. He lingered behind the stage curtain just long enough to catch the angry tone of the voices on the other side, then rushed directly to the podium, giving the crowd no time to react, and said in a loud voice, "Deutschland erwache!" (Germany wake up!), a political slogan often used by Hitler and his supporters. Caught by surprise at his way of getting their attention, they fell silent and let him proceed with his call for reconciliation and equally fair treatment of both German and French veterans of the Great War. He could not understand why this initially angry crowd of young men responded to his talk with cheers and applause until one of their leaders shook his hand and said, "You have precisely expressed what our Führer tells us every day: justice for all, equal treatment for all and peace for all" (291).

André would never forget this encounter and its sobering illustration of the way Hitler's populism had grasped the minds of a generation and persuaded them that the Jews and the Socialists were responsible for all of Germany's woes.

Things Fall Apart

The first half of the thirties was difficult in Sin-le-Noble, as it was throughout France and the entire Western world. The rise of Nazism was only one of the cancers growing on the body politic. A combination of two worldwide economic ripples, the Wall Street crash of 1929, and a pandemic tension between workers and their employers, made for an exceedingly restless period of cultural transition: from a world called into question at every level by the Great War toward a world where dreams of freedom and prosperity could be fulfilled.

Another transition involved a serious critique of the rationalism that had governed France's philosophers and policy makers alike. Many of the country's intellectual leaders saw the rationalist tradition as one of the paths that had led to the Great War, with the stubborn madness of the generals driving national pride to absurd extremes. Spiritual and emotional realities demanded a closer investigation, which could be pressed as much by poets and painters as by policy makers and professors.

Some focused on their personal frustrations and sense of ennui. Surrealist painters tried to reach for a new reality by merging the world of dreams and unconscious aspirations with the world of daily routines, and Sigmund Freud opened the gates of exploration to suppressed emotions, unconscious desires, and sexual fantasies. While those explorations were not on the agenda of most of André's parishioners, the bohemian community in Paris's Left Bank was happily trying them out and then writing about all the sexual behaviors from which Freud had lifted the lid. Paris had become a cultural refuge for Americans like Henry Miller, who wanted to write about the whole human experience including its sexual dreams and realities.

Sin-le-Noble parishioners had little time for either titillation or ennui. Most of them felt more trapped than bored, trapped in a web of hard work and minimal reward. The stock market crash of 1929 had inevitably eroded the money values that held the industrial world together. Desperate poverty for some and arrested prosperity for others would cast a shadow over most of the decade. Recovery would take five or six years before the run-up to World War II gave significant stimulus to the smoke stack industries and a stock market that took its cues from industry.

The appeal of socialist political thinking and the more radical communist doctrines had made elemental contact with a swollen and hurting class of laborers. During the same period, the IWW and other labor organizations had sharpened their resolve and expanded their numbers. Socialist doctrines had become a rallying point for most of the Sin-le-Noble workers. Christian Socialism of the sort shared by André and his theological contemporaries had shaped the ministry of the more liberal French Protestant clergy of his generation. When the communists in France echoed Lenin's contempt for religion of any sort, that contempt only further sparked the ongoing debate.

For the likes of André Trocmé, the communists were wrong, the socialists were more right than wrong, the Catholic Church was captive to the State, and the Église Réformée Évangélique was too bourgeois to recognize the changes in the air. No one strong group was driving the train toward social justice. It was no wonder that the director of a major mining company would feel the threat of strikes and violence within his own company towns, and no wonder that he would turn to priests and ministers to help keep things quiet and in good order.

Things were, in fact, falling apart. For far too many workers, alcohol was the path of flight from the grim reality of everyday life. That was a social problem on which everyone agreed. But the fundamental injustices of the workers' lot were still not a major focus of attention for André's mother church.

By the end of 1932, two other things surfaced that made it seem that the handwriting was on the wall and that André would not be able to serve indefinitely in Sin-le-Noble. One was the ill health of his family and the other was a spiritual development that ruptured some of his major sources of psychological support.

The health issue was the recurring illness of his children. The smoky, coal-dust-laden air of the dark winters was a hazard for all miners' families, and now it was becoming one for the four Trocmé children. Their parents were so concerned about the eldest, Nelly, that they sent her off to a children's residence in Switzerland and the care of a Doctor Rollier. There the clean air and decent Swiss cuisine would strengthen her. The family doctor had also sounded an alarm about the boys' health. He pointed out that silicosis and tuberculosis were on the rise in town, and that the children would be at risk if they continued to live there.

The spiritual issue was the slow collapse of André's circle of friends from seminary days. The Groupe du Nord was becoming unraveled and would cease to exist before long. Pentecostalism had just begun to wax strong among ministers of the Reformed churches, and some of his friends drifted off in that direction, where concern for social justice gave way to concern for personal holiness. Others had gone mainstream in

16. Four Trocmé children, July 1934. Unknown photographer.

their church affiliations and, for all intents and purposes, had shed their mantle of pacifism. It was time to look elsewhere to continue his ministry.

An Ecclesiastical Line in the Sand

André was visibly pleased when he was invited to be a candidate for assistant pastor in the church in Clamart. Clamart was one of three churches that operated under a single church council: Montrouge-Clamart-Malakoff (304). He had fond recollections of that little church, and even of the architectural disaster of the do-it-yourself parish house he and his friends had created out of a discarded army barrack. Clamart was a blue-collar suburb on a hill south of Paris, and had so far retained at least a touch of country living.

He responded to the invitation, went down to Clamart for an interview with the Church Council, and then returned in late February to give a sermon: the second step for vetting a candidate. The Council members already knew of his conscientious objection and were persuaded that he would not use their pulpit as his private platform for spreading pacifist ideas. At the end of the meeting they gave unanimous approval to his candidacy, and Pastor Finet wrote him a formal invitation to accept the job.

The Paris Regional Council of the Église Réformée Évangélique could install no one as a minister without a review, however. There followed an acrimonious exchange of letters between the president of the Paris council, Pierre Durand-Gasselin, and Pastor Finet. Durand-Gasselin told Finet that the appointment must be abandoned, citing Andre's pacifism as the reason. Appointing a pacifist minister would breach the peace of the church and cause irreversible divisions within it. Finet made the case that the church had the right to appoint whoever the church council, not the Regional Council, saw as the best candidate. Copies of this correspondence illustrate clearly the tensions between a congregation's authority and that of a regional bureaucracy. It came down to a question of who holds the purse strings.

Gasselin got in touch with André and told him the invitation would be discussed at the next meeting of the Regional Council, but that André should accept the fact that he would not be approved for the post. The council would meet *in camera* and would inform him officially of the outcome. Not one to sit idly by, André went to the Avenue Clichy headquarters of the church and asked to meet with the Regional Council in person. The president very reluctantly allowed him a brief audience with the council.

Then, with manifest anger, Durand-Gasselin allowed André to answer only one question: "In case of war, would you put on a uniform and defend the Fatherland? Answer Yes or No." Since the president already knew the answer, he announced forthwith that the invitation would not be validated, the appointment would not be made, and André was summarily excused. No account was taken of Montrouge-Clamart's unanimous invitation to bring André onto its staff.

It may sound strange to modern ears that an official Christian church council would take such an inflexibly negative position on the question of conscientious objection, but it was commonplace during the years between the two world wars. With Hitler's influence becoming increasingly strong throughout Europe, many non-German Christian theologians were speaking more and more forcefully about their anti-Nazi commitments. But their language was not often that of conscientious objection: it was rather the language of an institution striving diligently against being taken over by any state ideology.

In short order, it became mainstream Protestant doctrine that, while Christian believers must not promote violence, neither must they shrink from resisting evil, and by violent means if necessary. These were the Christians who tended to see conscientious objection as a form of pride, of avoiding getting "dirty hands" when resisting something manifestly evil (Von Klemperer 2001, 131–36). Many of the leading theologians in the Église Réformée during that era used Swiss theologian Karl Barth's *Barmen Declaration* as the bedrock of their policy not to let conscientious objection be preached from the pulpits of their churches. In the case of André and a few of his seminary friends, it was also a way for the church councils to vindicate their decision not to approve a known and outspoken pacifist for appointment to any of their churches.

André was undaunted, however. He was going to find a parish one way or another. With the help of a friend on the committee of oversight for the Evangelical Reformed Church, he was given another parish appointment to explore, this time in a French town near the Swiss border, overlooking Lac Léman toward Geneva. Once again, he had a thorough and satisfactory meeting with the council of the church at Thonon-les-Bains, and again he had their unanimous support of his nomination. There was one problem, however. A single member of the council had absented herself because she knew of André's pacifist convictions and did not like them at all. She got her message to Paris before André called in to announce that he had been given the post. Once again the Parisian church bureaucracy vetoed the invitation, leaving André with no option but to return to Sin-le-Noble to sort things out.

10

Le Chambon in the Thirties

Soon after André's return to Sin-le-Noble, a letter came from Roger Casalis, a minister friend who had begun to feel restless in this isolated rural parish. He had no car, nor would the parish provide him with a motorbike to get to his meetings and pastoral calls. By now he wanted out. To the church council, he presented urgent health problems as the reason for leaving. He did not want them to be without a minister, however, so he was searching for a replacement. Would André be interested? André knew only a bit about the area, and what he knew did not make it nearly as attractive an option as either Clamart or Thonon-les-Bains. A farming village three thousand feet up on the volcanic plateau Vivarais-Lignon seemed very far from any environment he knew or cared to know.

If he went to Le Chambon-sur-Lignon it would clearly be the church of last resort. Given the hostility to conscientious objectors in his own Église Réformée de France there was little likelihood that any other offers would come his way.

André and Magda set out to have interviews and get a first-hand impression of the place and the church. He preached that Sunday in the town's Temple, an imposing and austere Huguenot sanctuary that could hold a congregation of five hundred and echoed audibly when only a few were in the pews. The congregation that gathered to hear him that Sunday sat through the service and the sermon with totally unreadable faces. He saw their reception as "very lukewarm" (A. Trocmé 1953, 308). They clearly thought that any enthusiasm, theirs or his, would be out of place in the sanctuary. More animated conversations took place after the service in a meeting with the church council members. As part of those conversations, André made plain his pacifist convictions, but promised not to use the pulpit as a

17. Le Chambon-sur-Lignon Protestant Temple. Photograph by and courtesy of Richard Unsworth.

platform for proselytizing. Again nothing registered. It was as if they could not be bothered with such abstract matters. They just needed a minister.

This council, like the previous two, issued a unanimous invitation. The next big question was whether this invitation would have any better chance than the others of surviving review by the regional council and the church bureaucrats. However, this regional council was not in Paris. It was far away in the Ardèche, and its president, René Herdt, was a friend of André's. He solved all potential "administrative problems"—i.e., a probable veto—by acting directly and without consultation and giving André an interim appointment. The interim appointment was extended, but was only regularized by the church authorities much later, when it was too late to be threatened with death by committee. Thus began a parish relationship of sixteen years' duration, a relationship that included the challenging and turbulent years of the Nazi occupation of France.

The Happiest Years

Both André and Magda identified the years from 1934 to 1944 as the happiest of their long life together. During that decade, they became much closer to one another. They faced and weathered the tragic death of their eldest son; they established the important new Collège Cévenol that continues to this day; they gained widespread acceptance for their commitment to nonviolent resistance against the Nazi scourge (although they had more admirers than imitators). They were happiest, each of them, when they were busiest, and that source of inner satisfaction was never more nourished than in the late thirties and the years of World War II.

Theirs was a life in constant motion, a style that destroys many a marriage, but not theirs. What was it that made their marriage work so well? After all, both of them were given to being insistently outspoken about their disagreements, and one was deeply pietistic while the other was equally deeply skeptical about religious orthodoxies in general. Why did it work?

For one thing, their common passion for social justice was profound. Neither saw that passion as competitive with their personal needs. In this working blend of disparate personalities and beliefs, the Trocmés were poised on two ends of the seesaw: André the evangelical preacher on one end and Magda the frenetic activist on the other. They found the elusive goal of marital balance by complementing, and sometimes counterbalancing, each other; and if they had harsh words, they always made up before going to sleep.

Their other shared passion was their need to reject the bourgeois lifestyle they saw in their own families. This was the strong impression of André's nephew, Étienne Trocmé, a prominent and meticulous biblical scholar and dean of the theological faculty at the University of Strasbourg. Étienne saw his uncle as very proud of the Trocmé name and background, and in that respect hardly a renegade. But the issue of conscientious objection brought him into constant conflict with his church, a conflict not experienced by other members of the family. Perhaps, he asked, André was a bit overzealous and intolerant about his enmity for bourgeois convention? It was Étienne's strong opinion that André's pacifist stance, especially during the war years, was widely admired within the family and was regarded by them as very courageous.

Throughout their marriage, these two genuinely admired one another. André never got over the fact that a woman as beautiful, courageous, and generous as Magda could be his wife. She was refreshingly different from all those women the family had thought would make a proper wife for their André. For her part, Magda remained caught up by the aspirations she shared with André. Long after she had been widowed, she said in an interview with author Philip Hallie, "I am not a good Christian at all, but I have things that I really believe in. First of all, I believe and believed in André Trocmé. I was faithful to his projects and to him personally, and I understood him very well" (Hallie 1979, 152). She made much the same assertion to Pierre Sauvage in a later interview captured on film (Sauvage 1989).

Le Chambon was far from St. Quentin, geographically, economically, politically, religiously, and socially. For André, whose life had until then been lived in urban and urbane circumstances, life in a farming village high on a volcanic plateau looked as if it would be sharply different from anything in his prior experience. Life in Le Chambon would be different in another sense as well: the majority of its population was Protestant. Wherever he had lived in France until now, Protestants had formed a tiny minority of the population—less than five percent as a rule. The national proportion wavered between two and three percent.

When they arrived in Le Chambon in 1934, the town's year-round population was 990, eighty-five percent or more of them Protestants (Bolle 1992, 22). The town had been attracting rising numbers of summer visitors and summer residents from around the country, and the seasonal influx only increased the Protestant percentage of the whole. There were few other places in France that offered the multiple magnets of clear skies, clean air, and elegant mountain views, together with the cultural attraction of a large and lively Temple. Still another thing favored the growth of the seasonal population: the growing number of maisons d'enfants: children's homes designed to provide their enrolled youngsters with a healthy environment away from the city where they could live during the summer or the school year.

By 1940, the year-round population had grown to over 2,500. While the offices of government were not allowed to record religious affiliations, the Catholic diocesan records did include them, showing for the year 1940 that 2,543 were Protestants and only 165 were Catholics. By the early 1940s, the country was on a war footing and even more maisons d'enfants had sprung up to provide safe harbor for refugee children who were gradually being released from the camps at Gurs, Rivesaltes, and other locations throughout the south. The summer population was growing to over five thousand. In spite of that growth, Le Chambon was still a rural town at the center of a very traditional area, where farming methods had not changed for generations, where the economy was marginal at best and where there was no education available beyond the ninth grade level.

When André and Magda had settled into the presbytère, several things caught their attention about life in remote and rural France. One was the almost medieval relationship between the farmers and their animals. Both were sheltered against the bitter winter winds by living under one roof.

In a town with granite block houses dating back several centuries, there were other creatures sharing the quarters. Unwelcome rats were commonplace in homes built on the riverside. They lived safely behind the wooden paneled walls, occasionally rambling through the kitchen and dining room at night in search of any kind of food. For people brought up in fine urban homes, that kind of intimacy with the environment was neither familiar nor charming, but it was all part of the tableau of country living, and one learned to take it in stride.

At first, André was less sanguine than Magda about the prospect of building a network of friendships in this faraway place. He saw only a handful of people he reckoned to be cultured persons: the local physician, the matriarch of a wealthy landowning family, the director of the public school, a local teacher, and one or two others. He saw most of the peasant population as "heavy-hearted" people bound by outlived traditions, fatalistic about their circumstances, given to distrusting strangers, and preoccupied by death.

Intellectual Life in a Sectarian Stew

As he came to know more of his parishioners, and know them at closer hand, André found that their dour expressions often concealed a ripe sense of humor, true courage in the face of adversity, and a deep-seated adherence to fundamental principles. There emerged a deeper dimension to André's growing respect for the inhabitants of the towns, villages, and scattered farms surrounding Le Chambon.

The largest of these villages, Le Mazet-Saint-Voy, had long been the center of the Protestant movement known as Christianisme Social (Maillebouis 2004). It was much like the social action movements André had dealt with in his northern parishes, but with a major difference. In the Roman Catholic north, radical secular groups like the several socialist parties and the Communist Party generally dominated these movements.

In the heavily Protestant Plateau, it was not secular forces that brought the leftists together. It was the Protestant churches: most of the parishioners had been voting for left-wing parties for generations. On the Plateau, Christianisme Social functioned as a center of Protestant ethical thought, writing, and social criticism, some of it generated by the clergy, but as much or more by the intellectual laity. The organization had a wide reach in French Protestantism, and tiny Le Mazet-Saint-Voy became the site of the first National Congress of Christianisme Social in 1933 (Maillebouis 2004, 5), and of other conferences focused on issues of social justice.

The relationship with the local farmers also became warmer on their side, as they discovered that their new Pastor Trocmé was always walking out to parishioners' homes for pastoral calls or mid-week Bible study groups. He saw in these mid-week meetings that he had organized an opportunity to replicate the weekly kitchen meetings of Sous-le-Bois, the small informal neighborhood gatherings that had done so much to animate the spiritual and social life of that parish, at least until his boss had ruled them out of bounds.

In addition to adjusting to this very different sort of parish, André faced another challenge: the unique spiritual topography of the Plateau. The town and its surrounding communities harbored a stew of widely differing Christian communities. The Plateau and the neighboring mountainous Cévennes region had a long history of being home to separatist groups that treasured their religious liberties. The story of the Camisards and their resistance was the paradigm instance of that history (Bastide 1965). In 1702, these zealous Huguenot insurrectionists launched a fierce resistance against royal power after the revocation by Louis XIV of the 90-year-old Edict of Nantes, which had guaranteed religious liberty to the Calvinist groups that sprang up throughout France after the Reformation. The struggles of the Camisards still inspired Protestants in southern France two centuries later.

The Camisards left another footprint on the religious history of the area. They were "enthusiasts" in their forms of worship and favored inspiring preachers over churchly traditions. In the 1930s, the Pentecostal movement had those same characteristics. André's acquaintance with Pentecostals went back to his first days in the ministry, when he was a member of the Église Réformée Évangélique, the Church of the North. The merger of the Church of the North and the national ÉRF had not yet taken place. Under the leadership of Marc Boegner, the French Protestant Federation (FPF) had already been formed in 1909 to create an association of several French Protestant communities: Lutherans, Reform churches, free churches (represented in England and the United States by the Congregational churches), Baptists, Methodists and others (Maillebouis 2004, 14). The only actual merger was that between the Church of the North and the ÉRF, and that would not happen until 1938.

During that decade of change, some of his friends had given up on their organized churches and joined one or another pietistic group. They wanted to be part of a new awakening of Christianity in France, and they did not see that kind of spiritual energy emerging from the cluster of churches in the FPF.

André's course was different. He shared their pietism in many ways, but he chose not to leave the church of his family: l'Église Réformée Évangélique. When the merger took place, he remained in the Reformed mainstream. It simply did not occur to him to join a splinter group. The harder task was to stay within the church and seek its renewal through obedience to the Gospel in the practical works of peace and justice rather than the cultivation of personal holiness.

Another non-denominational group with a significant following in the Plateau was the Salvation Army, an outgrowth of the nineteenth-century revivalist preaching of an English Methodist layman, William Booth. Booth's twin foci were evangelism and ministry to the poor, aims that remain central to this Army of the Lord even now. When the Trocmés arrived in Le Chambon, the Armée de Salut was already a long-standing presence, with an office in town that had been established in 1885 (Bollon 2004, 32–37). André's only complaints with the Salvation Army were two: their focus on a personal morality and their simplistic condemnation of what they saw as the sins of their culture. It seems that a group of the Army's officers had once visited the presbytère and gone away saying that the Pastor had pornographic pictures in his study. They cited as evidence the nudity in his copy of Michelangelo's Sistine Chapel painting, *The Creation of Man*.

There was a third cluster of independent and unconventional Protestants in the area: the Darbyists, the spawn of another nineteenth-century revivalist, John Darby, an Irish Anglican priest who resigned his orders in search of a better way to serve his Christian ardor. The Bible was his anchor, not any church. Immensely affected by his reading of the Book of Revelation, Darby saw Christianity as a passing phase of spiritual development that was bracketed on one side by Jewish scriptures and on the other by the Jewish expectation of a coming Messiah who would usher in the Kingdom of God. Christians were simply gentiles who shared that expectation—honorary Jews, as it were. Christian faith, therefore, was but a step on the way to fulfillment of a Jewish expectation.

For Darbyists, therefore, Jews were the original People of God and their own spiritual kinfolk. Any attack on Jews was an attack on God's family and their own. So when Jewish refugees began to appear on French doorsteps in the Plateau, the normal thing for a Darbyist would be to offer them succor, a place to hide if necessary, or at the very least a sure passage to safer shelter.

In addition to their hospitality toward Jews seeking refuge, the Darbyists made another significant contribution to life on the Plateau. They established agricultural cooperatives and beneficial funds, one of which was created specifically to aid conscientious objectors (35). They were simple, straightforward people whose convictions served a multitude of groups in the population. But they had no tradition of going to church.

Life in and Beyond the Presbytère

The building that became the presbytère was built in the fifteenth century as a commodious winter home for the Counts of Fay. Its walls were made of three-foot-thick granite blocks, strong enough to protect the Counts' families against the winds of the Plateau and the predations of neighboring nobles. It did not yield easily, however, to the addition of modern amenities like central heating. But compared to their first presbytère in Maubeuge, it at least had running water and indoor toilets. Further, the church council recognized that Magda's call for central heating was a sensible one, and they sold off a piece of land in order to make that investment.

Once the Trocmés were established in the presbytère, it became a hub of parish activity. Occasional meetings took place in the all-purpose family room, with its handsome fireplace and wood paneled walls. Parishioners sought out their pastor in his study there. Guestroom space was cobbled together whenever it was needed, which was often. The great long dining room table served variously as a homework center for the children, a sewing table for the women who gathered to make clothing for needy people in the parish, or a hospitality site for whoever happened to be there at mealtime. Magda became an expert at watering the soup.

Jacques Trocmé remembers, during the war years especially, that there were often a dozen or more adults at the dinner table, often enough that his parents got a local carpenter to build a small table where the children could be seated on low stools at the end of the room. In all, it was a wondrously chaotic place, with animated conversations in which everyone participated, often simultaneously.

Although the children had few private hours with their parents, Magda and André tried to get the whole family out of the house for some time together as often as they could. Since André paid most of his pastoral calls by walking to parish members' homes, one opportunity for time with the children was taking them with him, one at a time, on the walk to and from those homes.

Nelly was with him one snowy day as they walked home. In the forest, they came on a patch of small and pretty pines in a clearing, each with snow bearing down the boughs and bending them into angelic shapes. André exclaimed, "Look, that's the paradise of little pine trees." His imagination could make magic of anything unusual, even a few snowy pine trees alone in a forest. His figures of speech were fine nourishment for the imagination of his children.

18. Dining room in the presbytère. Unknown photographer.

Periodically, they would crowd into the old Citroen C4 for a trip down to the valley of the Ardèche. Driving south from the Plateau is still a breathtaking trip, aesthetically and physically, with its endless sharp switchbacks and stunning views of the fields of fruit trees, vineyards, and vegetable gardens below, views that only those not at the wheel dare to enjoy.

The Plateau and nearby Ardèche also offered lots of interesting places for a day trip, so the Trocmés were likely to find themselves visiting an ancient ruin, like the medieval Château de Rochebonne, poised alone on a rugged outcrop in the mountains. From the walls of that ancient ruin, the view was a commanding sweep of the whole area.

There were also some memorable vacation months together, usually in June, before the summer tourists began returning for the season. Ministers often found ways to get away from their parishes by changing places with other clergy during their vacation month. Each could enjoy at least a modicum of peace and quiet and family time in another's parish, where they had few ties and were expected only to preach on Sunday morning. Occasionally these swaps brought the Trocmés to very attractive areas, like the Côte d'Azur. Other times they rented an old farmhouse close to the Lake of Annecy in Menthon-St. Bernard, near the Swiss border.

Life in the presbytère was lived at a high tempo. When an American Quaker staff member, Tracy Strong Jr., came for dinner with the Trocmés in 1941, he found them "a fine buoyant family with lots of life and naturalness. The kids are all active and each seems to know his [own] mind."[1] After-dinner moments were often salted with endless children's songs accompanied by André on his concertina, or with a performance by Magda of some of her wide repertoire of facial grimaces. She was famous for her talent for wiggling one ear at a time, or touching her nose with her tongue, or screwing up her entire face in a sequence of fantastic caricatures.

The presbytère was also home, for shorter or longer periods, to an unpredictable roster of paying guests and people in need. The paying guests might be students attending the newly founded École Nouvelle Cévenole, but the door seemed open widest to those who needed some brief shelter or help. At first, it was a neighbor, Mme. Robert, who cooked some of the meals and helped run the household in spite of her multiple ineptitudes. Later, of course, it would be that steady stream of Jewish escapees from the Nazi-occupied north.

André and Magda had always taken for granted that theirs was a partnership of equals in which both could realize their callings. The point was made quietly but unmistakably in Le Chambon when André wrote parish notes for the ministers' weekly page in the *Echo de la Montagne*. All the clergy were invited to submit to that page a brief report of what had happened and what was forthcoming in their parishes. In issues of the early thirties one thing strikes the eye. All the ministers except André signed their reports with their own names and titles. The Trocmé parish notes were often followed by both their names, and without the addition of titles.

Magda certainly took seriously her responsibilities in the home, but given the incessant demands of her teaching and of the refugee traffic that

---

1. Strong's diary; entry of October 5, 1941.

coursed through the house, she had much needed help with those responsibilities from women hired for the purpose, and later from Jispa, who had arrived on their doorstep when the flood of refugees became a torrent.

Their help was also important both to the family and to Magda, because housekeeping was not enough to satisfy her sense of the purpose of her life. That had been clear since childhood. She did not want to save the world, just those people in it who were victims of injustice, hunger, repression, neglect, and the host of other woes too easily accepted by the world. So when she arrived in Le Chambon, she continued to do what she had been doing all the while in their first two parishes. She was able to make it clear in the community that she was a woman who would rise to meet the human needs she knew about, and she took it for granted that others would do the same. When a need was obvious to her, she assumed it would be equally obvious to others and they would, of course, pitch in to help ameliorate the hurt. She took charge without thinking that she was taking charge, a trait that made her admirable to some and irritating to others.

Examples abound, whether it was organizing a big Christmas party for the elderly of Sin-le-Noble or offering classes on childcare to wives of the Italian immigrant miners. These were displaced persons, after all, and they would not learn the art of child rearing from their parents or aunts and uncles, so Magda decided she would remedy the situation as best she could.

In Chambon, she created her own illustrated "how-to" brochures for young mothers. She found there was a place for such learning in the gatherings of Jeunes Aînées, the young women's group in the church. She taught them a course that included issues of pre-natal care, the health needs of pregnant women, and some common medical questions, even tips on proper clothing for infants and young children. In her way it was well and thoroughly organized.

Her teaching repertoire also included short courses designed to broaden the intellectual horizons of the Jeunes Aînées. One of them focused on a favorite historical figure of her own, Pierre Valdo, the pre-Reformation reformer who established the Waldensian community in a remote valley of northern Italy. It was a community that had captured her own imagination as a young woman because of its devotion to the needs of the poor.

The Teaching Preacher

One of the fruits of André's classical French education was an extraordinary ability to study his material carefully, frame its presentation in a few notes, and then speak directly to his audience while only occasionally glancing at his notes. Although he gave the impression of utter spontaneity, his teaching and preaching was the product of disciplined thought. He thought in whole concepts, structured them in outline, and then spoke them in paragraphs. He did this routinely, as much in conversation as in any public venue. It should be added that this lent an air of authority to his speaking, even when he was wrong.

As a result, his Sunday School and Confirmation lessons were as well organized as any good class designed for bright lycée students. At least two of his Sunday School students retained notes of those lessons into their advanced years. They make exceptional reading for two reasons: they reflect André's high respect for the intellectual potential of his students, and they include abundant and accurate information about religious traditions other than Christianity.

André also had a talent for addressing the relationship between religious and scientific ideas in accessible terms, something not often found in a Sunday School curriculum of the 1930s. His students typically described André as an unforgettable teacher and as an evangelical minister with liberal ideas, a description widely shared by others in the parish of Le Chambon.

André brought a large presence to his teaching and preaching. He was unusually tall for a Frenchman of his era, well over six feet. His face was broad and animated, his voice strong, and on his entry or exit from a room, the floor shuddered a little under his footstep, his stride giving no hint of the increasingly severe back pain he lived with daily. The handsome wooden pulpit in the Temple, raised several steps up against the front wall, combined with his own height to give a commanding appearance.

19. Sanctuary, temple in Le Chambon-sur-Lignon. Engraving by Evelyn Bridge, February 1935.

His teaching from the pulpit was different in both tone and intent from the teaching in Sunday School. The latter was akin to any good schooling experience, but in the pulpit, his intent was to be the evangelical interpreter of Christian faith, persuading his listeners to participate in its joys and heed its duties.

Given his habit of speaking from brief notes, it is hard to find written copies of his sermons from the Chambon years. There are a few, however. One is his first sermon upon arriving in Le Chambon in 1934, where he laid out his pacifist convictions for all to understand, especially in the face of Hitler's rapidly rising power in Germany. He said, "No government can force us to kill; we have to find the means of resisting Nazism without killing people" (Bolle 1992, 390). Another is the often-quoted sermon preached, together with Edouard Theis, on June 23, 1940, the day after the French signed their armistice with the Nazis. In that sermon as in daily life the two pastors took the same position: "The duty of Christians is to resist the violence brought to bear on their consciences with the weapons of the spirit—we will resist whenever our adversaries try to force us to act against the commands of the Gospel. We will do so without fear, but also without pride and without hatred" (597–99).

Although the written texts from those years are rare, there is an abundance of testimony from Andre's hearers to the quality of his preaching. One of the young people in the parish said, "We lived from sermon to sermon—I took notes, which I kept." The most eloquent comment on Trocmé's preaching occurs in a letter from his eldest brother, Francis, to another brother, Robert. While vacationing in Le Chambon one summer, Francis found himself very moved by one of André's sermons, which he then tried to describe to Robert:

> It was an extraordinary sermon—formidable. He is an absolutely striking pulpit orator with an authority surpassing any preaching I have ever heard. He begins in a simple, familiar tone of voice speaking about recent events, both secular and religious, with a clear-sightedness that is almost disquieting. . . . He uses the people's language, even if occasionally coarse. . . . Where is he going? Where is he leading us? Is he going to succumb to trivialities? But no, that is where the tone rises, his voice becomes grave, the phrases roll out in larger and larger scope, in great spirals, mounting higher and still higher with superb gestures and a magnificent assurance, higher, always higher. He leads you up to the summit of religious thinking, to the boundaries of the ineffable; and once there, he makes you soar in a veritable ecstasy. Then slowly his voice becomes softer, the tone more intimate as he gently brings you back to earth with a feeling of peace and an "Amen". . . . Surely not all his sermons are as deeply inspiring; but in the ones I have heard, what strikes me is the tone of absolute sincerity . . . a facility and vigor of expression, a spontaneous richness of language.[2]

---

2. The letter was saved by Robert's widow, Germaine, who sent it to Magda after André's death.

A Protestant Collège for Le Chambon

One of the lasting monuments to Magda's restless efforts to help others have better lives was her promotion, together with André, of the idea that Le Chambon needed its own secondary school. She looked at the futures chosen by or forced upon the young people of their larger community and realized that most of them had no chance to move beyond schooling that would only offer them opportunities as lower level government workers or primary school teachers.

She thought about a model that just might work for Le Chambon: a school in Torre Pellice, a valley in northern Italy which had been settled by the French-speaking Waldensians more than two hundred years before Martin Luther sparked the Reformation. She had visited there for a few weeks while still living in Florence and was very much taken by the spirit of the place and the fact that the Italian government honored the diploma earned by its graduates.

She proposed to André that they should take it as their model for a secondary school in Chambon. André responded enthusiastically to the idea and during the summer of 1936 laid it out with the other clergy in the regional council. Its gestation took a long year of consultation with a great many people in the Chambon area and another year of formal planning by a few key people with some direct knowledge of the finances such a project would involve. That group, fortunately, included Roger Darsissac, the director of the local public school (Hatzfeld 1989, 11–12).

The Trocmés were not the only ones who wanted to see the growth of opportunity for the young people of the Plateau. Charles Guillon, the former pastor and then long-time mayor of Le Chambon, wanted to establish a summer camp on the model of the American YMCA camps, and then be able to put the buildings to work as a secondary school for the town during the rest of the year. Someone else wanted to establish additional maisons d'enfants to accommodate the growing need. There were other such projects in either the dream stage or the planning stage, and the question was how these interests could be developed to serve the needs of the rising generation. André proposed that a new secondary school would be the best means of meeting their most important need, a stronger education, effectively and efficiently. He noted an important supporter of the idea in Charles Schmidt, the Inspector General of Libraries, who summered regularly at the Luquet farmhouse, a building that would later become the headquarters of the Collège Cévenol when the Luquet farm became its campus.

A consensus emerged that the secondary school was the most urgent of the several proposed projects. Finding a director would be the first and indispensable thing. Guillon suggested that André invite Edouard Theis to consider coming to Le Chambon, dividing his time between two important roles: assistant pastor at the Temple and Directeur of l'École Nouvelle Cévenole. The two men already knew one another very well: in Paris, Theis had been André's contemporary at the Faculty of Theology and then in New York, his predecessor as French tutor to the youngest Rockefeller sons.

The school's founding team laid out a challenging goal. They aspired to create an educational community for which there was but one even partial parallel in all of France: the Protestant lycée at La Rochelle, and that was a much more traditional school established in a prosperous city, which dealt chiefly with students from the haute bourgeoisie families there.

The goal in Le Chambon was different. The planners were aiming at students in a remote area, most of whose families had modest educational backgrounds. Furthermore, they had fashioned a unique mission. André put it this way in his memoir: "We wanted to be laymen in spirit, but Protestant and international in practice. A means of expression of the ancient Protestant left, still so much alive in the region, had to be invented, and I insisted on the promotion of pacifism" (A. Trocmé 1953, 326). It came down to a mission that rested on ancient Huguenot tradition but tested the conventional thinking behind conventional behavior at every turn. It was, however, a perfect institutional expression of the founders' own habits of mind and conviction.

Several unique educational characteristics emerged as the school took shape. Its Protestant character meant forging an alliance with the newly united ÉRF. That link came through the Fédération Protestante, a catch-all organization designed to oversee schools, hospitals, military chaplains, youth camps, prison ministries, ecumenical relations and any other Protestant organizations that were not parish churches.

It was unique, too, in being privately owned, a decision that meant exclusion from government funding but not from government regulation. The Education Ministry would require that the Collège have two governing boards, one to own the land and assets, the other to run the daily curriculum and residential life.

Its international outreach was also a hallmark of the school. It was a new concept in French education. The commitment to internationalism had the powerful backing of André Philip, a Christian pacifist and an influential member of the *Chambre des Députés,* France's national legislature. It affected the makeup of the student body and of the faculty. It meant having at least a few non-French faculty members on its permanent staff, people who had not run the gamut of official French academic accreditation. The first two of these were Lesley Maber, an English teacher who joined the faculty before the war and remained there throughout her career, and Mlle. Hoefert, an Austrian Jewish refugee who came to teach German.

The Collège was venturesome in another respect as well. It would install an honor system. It only worked for a while, while the early idealism still had a grip. By contrast, the decision to be co-educational has continued. That would be one of the biggest challenges, one that could only be met if there were two directors, one male, and the other female. In preparation for the opening of its second academic year in 1939, the regional educational authorities were officially notified that the school would have two directors: Mlle. Lucy Pont and M. Edouard Theis. Mlle. Pont had come from her regular appointment at the Collège Lucie Berger in Strasbourg to direct a summer studies program, and stayed on until 1946 as co-director with Theis. She was succeeded by Antoinette Lavondès, who remained in this titular position until her retirement (Hatzfeld 1989, 169).

In the final analysis, Edouard Theis carried the title and the tasks of Directeur, and Mme. Lavondès, although officially a co-director, functioned as dean of students. She developed the appearance of severity that suited her disciplinary role. One of her students described her thus: "She had the expression of an ant, always dressed in black, black hair tied in a chignon, often wearing a black scarf. She had piercing black eyes and a reputation of severity." As a teacher of French, however, that same student found Mme. Lavondès had her softer side. The student had not prepared for a test on the disputes between Ancients and Moderns in seventeenth-century France, so she filled her paper with colorful but irrelevant snippets, on which Mme. Lavondès wrote only, "This is a little short" and let the matter pass. The office and the classroom required different demeanors, and Mme. Lavondès had room for both.

In the thicket of problems that stood in the way of realizing the goals of the Collège, two were most challenging: many in the town were very skeptical about the viability of the project, and everyone assumed that war would break out any day—not a propitious moment for mounting such an expensive and idealistic project. These were dark years for finding the funds and the faculty that would make such a utopian dream come true.

It was against that backdrop that Theis took up the challenge and, in the fall of 1938, began his term as director of the new school, a term that would last until his retirement twenty-five years later. When he began, the student body of eighteen was taught by a faculty of four: Edouard and Mildred Theis, Magda Trocmé, and the Jewish refugee, Mlle. Hoefert. Among them, they mounted courses in French literature and four foreign languages: Latin, English, German, and Italian. Teaching spaces (they could not be called classrooms) were scattered about the town, three of them improvised by using the all-purpose screens in an assembly room of the Temple. A local woodworker crafted tables and chairs, one for each student. Magda described one of her own classrooms with typical color: "My Italian class was held in one of Mme. Marion's bathrooms. . . . I had from four to six pupils and I had great fun teaching in an oversized bathroom. I also used two rooms in the Hôtel Sagnes, which was closed during the winter. These rooms were as cold as a dead duck. There was no central heating, and we used wood stoves" (M. Trocmé 1946, 223).

For American-educated and quiet-spoken Mildred Theis, being an unpaid English teacher had to compete with the everyday work of bringing up her seven daughters, soon to be eight.

For Edouard Theis, the demand and the risk were perhaps greatest. He had made the move to Le Chambon primarily to become director of this fledgling institution. It needed to succeed if he were to stay there, and he needed to stay there because, as a conscientious objector, there would be few if any other opportunities coming his way from the Église Réformée. Furthermore, the regional council had approved only half a salary for his post as assistant pastor, hardly enough to provide for a family of ten.

As that first year moved along, it became obvious that the idea had a decent chance of catching on. Other teachers came to join them, in large part because they believed in the school's mission.

By the opening of the second school year in the fall of 1939, the German army had marched into Czechoslovakia without opposition and had launched its attack on Poland. That fateful fall, the new school had

20. Edouard and Mildred Theis. Unknown photographer. Courtesy of Jeanne Theis Whitacre.

forty students and enough teachers to offer the courses necessary to gain accreditation. By the spring of that second academic year, the Nazis would overrun France itself. The Débacle, as it was known, took only six weeks, and in June of 1940 France surrendered to its old rival nation-state.

Le Chambon and its surrounding villages exhibited a kind of corporate moral heroism around the emergence of its new school. No one seemed inclined to turn this new institution to his or her own profit. Local merchants went out of their way to keep their charges as modest as possible. Teachers came to work there because they shared the school's commitment to stem the exodus of youth from the Plateau and to raise a generation of children who would value a good education as the best guarantee of religious liberty (Hatzfeld 1989, 12–13).

From the outset, its international outlook was central to the school's curriculum and way of life. When it came time to adopt a descriptive phrase to convey the unique vocation of the place, Theis and Trocmé came up with "An international center for peace." After the war, when the major classroom building was finished, that legend was carved into a large wooden plaque in the foyer, and no student went to class without passing under it.

The Nazi domination that came in 1940 would quickly add an important dimension to the school's mission. It would take in any number of students who found their way there by virtue of being refugees. Because of the large flow of refugees to the Plateau, and the enrollment of many of their children in the new school, the "international center for peace" would be just that, and the legend that later hung in the classroom building would become the stuff of daily experience as its students learned that resistance can be solidified around strategies of nonviolence and noncooperation.

For André and Magda Trocmé, the thirties ended in confrontation with the monumental task of keeping a peace witness alive, keeping the new school from being still-born, and insuring that Le Chambon-sur-Lignon would become the City of Refuge that would soon be desperately needed, all while bringing up four young children in a strong and nurturing family environment.

11

Understanding Catastrophe
1939–1941

The years from 1939 to 1944 are sometimes referred to as the heroic period in the story of Le Chambon-sur-Lignon and its surrounding towns. Yet the very word "heroic" is one that local people would never use to describe their own actions in creating a city of refuge. It goes against the grain of their Huguenot heritage.

The same was true for Magda and André Trocmé. In their view, being true to the principles of nonviolence was nothing heroic. Yet there were some courageous undertakings, some which involved high risk and others that involved little more than stubborn refusal to collaborate with the demands of the Vichy government.

There is no question that the Trocmés were among the people most engaged in resisting these assaults on persons and on conscience. Nor is there any question that André Trocmé, for all his uncompromising qualities, was unique. He was an original. So it was no surprise that he emerged as a leading spirit in the town and a force to be reckoned with throughout the region. André had a more thoroughly examined conscience than most and was intransigent in the face of any threat to his principles. Yet there was a deep self-knowing about the man, as there was about his indomitable wife. With a hint of a grin, he once offered me a little friendly advice: "Beware men of principle; they're the worst kind."

Three Deciding Moments

By the end of the thirties, the only real question was what to do when war came. Like it or not, everyone had a stake in the question. The stakes were particularly high for André and Magda. They were enemies of war itself, not just of the conflict now on the horizon. How would they keep faith with both conscience and country? Furthermore, André was an activist at heart. A friend and former professor at the Collège Cévenol, Olivier Hatzfeld, described him as "essentially a man of action. In every situation, happy or difficult, his first reaction is always 'What's to be done about it?' ... He asks, 'Who needs to do what?' and 'How can I persuade him to do it?'" (Bolle 1992, 22). Any answer to that question would involve sorting out the right actions and then persuading others to join him.

Persuasion was one of André's long suits. Another friend and former professor, Tom Johnson, recalled a life-changing encounter with him during a 1945 train trip in California. By the end of the trip, he was so persuaded by André's vision for his school that he accepted on the spot an offer of a year's appointment there, even though he had never entertained the thought of teaching abroad until that moment. He ultimately spent the whole of his very fruitful teaching career and his retirement in Le Chambon.[1]

In the summer of 1939, André the activist became increasingly obsessed with the question of what exactly would be his way both to serve his country and to honor his conscience. He knew that he could not compromise the Sixth Commandment, "Thou shalt not kill." There was nothing in the Commandment that said "except in the following circumstances." But neither could he turn a blind eye to the horrors that Hitler was inflicting on innocent civilians in the name of eugenics and the Master Race. Jews, Romani (Gypsies), Blacks, homosexuals, the mentally ill, and the physically impaired: all of them were groups tagged as genetically defective and therefore candidates for sterilization or death. It was simply a matter of weeding the garden of humanity. The Nazi doctrine of the inherent inequality of human beings embraced a form of eugenics gone totally mad. André understood the implications of the widely accepted pseudo-science that supported emerging German policies under Hitler. How could he remain a conscientious objector when his world was faced with a force he recognized as the quintessence of evil?

---

1. Johnson told me his tale in a conversation in Le Chambon in 2003.

Before the summer was over, he attended a conference in Geneva on "the churches and a world at war." The topic and the conversations set him thinking about modes of service to his country that would not call on him to kill young men he saw not as enemies, but as victims of other people's lust for power. He even asked himself why, with his excellent command of the German language, he could not sneak into Hitler's entourage and assassinate him before he threw the world into utter chaos (A. Trocmé 1953, 330). But he could find no way to reconcile assassination, even Hitler's assassination, with his commitment to nonviolence. Some major decisions had to be made about himself and his way forward.

The First Decision: Resign the Pastorate?

By September of 1939, the questions had turned critical. France had already begun mobilization and by August 30 had evacuated some 16,000 children from Paris, so certain was the prospect of a German invasion.

André and Magda had always tried to take some time together on Mondays, the pastor's traditional day off, taking a walk in the hills or otherwise escaping from the demands of life in the presbytère. The first Monday in that September, they used their time together to talk about this, since anything that André decided to do would have to rest on their mutual commitment.

The next morning, September 5, he sat down to pull his thoughts together in writing. He found writing a clarifying way to examine what he might have to do when the storms of war would finally break. He put a title to his paper, *Mise au point concernant mon attitude en temps de guerre* (Clarification of my position in a time of war) and wrote openly: it was only for his own reading after all (Boismorand 2008, 111–16).

The document was a fresh look at his convictions and their consequences now that war was inevitable. In it, he tried to weigh and balance two moral obligations that might appear to be at cross-purposes. He condemned no one who, in good conscience, felt a responsibility to serve the country in the military. He too had felt that responsibility and had responded to it when he enlisted in 1921. But he had also learned from his army experience that no matter what your assignment, the military is always the branch of government in charge of violence. If forced to choose between his country's call to go to war and loyalty to God's word, he knew he could not take up a rifle and kill an enemy soldier. He would have to find his calling in some new nonviolent action that would serve his country in its hour of overwhelming need.

Once having laid it all out on paper, it seemed clear that he could not go on living a protected life in a country town. He also realized that any concrete response he made might mean leaving the parish of Le Chambon. That afternoon he gathered his church council together and shared his dilemma with them. He did not want to abandon his work with them, but neither did he want to draw them into a divisive public debate by whatever decision he made. He offered his resignation as their pastor.

Thursday evening, September 7, he composed a long letter to Marc Boegner, the president of his church, telling him about offering his resignation and why he felt compelled to do that (116–17). Although he could not respond to a call to military duty, and he was not trying to avoid being put in danger, he wanted very much to be of service in a civil capacity and was more than willing to take the risk of a dangerous assignment.

A little over three weeks later France and England declared war on Germany, and there was more than enough for a minister to do in a church whose families were bound to be touched by the risks and tragedies of war.

On October 4, Boegner replied to André's letter, saying that he had done the right thing by offering his resignation because of the pacts he had made not to use his pulpit for proselytizing others to his pacifist position. He had made the same promises to the church council, the regional council, and the national church body that had (belatedly) confirmed his nomination to the Temple in Le Chambon. What Boegner did not know was that the church council had promptly refused to accept his resignation. They supported his concern and would adapt to whatever might be required by any decision he finally took.

The Second Decision: Serve His Nation Without Killing?

André stayed in Le Chambon that winter but continued to fret over the right course of action. Germany's main energies were being spent in

Eastern Europe during those months, but the spring of 1940 would bring a massive invasion of France by way of the Netherlands and Belgium. On May 25, André posted a letter to the American Red Cross at its headquarters on the Champs Élysées, asking whether "the American Red Cross would need my services as a nurse or as a chauffeur, in order to help the civilian population in the war zone, and at a dangerous place, of course with no salary." He gave two references: John D. Rockefeller and the president of the Église Réformée de France, Pasteur Marc Boegner.

In fact, André and Edouard Theis were both ready for the risks involved in working in a dangerous place, as long as they would not be required to carry guns. Boegner had arranged for them to have a meeting with Red Cross officials to explore this possibility. They went to Lyon to follow up with the Red Cross office there. Alas, they were told that the French government had limited Red Cross recruitment to volunteers from neutral countries (Switzerland and Sweden, at that point) or other non-French volunteers whose nations would excuse them from any future call to military service. Only those French men who were exempt from military draft could be enrolled in Red Cross service. Edouard Theis was one such person because, with eight daughters, he had the status of head of a very large family (a *famille nombreuse* in bureaucratic lingo). With only four children, André could still be mobilized in the Home Guard if not in the regular army. Theis realized that he could not abandon financial responsibility for his family. They would have literally nothing to support their daily life. The two men returned crestfallen and uncertain about what to do next.

A Third Decision: Serve in the Refugee Camps?

By mid-June, sooner than anyone had anticipated, the Germans were marching down the Champs Élysées and Marshall Pétain had signed the armistice that divided France in half. The situation in France would spiral downward very quickly in the following months.

Once again, André asked the church's permission to go in search of a non-military service he could perform. He had heard tales of the massive overcrowding of the internment camps operated by the Vichy government, camps that would soon become known simply as concentration camps. This time he asked the church council to consider designating him as its representative to the camps, charged with supplying and distributing food, health necessities, and other forms of relief that the church would provide. The council readily concurred. But neither the council nor the pastor had any idea how overcrowded and devastating conditions really were.

It was common knowledge that the internment camp at Gurs, built in April 1939 by the French Third Republic government some fifty miles from the Spanish border, had long since been filled to capacity by Spanish refugees in flight from Franco's Nationalist army. But in early 1940, the French government rounded up and added about 7,000 German Jewish refugees to the camp's population, justifying the act by holding them as "enemy aliens." After the Débacle, the Germans added still another 6,500 German Jews to the Gurs population. The task of providing food and drinking water for the internees was impossible, and the rate of disease and starvation climbed quickly (Marrus and Paxton 1995, 173–74). A similar story describes the camp at Rivesaltes, where Jewish families were interned (although with men, women, and children housed apart from one another). Two years later, this camp became a launching point for Jews to be transported to Drancy and ultimately to the German death camps.

André's search for a mode of nonviolent service was taking place against a political triangulation that was becoming daily more complex. His own goal, the grim realities of the camps, and the gross anti-Semitic policies of the Vichy government made any decision difficult.

Defeat, Repentance, and Collaboration

Serving his country through some nonviolent role implied serving the Vichy regime and its heroic leader, Marshal Pétain, for it was he who had signed the armistice and ultimately established his role as Head of State, and it was he who sought from the outset to establish a highly personal relationship with his constituency, saying in his first radio address to his people that he had given to France "the gift of my person" (Paxton 1972, 37). Pétain had a moral explanation for France's defeat and a moral framework for its recovery. The moral explanation was simple, and one Pétain had affirmed for years: France's crisis was spiritual, not material. The "spirit of enjoyment" had prevailed over the "spirit of sacrifice," and it was now time for "an intellectual and moral renewal" (Jackson 2001, 124–29).

The moral framework would have to be a national program that could bring a defeated population together around compelling common goals, and thereby restore the moral, economic, and political integrity of "free" France. The program was given a label, *La Révolution Nationale,* and a succinct list of goals: *Travail, Famille, Patrie* (Labor, Family, Fatherland). Serious attention to those core values would help the French people recover from the defeatism that seemed to be everywhere. The path toward success would necessarily involve collaboration with the German forces, but collaboration was a touchy matter. Pétain presented collaboration as a necessary element of the relationship between the Vichy regime and the German forces, necessary but not always desirable. It was therefore a field of diplomatic political activity open to a measure of negotiation.

Pétain was seen, at least by those on the political right, as the one who "saved us from the abyss" (Paxton 1972, 142). With such a reputation, his ministers were able to portray him as the incarnation of patriotism itself: the man who had promised to heal the wounds of war in the Unoccupied Zone and to see that every French citizen had his concern and support. It was a view of things that held together at the outset and then rapidly came apart as one after another government policy signed by the *Marechal* was issued. Although he was increasingly anxious about the general circumstance of Jews in France, even the Grand Rabbi, Isaïe Schwartz, was inclined at the outset to regard Marshall Pétain as "beyond suspicion" (Poznanski 1997, 27).

Pétain's role as Head of the State permitted him to seem above the political fray, a leader who personified the nation's welfare, but not the person in charge of the politics that made it run. That person was Pierre Laval, an important figure in the Third Republic and one who moved from left to right as the political deal-making might require (Jackson 2001, 129–33). Pétain appointed him as Minister of Foreign Affairs and Prime Minister, effectively the head of government. During the first months of the Vichy regime there was relatively little public dissent from the beloved Marshal's plan for the regeneration of his France, although Laval was hard at work bringing the regime into line with German expectations, including its commitment to rid Europe of the Jews. Both men were vested in the success of the *Révolution Nationale,* but Julian Jackson sums up their differences thus: "For Pétain, collaboration was the instrument of the National Revolution; and for Laval, the National Revolution was the instrument of collaboration" (141). The result was a cabinet shuffle in December 1940 that removed Laval from his role in the cabinet, a position he would resume two years later.

His ministers made a project of promoting a cult of personality around Pétain. Thousands of his portraits were printed and sent off to schools, hospitals, and businesses, everywhere that they might be hung. By the opening of the 1940 school year, the Marshal's portrait was expected to be hung in every school classroom. Teachers and civil servants alike were required to sign an oath of personal allegiance to him. That is where early resistance to the Vichy regime occurred in Le Chambon. Beginning with their director Edouard Theis and supported by their pastor André Trocmé, the teachers at the École Nouvelle Cévenole refused, as a matter of conscience, to sign such an oath to a secular authority. Theis also refused to hang the Marshal's picture in every classroom, or anywhere else for that matter. Then a further demand came down. Students were expected to gather every morning and salute the Vichy flag and recite an oath of allegiance. Theis devised a policy that would be hard to assail. He would not require students to gather for the flag ceremony, but he would permit all who wanted to do so to cross the street to the grounds of the public school and share in their morning flag ceremony. A number of them did so at first, but as winter came on and the walk got colder and colder, the file of Cévenol students got smaller and smaller.[2]

The intense loyalty to Pétain did not remain undivided for long. It began to crumble when he showed his hand with the passage of the Jewish Statute of October 3, 1940. It called for the registration of all Jews in the Unoccupied Zone, just as the Nazi occupiers had ordered in the north.

---

2. Edouard Theis described these events in a personal conversation with me in Le Chambon, 1961.

Once registered, Jews could be eliminated from public roles in education, civil service, and the press, and deprived of non-commissioned or commissioned officer rank in the remaining military structure. Every registered Jew—whether male or female, whether French, German, Italian, or any other nationality—was a potential victim of this law. The ultimate purpose of that registration began to dawn on the public, and a resistance movement began to awaken.

The law of October 3 and the refinements established in a follow-up law of June 2, 1941, established tiny job quotas for Jews in law, public service, education, and other fields—two or three percent in most cases—and deprived the rest, wherever possible, of earned income, property ownership, and other personal rights. The armistice with Germany permitted the Vichy state to maintain a total military force of 100,000 to be used only in maintaining public order (Marrus and Paxton 1995, 142–43). The responsibility for faithfully carrying out the law's provisions was handed over to the business and professional communities. Vichy was doing the Nazi bidding even before the Nazis required it. A long list of such laws was promulgated over the next months, each one finding a new nook or cranny of persecution that had been overlooked.

In order to placate the more liberal wing of the political spectrum without abandoning the conservatives, Pétain created, in January of 1941, a National Council, with vaguely defined goals and structures. Its function was consultative and its mode of exercising that function was bizarre indeed. The Council was never to meet as a body, but only in commissions that had been assigned particular tasks. Members would take their opinions and recommendations directly to the Marshal and he would decide what to do with them (Jackson 2001, 153–54). In spite of this unconventional structure, many members of the Council had frequent accidental or deliberative meetings with Pétain. Boegner learned of his membership in the Council by listening to the morning radio news on January 25 while in Grenoble (Boergner 1992, 71). Still, he was one of those who communicated with the Marshal often.

Boegner began his service on the National Council out of genuine admiration and respect for Pétain. As the Vichy's anti-Semitic legislation began to dominate the scene, however, Boegner saw that his presence could do little or nothing to constrain the anti-Semitism that was being pushed by major officers of the Pétain government. On March 9, 1941, therefore, Boegner made a "long and sad" visit to Isaïe Schwartz, the Grand Rabbi of France, concerning the Vichy government's anti-Semitic policies. The personal visit was followed, on March 26, by an open letter to the Grand Rabbi, expressing his church's deep resentment at seeing such racist legislation embraced by the Vichy government and assuring its "ardent sympathy" for the Jewish community. He had directed his clergy to see that this letter was distributed at church doors and city market places throughout the country.

The Revolving Doors of Marseilles

As this more sinister side of the Vichy was unfolding, Trocmé went to Marseilles to connect with the American Quakers and the French CIMADE, relief organizations working in the internship camps there. During 1940–41, Marseilles became a kind of revolving door, with several international relief organizations bringing aid to the camps and at least one of them, the American-based Emergency Relief Center,[3] enabling a host of refugees to escape to Spain, Portugal, and the United States. In a matter of thirteen months the Center's Director, Varian Fry, used every means he could, legal or illegal, to enable the escape of 1,200 or more of Europe's refugees, among them many of its key intellectuals. Among those he rescued were historian Hannah Arendt, artist Marc Chagall, and pianist Wanda Landowska. The Vichy government finally withdrew his permissions and he returned to New York in September of 1941.

André's account of his visits to some of the camps is harrowing and coincides with the description given by relief workers like Pastor Pierre-Charles Toureille of the Comité de Nîmes (Zasloff 2003, 99), Burns Chalmers of the American Friends Service Committee (Rose 2004, 162–68),

---

3. Varian Fry's Emergency Relief Center was the product of the Emergency Rescue Committee (ERC), an American group determined to save a group of Europe's major intellectuals from Hitler's predations. Among its leaders were William Allan Neilson, president of Smith College, and theologian Reinhold Niebuhr.

21. Burns Chalmers, 1940. Unknown photographer. Courtesy of Smith College Archives.

Madeleine Barot of CIMADE, and others. In November of 1940, more than 50,000 internees were living in filthy conditions and were completely destitute (Poznanski 1997, 262).[4]

On this trip André found a need he could fill, but not the one he had expected. It would not be carrying food and supplies to the camps; it would be providing refuge in Le Chambon for children from the camps. He met with Burns Chalmers, explained his proposed mission, and got a reply that countered his offer with an unanticipated question.

Chalmers said the camps were becoming something of an albatross around the neck of the Vichy bureaucrats, and it was therefore a little

---

4. The collective records of several international aid agencies put the total of camp populations in November of 1940 at 53,160. The source of that precise figure is Poznanski in a reference quoted in Horesnyi 1997, 28.

easier to get permissions for release from the French doctors. For Jews and "undesirable aliens," the doctors would certify that they were not fit for the forced labor assignments to which they would be transported in Germany. Now the relief organizations needed major help to find places for these people to live. The most difficult to place were the children whose parents had been deported to forced labor. There were too few towns in France willing to take the risks associated with an influx of foreigners, especially the children of Jewish deportees. Something had to be done to save them. The relief organizations desperately needed towns they could work with.

Chalmers asked André directly whether Le Chambon would be able and willing to accommodate some number of those children being released from the camps. It was just the sort of challenge André was adept at meeting. In answer to his questions about the means to house and feed and educate such children, Chalmers promised that the Quakers and other relief organizations would provide the funding if André could find the housing and the people to volunteer for such a venture. André thought it reasonable to hope that the town would respond to such a challenge. It had both tradition and experience in such matters. The tradition went back at least to the seventeenth century, when Reformed Churches in the region were formally charged with a policy of being solicitous toward the poor and ready to provide protection and help to the persecuted. Then in 1893, a charismatic minister from industrialized St. Étienne, Louis Comte, came on the scene and organized L'Oeuvre des Enfants à la Montagne, whose purpose was to bring children to the Plateau for a summer or a year of clean air, vigorous exercise, and nourishing diet (Bolle 1992, 151–55). In 1893, the organization served fifty-two youngsters. By 1935, the participants numbered more than 3,700. The long history of Louis Comte's organization was a good foundation on which to build the help that Chalmers was asking for. So was the more recent experience of providing for children when the townspeople were asked by town leaders to receive a group of about thirty Spanish children and their mothers, all of them refugees from the Spanish Civil War (413).

Chalmers' challenge to André had turned into a well-prepared and specific opportunity for Le Chambon to become a City of Refuge. With all that in mind, André set out for home immediately to give the church and the community this challenge. When he arrived in town, he found his church council members and most of his parishioners entirely hospitable to the idea of receiving Jewish children from the camps, although many had their doubts about receiving whole Jewish families, especially non-French Jews. By contrast, the Darbyists did not share that hesitation. Jews were Jews, whether children or adults, French or foreign, and all were God's special people. In due course, the distinction between refugee children and refugee adults melted away.

The City of Refuge

The concept of cities of refuge is discussed several times in the Hebrew Scriptures and is identified with six specific cities in the Book of Joshua, chapter 20. In the Haute-Loire, there would emerge multiple cities of refuge including Le Chambon and all of its surrounding towns. Becoming a city of refuge meant taking the risks of hiding individuals and families for shorter or longer periods. For those likely to be hidden for the duration of the war, it also meant providing a proper education for the children. Those being hidden for a shorter time, for whom Le Chambon-sur-Lignon was a stopover on the longer journey of escape, would require knowledgeable guides who could lead small groups safely to the border of Switzerland or elsewhere. A city of refuge also needed skilled and reliable sources for false identification papers and food ration stamps.

While many people were involved in the effort to provide false papers, the most skillful and prolific was Oscar Rosowsky (Fayol 1989), a young French Jew whose parents were already imprisoned in the camp system. When he arrived in town, he carried his own self-manufactured false documents. He was soon turning out papers for others daily, while living in hiding in the barn on Henri and Emma Héritier's farm. M. Héritier was party to Rosowsky's effort, regularly storing bundles of the false papers in the farm's beehive.

One of the greatest challenges was managing these multiple tasks of hiding numerous refugees: safe houses, false papers, escape routes, schooling for children, and all the rest without using conventional means.

When asked by a postwar interviewer how the townspeople managed to organize these complex requirements of illegal refuge, Magda Trocmé replied simply, "Organization? There was no organization." In fact, the risk of having any written records was too great, so the participants in the effort had to depend on face-to-face conversation, clever encryptions, and very accurate memories.

For instance, the pastors involved needed a way to let a pastor in a neighboring village know that some Jews were on the way to his village in search of safe harbor. Edouard Theis solved the problem by printing up some postcards showing a picture of the Tower of Constance, a fortified tower in the walls of the ancient city of Aigues-Mortes. All Protestants knew that story. The Tour de Constance had been used for centuries as a dungeon. In the seventeenth century it held a large group of Huguenot women who had refused to submit to the king and become Catholics. Marie Durand became the storied figure of this dungeon, where she spent thirty-eight years. When she was finally released, officials found the word "Resister"[5] scratched into the curbstone surrounding the dungeon's well. What better way to pass the word from one village to the next than to send a Tour de Constance postcard to that town's pastor, saying "I am sending you five Old Testaments today"? (Boulet, quoted in Bolle 1992, 415).[6]

Even with the best of precautions there would be risks. The Vichy government included plenty of outspoken anti-Semites, many of them in high places, and there were more than enough in the police forces that would be sent to round up Jews. Still, the townspeople had made their inward commitment to cooperate in the tasks of refuge. They were ready to resist by employing only the "weapons of the spirit" and learning to "love the sojourners, for you were sojourners in the land of Egypt." Two years later, the armed resistance forces of the Maquis became a new choice that some of the men would make, and the risks were elevated.

---

5. The inscription was actually written "Registez," a spelling used in the ancient dialect of the region known as Oc.

6. First heard in an interview with Edouard Theis in 1961.

Chalmers' question to André Trocmé had been urgent and concrete. There was so much suffering by so many, and the heaviest weight was falling on the most vulnerable: the children. Fortunately, some of the facilities for refuge were already on hand in Le Chambon, among them the *maisons d'enfants*. Almost without exception, the directors of these homes stepped up to the challenge of a large influx of refugee children. In 1939 there were at least a dozen such *maisons d'enfants* ready to be mustered, but that was too few. More were urgently needed to take in the rising number of children. The *Secours Suisse aux Enfants* and other agencies were quick to rent new properties and to staff them for the growing number of refugee students. During the two years after December 1940, nine more were added, providing another 275 places for children.

Auguste Bohny

The person dispatched by the Secours Suisse aux Enfants to create additional children's homes in Chambon was Auguste Bohny, a German-speaking Swiss army veteran from Basel. He was thirty-three when he arrived, and already had experience directing such a home in Talloires, on the Lake of Annecy. The American Quakers who were financing the Talloires children's home had petitioned the Secours Suisse to transfer him to Le Chambon for this larger task. He was imaginative and gifted, and he could improvise solutions to problems of food or clothing or even escape. After establishing two homes for refugee children in the fall of 1941, La Guespy and l'Abric, he went on to establish two others in 1942 and 1943: Faïdoli and the Farm School (*Ferme École*) as well as a carpentry training center, *l'Atelier Cévenol* (the Cévenol workshop). He lived in one of the children's homes and used that as a base for the many trips he had to take outside of Le Chambon in search of critical food and medical and other supplies.

Bohny and the Trocmés became very good friends, each supporting the other whenever possible, especially now that the pressure to accommodate more refugee children was rising. One thing that Magda and André could do for these children was to help them feel secure and welcome in their new environment. For most of them, that alone was different from their experience at other stops along their way to refuge.

Jacob Lewin's story is a case in point. Lewin, a teenage German refugee, was being held at the camp in Gurs with his family during Chalmers' months of service in the area (Bolle 1992, 212). Jacob described the camp as "a horror. The food was rotted, the buildings were dilapidated and cold, infested with insects and swarming with fleas and swarming with rats as big as cats. . . . People were dying of malnutrition and other maladies" (Horesnyi 1997, 14). Fortunately for him, he was still young enough to be released from Gurs and sent off to Le Chambon-sur-Lignon. He learned later that his parents had been sent to the assembly point at Drancy, outside Paris, and carried off to Auschwitz, never to be seen again (Marrus and Paxton 1995, 227).

Once in Le Chambon, he was lodged in La Guespy, where he got to know the key figures in the Chambon rescue network: pastors Theis and Trocmé, Mme. de Félice, the patroness of La Guespy, and Mireille Philip, the organizer of escape routes, as well as his fellow students in La Guespy. He saw M. Bohny more often than the others and soon found him a valuable friend who might be a father figure, now that his own father had disappeared on one of the death trains. Indeed Bohny saved Jacob's life more than once.

Bohny's ebullient spirit endeared him to many of the students, who referred to him as "Papa Gusti." For one thing, he was an accomplished pianist whose repertoire included Dixieland jazz as well as classical and religious music. He had a totally practical side too. He persuaded a local farmer to rent him the use of several fields, so that students could raise at least some of the food needed by the seventy-five or eighty pupils in the Secours Suisse homes. He even persuaded his Swiss bosses to come up with the money to establish the farm school, where older students would learn the skills of milking cows as well as raising carrots and potatoes.

Bohny found the perfect directrice for this Ferme École in the person of Friedel Reiter, a young Swiss pediatric nurse who had been posted by the Swiss Red Cross to serve the children of another notorious camp, at Rivesaltes in the eastern Pyrenees. Thanks to Reiter, Rivesaltes became something of a shrine. Friedel Reiter had been spiriting children out of

22. Jacob Lewin (second from left) and students of La Guespy. Unknown photographer. Courtesy of United States Holocaust Memorial Museum.

the camp, sometimes with and other times without authorization, and bringing them to the safety of Chambon. Finally, the Rivesaltes camp was closed altogether and its remaining population deported to the death camps. Friedel then came to Chambon at Bohny's request and took on the job of directice of one of the children's homes, Faïdoli. Her responsibilities expanded when Bohny added supervision of the Ferme École and l'Abric to her duties. She later married Auguste Bohny. Both Friedel and Auguste were recognized as among the Righteous of the Nations by the Yad Vashem in 1990.

The role of the Secours Suisse aux Enfants was unique. Its roots were in a comparable collaboration of Swiss agencies that had been gathered by the Swiss Civil Service to deal with the post-1936 chaos in Spain. That model led to the creation of the Secours Suisse aux Enfants when the French camps multiplied at the outbreak of the Second World War. These camps were initially seen as a humanitarian response to the mix of

23. Auguste Bohny, 2001. Photograph by and courtesy of Richard Unsworth.

internal refugees from the Anschluss in Alsace-Lorraine, both French and foreign Jews, and leftists, Gypsies, and others from central and Eastern Europe. They quickly became "assembly points" for undesirable persons: foreign nationals, Jews, Gypsies, and Communists, groups that might be dealt with through resettlement in France, or forced labor shipments to Germany or deportations to death camps in middle and Eastern Europe (Kotek and Rigoulet 2000, 25).

Representatives of some twenty Swiss humanitarian aid organizations collaborated, under the leadership of the Swiss Red Cross, to create an agency that would focus on the needs of children. It was the only non-French agency in charge of homes for children. It was also an agency already known to André Trocmé, who had promptly contacted the Swiss Civil Service and through them proposed collaboration between the Secours Suisse and the town of Le Chambon to provide refuge for Jewish children interned in Gurs and other similar camps. By May of 1941, the first of those homes, La Guespy, was opened to sixteen Jewish children, most of them from Gurs. By October, a second home, l'Abric, was opened to receive thirty-five malnourished children from major urban areas for periods of three to six months. During the years leading up to the liberation of Le Chambon in 1944, about eight hundred youngsters had been hidden and educated in these Secours Suisse establishments (Bolle 1992, 192–215).

Even though the maisons d'enfants were places of refuge to many Jewish children and young people, the French police did not immediately harass them. In fact, the existence of the homes took a certain measure of pressure off the Vichy government and its miserable internment camps.

In the waning months of 1941, however, pressures were building between Pétain's government and the German occupiers in the north. A steady diet of agreements and negotiations between the two forces was under way. The Vichy government would be expected to take a tougher stance with regard to its internal Jewish refugees, as well as the foreign Jews that Germany itself had unceremoniously dumped in French territory.

Vichy police forces stepped up their presence markedly in areas like Marseilles, where Jewish refugees had at least some chance to get out from under the German boot. But that was not enough to satisfy the German occupiers in the north. Their intelligence systems told them that Pétain's government, for all its anti-Semitic laws, was not a satisfactory collaborator. So more German administrators, army officials, and troops were posted to Vichy areas to insure enforcement of Germany's Master Race policies. The plight of the refugees and their protectors in the City of Refuge would worsen considerably.

12
The War Worsens
1942–1943

In the opening months of 1942, Marshal Pétain was still popular in sectors of this new French State. Church authorities were still willing to regard some of the more odious actions the government took (e.g., the Jewish Statute of October 3) as necessary compromises made in exchange for the Vichy government's independent status. Pétain's emphasis on the three virtues of work, family, and fatherland was accepted as a commonplace template for the moral reform of the French nation. Church publications made repeated favorable comment on this celebrated triptych. The president of the ÉRF, Pastor Boegner, was still in support of Pétain and still a member of his National Council, even though critical of many of the Council's ministers.

During 1941, the Vichy government had often expressed its gratitude to those relief organizations that had arrived on the southern scene to help manage the increasing burden of the internship camps. In one early letter from Pétain to the head of Quaker relief operations in Europe, Howard Kershner, the Marshal expressed his own and his nation's gratitude for "these activities which you have undertaken in favor of France" (Horesnyi 1997, 5). Six months later, Kershner returned the compliment in his annual report to the American Friends Service Committee, writing, "No nation in the history of the world has ever been so hospitable and generous in its dealings with foreigners who have been unwanted and have come without invitation . . . [France] has generously allowed the persecuted of all lands to seek asylum within her borders" (Kershner 1941, 21). Those estimates of benign intent would be turned inside out during 1942.

It is not surprising that the nonviolent resisters of Le Chambon found fulfillment in what they were doing and the values they were serving. It should not be surprising either that André Trocmé could refer, in his memoirs, to 1942 as the happiest year of this period. Magda and André had unmistakable duties of conscience to fulfill, for which their reward was simply having kept faith with their beliefs and with those who came to the Plateau for refuge.

The first Jew they had taken in was a German woman who had heard that she might find refuge in this remote town. She arrived on their doorstep on a snowy night in the winter of 1941–42 with no suitable clothing and no money. Once the woman was warm and fed, Magda wondered what she should do next. She went to the mayor for advice. He warned her that housing a non-French Jew was a risky thing, especially because there were already French Jews who had been taken in, and the presence of a non-French Jew would put the French Jews at risk. Discouraged by that advice, she sought out an important Parisian Jewish woman who had come to Le Chambon because life for a Jew was so dangerous in the city. Her advice was the same as the mayor's: an influx of foreign Jews would put the French Jews like her in danger. Magda and André finally got false papers for her and put her in touch with someone they thought could get her into Switzerland.

During 1942, the influx of foreign Jews did in fact increase, but most of the people of Le Chambon simply could not turn their backs. They did whatever they could for whoever arrived. Soon enough it was clear that Pétain had agreed to have foreign Jews rounded up in the Unoccupied Zone, and before the year was over, Jews of any and every nationality were being rounded up and sent to Drancy, and thence to the death camps in the East.

The Trocmé family, like so many others in Le Chambon, took in the refugees, the French and the foreign, the grateful and the annoying, the whole pastiche of humanity. They took in Madame Berthe, a German Jewish woman known by the name on her false papers, who was to serve as Magda's helper. Her talents were limited, but they clearly included complaining about her lot and excusing her ineptitudes as a cook. And there was M. Colin, a cabinetmaker from Berlin, whose birth name was Cohn. He was good at building furniture for the household but equally good at throwing fits of anger.

On the brighter side of the ledger was the friendship between the Trocmé family and Roger LeForestier. LeForestier had come to Le Chambon early in 1936. He had finished his medical training and after his term of required military service had become a medical missionary working with Albert Schweitzer at his hospital in Lambaréné, a then small town in central Gabon. After some months he took sharp issue with Schweitzer over the doctor's harsh disciplinary treatment of an African patient and left Lambaréné to establish his own clinic in the Cameroun. That ended when he contracted an invasive parasitic disease and had to give up tropical medicine altogether. Now he was the one in need of a healthy living environment, and that led him to establish his practice in Le Chambon-sur-Lignon.

Having heard of the Trocmé family, he thought the presbytère would be a good living situation while he got his practice going. Before long he had moved in with the Trocmé family, much to the delight of the children, and there spent his first year in Le Chambon-sur-Lignon. His imagination was irrepressible as was his sense of humor. He became very much a part of the family, to the point that Magda Trocmé regarded him as one of her own sons (M. Trocmé, 211).

In those first years of the war, the German occupation and the Vichy government would cause him great grief and ultimately cost him his life. In spite of his very high regard and affection for André, he could not share André's absolute commitment to nonviolence, although he saw violence as repugnant. He was bound by his Hippocratic Oath to do no harm and to heal any and all who came to him. He did not take sides and he did not carry a gun, even in the most dangerous of circumstances. His private car became the town ambulance, and he carried out his obligation as a physician, readily serving anyone in need, including members of the Maquis, German soldiers on leave being housed in two downtown hotels, or refugees hiding in local homes.

Rounding Up the Hidden in Le Chambon

As it wore on, 1942 became a far worse year than 1941. Four events signaled the change. The first went largely unnoticed by the population in general: Hitler called for a showdown with the Vichy government in April, giving Pétain's head of government, Pierre Laval, 24 hours to make changes in the cabinet and have them approved by Hitler's high officers.[1]

A second signal came in March of 1942, when the German authorities imposed the visible identification of Jews by the Star of David in the Occupied Zone. The public reaction of non-Jews in the Occupied Zone was negative and grew steadily. While the French Police dutifully enforced the use of the Yellow Star, others often regarded it with contempt or ridicule. A group of students at the Sorbonne even wore badges inscribed with JUIFS, which they explained stood for "I am a Jeunesse Universitaire Intellectuelle Francaise," Young French University Intellectual (M. Trocmé 1946, 239). So when the Germans pressed the Vichy regime to follow suit, a host of reasons came back why such a thing would be counter-productive in the Free Zone. A wide range of protest came to Pétain from sundry quarters of his citizenry, among them the Council of the Protestant Federation of France, whose president was Pasteur Marc Boegner. Ultimately, the roundups and deportations of Jews from both the Occupied and Free Zones, all going on at the same time, overshadowed this effort to label Jews, and the demand on Pétain's government faded away.

A third and most disquieting signal came in July with the roundup at the Vélodrome d'Hiver in Paris. Now the population in the Free Zone began to wake up to what was going on.

The fourth event came on August 4, when strictly confidential instructions were sent to the regional Prefects in the Free Zone. The Secretary General of the Police instructed them to transfer to the Occupied Zone all foreign Jews who had come to France after January 1, 1936. Next came instructions to the Prefecture of the Haute-Loire to begin surveillance operations for certain Jews and others, and finally the roundups of non-French Jews in the Free Zone began on August 26. By the end of the month, 5,885 Jews had been arrested and transferred to Drancy for deportation (Horesnyi 1997, 78). The "Final Solution" was under way in the Vichy region.

---

1. *New York Times*, April 26, 1942.

By mid-1942, roundups had begun in the Free Zone as well, but in small incremental numbers by comparison to the spectacular 13,000 at Vélodrome d'Hiver. Those who were swept up in the action were scattered among fourteen camps and were, to most of the Free Zone population, out of sight and out of mind. But for Trocmé and Theis and others in Le Chambon, the threat of roundups was not a distant something that could happen to someone else. It was bound to happen in Chambon, the only question being when and how.

Trocmé wanted to take every precaution possible in advance of an event. He went to the chief of police to lodge a warning: three projects in town would have to be given diplomatic immunity. The O.S.E. home was under the protection of neutral Sweden; two others—Les Roches and Coteau Fleuri—were under American and Swiss protection. The chief promised to send this information along to the authorities. It seemed ominous that there was never any reply.

The first attempt at a roundup in Chambon came at 4:30 on a Tuesday morning, August 25 (Bolle 1992, 200). About eight gendarmes and the Inspector of Security for the region were in charge. When they asked to see M. Steckler, director of one of the homes down the road, to check his papers, Bohny led them down to that other house and woke M. Steckler, while back in l'Abric, one of his staff made sure that any pupils under the least suspicion got out of the house and into the woods.

Meanwhile, Bohny warned the officers that they could take no action with any students unless they had the express permission of the chief of police. They left to find the chief and came back at 9:30. While they were gone, Bohny had his students put together some breakfast and head out to the woods. When the officers returned there was no one home but Bohny. The commandant was furious and threatened to arrest him on the spot. Bohny made sure the commandant knew that, were he arrested, a report would go to his Secours Suisse superiors in Paris, and would likely result in the agency's refusal to continue caring for the 10,000 or more Jews in Paris who were in their jurisdiction.

The whole story is a testimony to the virtues of a clumsy bureaucracy, where everyone has to check up and down the line before taking action. The authorities came with only conditional authority and a bus they were to fill with Jewish children and adults. They left with one prisoner, M. Steckler, and drove the bus to le Puy to book Steckler, but only after an embarrassingly heartfelt farewell from a large group of Chambonnais. As if to cap the tale, Steckler was held overnight and then released because of a letter indicating that he was only one-fourth Jewish. It came from a Vichy Social Service agency and had been rushed down the mountain roads that morning (Bolle 1992, 200).[2]

Jacob Lewin and his brother were evidently on a continuing list of Jewish refugees in Le Chambon, because they were the objects of another search for Jews in February of 1943. This one could not be called a roundup. It involved only these two boys and one other person. They were taken to le Puy to be booked, but Jacob was released because he was under age. André Trocmé and Roger LeForestier followed them down to le Puy and were able to bring back two of the three. Martin Lewin was booked and sent off to Gurs for another round of mud and wintertime starvation.

This time Jacob was moved to les Barandons, a chalet outside the town which belonged to the Salvation Army. There he remained for another two months. The inactivity of hiding was getting on his nerves. He needed to go join the Free French Forces in North Africa, or at least to get to Switzerland. Both goals would involve long travels and more help from hiders along the way.

Pastor Theis got the false papers, and the son of the schoolmaster, Marco Darcissac, arranged the escape plan together with some friends. They dressed themselves and Jacob in the uniforms of the Boy Scouts and took off by bicycle down the mountain road to Valence, where they delivered him to a minister who was part of the underground network of filières, the secret pathways to freedom. He was handed over to other guides who got him over the Swiss border. There he would be picked up and settled into the Swiss population with yet more false papers.

---

2. One peril of recollections after many years is conflicting accounts of the same event. The recollections of M. Bohny and those of Jacob Lewin differ in dates and details, although the thread of the story is the same in both accounts. Where details differ, I have chosen to follow the account of M. Bohny as it appears in Bolle.

All these very public confrontations stiffened the resolve of the rescuers of the Plateau, whose reaction was to secure the safety of the persecuted. The escape routes increased, more escorts appeared, and the number of the hidden increased sharply.

One more chapter of this story concerns the daily insecurity of young children, teenagers, and adults who were at the center of the rescue and refuge efforts. That insecurity was an emotional challenge that had to be faced and overcome. Here is Auguste Bohny's description of that part of daily life: "I hope one can feel a little of the ambience of that time. Worries about what would come next were the 'daily bread' of every day. 'Will there be a checkup by the police? Will there be a roundup? Will we still have all the children at the end of the day? All those questions cannot express sufficiently the daily anguish of that period'" (Bolle 1992, 25).

The other side of that common anxiety was the strong bond that grew up among those involved in the refuge and rescue. It was a unifying experience as well as a worry.

Lamirand Comes to Town

Almost immediately after the Armistice, Pétain had focused attention on the youth in the Free Zone. It was all part of his larger plan to dispel the humiliation of the defeat and give a new generation the sense of pride that ought to go with serving their nation in its process of reconstruction. Taking a leaf from Hitler's book, he called for the national organization of a group of reliable young patriots. They would be called Les Compagnons de France. The aim was to have at least 25,000 boys from thirteen to twenty involved as volunteers in projects set out for them: working on farms, in homeless shelters, even joining one of the theater groups that toured the country with a positive message of progress and unity in creating the new French State. By the middle of 1942, it was clear that Pétain's aim was not being fulfilled. Instead of 25,000 participants, German intelligence could account for no more than 3,350 in the volunteers' camps.

When Hitler's gauntlet was thrown down in April, it was clear that the whole scheme needed more prominent and more skillful leadership. The management and development of these programs was put in the charge of George Lamirand, the Under-Secretary for Youth Affairs in the Education Department. He saw his new task as providing "a new order built on justice and solidarity, calmly and peaceably" (Paxton 1972, 163).

In mid-August, the Marshal was scheduled to be in le Puy, the Haute-Loire capital. His visit was to be part of a grand pilgrimage, scheduled for Assumption Day, when Catholics worship at a particularly popular shrine of the Virgin. It was also the occasion to muster all Catholic youth groups in the Unoccupied Zone. Le Puy was selected because it was the home of the famous Black Virgin. The cardinals and bishops were to be in attendance, as were key members of the Vichy leadership, including Georges Lamirand (270).

Haute-Loire officials urged the Marshal to add Le Chambon to his agenda, since it was nearby. He would see what good things were happening with youth organizations in the town and would have an opportunity to strengthen his image among the Protestants in the remote Plateau towns. Knowing the growing disquiet about the Marshal in the Plateau, the Vichy leaders thought better of the idea and assigned the visit to

24. Lamirand visits Le Chambon-sur-Lignon. Unknown photographer. Courtesy of the Chambon Foundation.

Lamirand. He would represent the Marshal. He would also use the opportunity to promote interest in the Compagnons de France (Bolle 1992, 419).

Lamirand's office was in touch with town authorities in advance, laying out in detail their expectations about the welcome: an attention-getting arrival of his official party, townspeople lining the sidewalks waving Vichy flags, a formal gathering in the church with all the notables, local and national, in attendance, and a cordial feast to top it off. Most of the power holders in the ÉRF were on board with the plans. When they learned of the refusal of Trocmé and Theis to cooperate in the planning, they dispatched Jean Beigbeder, head of the Protestant Boy Scout organization, to take the planning into his own hands (393).

As the day moved along, the Under-Secretary's morale-raising visit did nothing to raise his own morale, and to the extent that it raised the morale of the young people of Chambon, it did so for all the wrong reasons. There were no flags flying, only a few people looked down at the motorcade from their windows, and the luncheon menu consisted of Spartan dishes that were typical of the food available to the townspeople, served not in a fine hotel dining room but in a rustic all-purpose building on the grounds of *Joubert*, the YMCA camp. The Boy Scouts and Girl Scouts, including fourteen-year-old Nelly Trocmé, were assigned the task of waiting on table. Nelly was carrying an over-full tureen of soup when she accidentally spilled soup down the shoulder and back of M. Lamirand's newly tailored quasi-military uniform (A. Trocmé 1953, 285). It was a great embarrassment to Nelly, even though Lamirand, ever the gentleman, reacted with dignity. But there was silent hilarity around the room, adding ironically to the spirit of the day.

When the assembly gathered for a service in the Temple, neither Theis nor Trocmé was in the pulpit since neither wanted to give the impression of honoring the Vichy government's representative. The minister from nearby Mazet-Saint-Voy, Marcel Jeannet, spoke instead, reminding the congregation that they must respect the authority of the State, provided only that the State did not ask the church to disobey God's law. Jeannet was one of the Swiss preachers who came to the Plateau during these years; here was the anomalous situation of a French church asking a Swiss preacher to welcome a representative of the French government.

After the service in the Temple, Lamirand was greeted by a delegation of older students from the École Nouvelle Cévenole. Led by René Chave, a student in the special curriculum for future theologians, the group presented a written document to M. Lamirand and asked him to read it. George Menut, another of the students present, later reconstructed the manifesto as follows:

> Monsieur le Ministre,
>
> We have learned about the horrifying events which took place in Paris three weeks ago, when the French police, obeying orders given by the occupation forces, arrested in their homes all of the Jewish families of Paris and shut them inside the Vel d'Hiv. Fathers were torn from their families and deported to Germany; children were wrenched from their mothers who suffered the same fate as their husbands.
>
> Knowing from experience that decrees of the occupying forces are, in a short time, imposed on non-occupied France where they are presented as spontaneous decisions made by the head of the French State, we are afraid that the deportation of Jews will soon be applied in the southern zone of France.
>
> We want you to know that there are, among us, a certain number of Jews. Now, as far as we are concerned, we do not make any distinction between Jews and non-Jews. That would be contrary to the teaching of the Gospel. If our friends, whose only offence is to have been born in another religion, receive the order to let themselves be deported or even be subject to a census, they will disobey those orders, and we will do our best to hide them in our midst. (Bolle 1992, 393)

Lamirand's response was barely contained anger at what he regarded as uncalled-for defiance. His host, the Prefect of the Haute-Loire (and a Protestant) M. Bach, was equally upset and warned Trocmé that if asked for a list of Jews in Chambon, he had better comply or it would be he who would be deported. Bach's belligerence struck a nerve, and Trocmé replied, "We don't know what a Jew is, we only know men" (A. Trocmé 1953, 361).

There was every reason to think that some kind of additional pressure would be put on both the hiders and the hidden in Le Chambon. While there is no direct evidence that two important events were connected, it is the case that Lamirand's visit took place on August 10, and the first (but unsuccessful) roundup of Jewish students at La Guespy happened five days later. In any case, some students were feeling the pressure intensely, quite apart from any encounter with Lamirand.

One of those was a student named Hans Hoffman, a German Jew sent to Le Chambon from the internment camp at Rivesaltes, where his parents were still being held. Just before the formalities were to begin, he was handed two letters from his parents. The more recent of the two included this news: "Tonight we will leave Camp de Rivesaltes to be transported to a camp near Paris. The name of the camp is Drancy. Drancy is the last stop before deportation to Auschwitz in Poland. And dear Hans, you know what that means. Be strong and pray for your mother and father, as they love you forever and ever" (Hoffman 1989, 21).

New Families

For some refugees, especially the eight hundred or more who arrived in Le Chambon as members of intact families, their protection involved longer stays as tenants or guests or adopted members of a local family. Some were able to rent properties and set up their own private quarters, but the great majority arrived in need of help. Pierre Sauvage's parents were helped by a farming family: Henri and Emma Héritier and their daughter, Eva. Young Sauvage arrived in his mother's womb. He was born in refuge, and delivered by Dr. LeForestier, who saw to it that his mother had the services of the hospital at nearby St. Agrève. His father was a Jewish journalist and theater director who had early on seen the benefits of a non-Jewish pseudonym (his real name was Léopold Smotriez). When the Nazis took over Paris, he and his Polish Jewish wife, Barbara, had fled to Marseilles and Free France because they were Jews and the Nazi repression had already begun.

When Marseilles was no longer a safe place, they looked for a small town where there might be less risk of being identified as Jews and thus as candidates for deportation. Léo and Barbara took their false papers' name, Sauvage, when they arrived in a hamlet called La Fayolle, just outside

25. Henri and Emma Héritier, 1944. Unknown photographer. Courtesy of the Chambon Foundation.

of Le Chambon. There they found small quarters in the Roche family's home. They too were a farming family.

Four years later, the Sauvage family came to New York, where Léo went to work as the correspondent for *Le Figaro*. Pierre grew up still speaking French, and attended New York's French Lycée. He knew that he had been born in a little town in the Massif Central, but that is the extent of what he knew about his earliest days. He did not know he was born Jewish, or that the family was in a town where countless other Jews were hidden for shorter or longer times. Nor did he know that he was one of that small number of European Jews who survived the Holocaust. He only discovered those things at age eighteen.

Later he made it his business to understand how and why some farmers in the hamlet of his birth had made his survival possible. He went to Le Chambon, found the Héritiers and asked them, among other things, why they risked their lives as they did for total strangers. Their taciturn response was "J'sais pas. On étaient habitués" (I don't know. We were used to it). It was nothing exceptional. They only did what anyone would have done. In fact they were already hiding another Jewish refugee, Oscar Rosowsky, the prolific producer of false identity papers. In 1987, the Héritiers were recognized by the Yad Vashem as belonging to "The Righteous Among the Nations." In the view of Yad Vashem their action was not at all the ordinary thing that anyone might do; it was what only a very tiny minority of French citizens had done.

In the 1980s, Pierre Sauvage set out to make his now famous documentary film, *Weapons of the Spirit,* a steady-handed and well-told film that has done much to broaden awareness of the story of the hiders and the hidden in the Plateau Vivarais-Lignon.

Treks and Other Escapes

In the archives of the Vichy's Commission on Jewish Questions, Le Chambon is referred to not as a refuge for Jews but as "the head of the escape route for Jews into Switzerland" (Bolle 1992, 114). Clearly it was both, but the government seemed to take the latter identity more seriously than the former. In an identified place, the police at least knew where to look for their prey. When it came to escape routes, however, those trying to intercept a handful of escapees in sparsely populated hills near the Swiss border faced the greater challenge.

Several people in Le Chambon participated in leading little columns of refugees to freedom. One participant, Pierre Piton, a seventeen-year-old refugee in the Future Theologians program, described a filière in the mid-winter of 1942–43 (262). Everyone had a role, said he. According to Piton, André Trocmé was "the brains behind the operation," and Edouard Theis and Mireille Philip were the master planners, setting up short-term hiding places on one of the farms in the area in preparation for the escape. School principal Roger Darcissac prepared the necessary false papers for each one.

It would not be an easy trip. The winter was a harsh one, and when the day came for their trip, Piton came to the rendezvous pulling the meager possessions of the escapees on a toboggan. In the middle of the night, he gathered the three refugees he was handling on the trip, meeting them at one of the farmhouses. There he gave each one Darcissac's false papers and saw to it that any real identity papers were sewn in the lining of their clothes. The farm family had a good midnight meal ready to serve them. Then, at one or two in the morning, when the neighbors were sound asleep, they slipped out and were on their way. They traveled by rail when possible, buying tickets at each stop only as far as the next, a ploy for hiding their ultimate destination from the gendarmes. When they got to Annecy, Pierre paid a call on the Catholic curate there, who directed him to take the group onward via the 9:00 a.m. bus. The driver was in the know and left them at the top of a road leading to the home of another Catholic clergyman, who met them and hid them in a granary.

So it went with such trips: the fewest people possible knew the whole story; elaborate precautions and discrete communications got them from place to place along the way. The tactics parallel those of the Underground Railroad in pre-Civil War America that brought so many escaped slaves to safe places in the North.

Edouard Theis made similar treks himself. On one occasion he hiked a large part of the distance to the Swiss border alone in order to get funds for the maisons d'enfants awaiting him there. He was arrested by a Swiss patrol and jailed overnight, but fortunately was set free the next day. The goal of his most memorable solo trip was to pick up funds intended to enable the purchase of a parcel of land that would become part of the campus of the Collège Cévenol. The International Protestant Loan Association had agreed to a loan of a million francs, which large sum he carried concealed in his clothing on the return to Le Chambon. On another occasion Theis and Mireille Philip made that trek together, going a large part of the way on foot and camping out in the mountains until they saw their refugees cross the Swiss border.

The Vichy dispatches were right. These various back channels originating in Le Chambon accounted for a large number escaping into Switzerland. There are no records, only recollections, so there is no way to determine that number exactly.

1943: Detention at Saint-Paul d'Eyjeaux

In February of 1943, both Trocmé and Theis were arrested, along with their friend and colleague Roger Darcissac, and sent to a detention camp in Saint-Paul d'Eyjeaux[3] near Limoges, more than four hundred kilometers from home. It was the first time they had both been absent from the Temple and its pulpit at the same time. Roundups of Jews and those disloyal to the Vichy were on the rise, and both Magda and André knew he might very well face arrest at some point. Magda's first instinct was to pack a suitcase full of basic necessities and store it away, to be ready if and when needed.

The day of his arrest, there was a knock at the door and Magda was greeted by two police officials who said they wanted to see André on a personal matter. That was not an unusual request at the door of the presbytère, so she ushered them into his study and said they could wait for him there; he was out of the village presiding at a neighborhood meeting and would be home before long. By then it was suppertime, and being Magda, she invited the officers to sit down and share a little supper with them. For the officers, it was a very awkward moment, but they sat down at the table even though one of them said he didn't really feel like eating. When André returned and met with the officers, he came out of the study to say to Magda, "Well, this is it." It was time to get that suitcase out, but when the weather got cold, Magda had emptied it. So she asked if she could get it ready once again, a request the officers readily granted.

---

3. The particulars of this account are paraphrased from multiple sources, including both André's *Mémoires* and Magda's *Souvenirs*, the testimony of George Menut's article (Bolle 1992, 378), the research of Pierre Boismorand in *Magda & André Trocmé, figures de résistances,* and a letter of Pastor Boegner, dated March 18, 1943 and excerpted in Bolle 1992, 396.

The whole encounter was unique for both the Trocmés and the officers. Magda remembered one of them with a tear in his eye, telling them that he really found this a very difficult assignment (M. Trocmé, 231). He did not mind arresting criminals, but an honest man and a minister, that was another story. Nonetheless, the officers could not disobey their orders, so they led André out to the car to go on to their next arrests: Edouard Theis and Roger Darcissac. What none of them knew was that André's goddaughter, Suzanne Gibert, had come to tell the Trocmés something, but seeing from the foyer the police officers inside, she immediately left to pass the word in the village about what was going on.

When the police and their prisoner left the presbytère, they found a large gathering of villagers who had come to bring food and other gifts for André to take with him. As they got into the car to leave, the villagers broke into singing Martin Luther's hymn, "A mighty fortress is our God." The police moved on to arrest the co-pastor and head of the École Nouvelle Cévenole and the principal of the public school in town. Trocmé, Theis, and Darcissac made a most unlikely clutch of prisoners. They were carried off to nearby Tence, where they were booked, and from there to Lyon, where they and their two guards boarded a train for Limoges and the detention camp at Saint-Paul d'Eyjeaux. For André, at least, it was an eye-opener to see passersby look at these three men and their police escort with faces that assumed the men were criminals.

The detention camp was a surprise. The Vichy authorities referred to it as the Centre de Sejour Surveillé De St-Paul-D'Eyjeaux, a "supervised holding center" for undesirable French persons and foreigners. During the Trocmé, Theis, and Darcissac sojourn, the majority were communists. The police were in charge, freedoms were severely limited, barbed wire formed the borders, there were armed guards at the watchtowers, and the barracks were crude and overcrowded. Yet none of those things put this camp in a class with Gurs or Rivesaltes or the other concentration camps. The prisoners could receive visitors, albeit under the same sort of supervision that would pertain in a prison. They could also send and receive mail, including packages of food and personal supplies. A particularly touching letter came from Dr. LeForestier, who tried to reassure them, saying, "The church of Le Chambon may not be the dove of the

Holy Spirit, but it is like a duck: even when you chop off its head, it keeps on walking automatically" (Bolle 1992, 257).

The population was also a surprise. Their fellow captives were not typical criminals, but dissidents. Most of them were communists whose beliefs had been criminalized: a classless society, the overthrow of rule by the wealthy, resistance to authoritarianism of any sort. There were a few Catholic priests and others guilty of helping refugees. André found them interesting people and made friends with many of them, including those who thought Christianity was ridiculous and the opiate of the masses.

The commander of the camp was a more open person than the three Chambonnais expected to find. Darcissac, Theis, and Trocmé proposed that they be allowed to conduct Protestant worship services. The commandant's response was a fair-minded one. He had given permission to a priest to say mass, so he felt compelled to give equal treatment to these Protestants. Darcissac took care of the music, Theis did the liturgy and prayers, and Trocmé was the preacher. A handful attended, mostly out of curiosity, but then there were ten and twenty and more, so the commandant gave them permission to meet three times a week for discussions and prayers. Why? One can only speculate, but certainly the center of the Protestant message for all three men was justice, human dignity, and freedom, hardly things that communists would reject out of hand. Gradually a coded language emerged that permitted all sorts of sensitive issues to be discussed, developing a mutual respect, if not always agreement, among the interned men.

On one occasion, the three prisoners had visits from their families, one of which included Nelly Trocmé and Marco Darcissac. Darcissac's son smuggled in a small camera so that the threesome could have some photo record of their experience. Add to that the fact that Trocmé had a real talent for drawing and made many sketches of the place and of fellow detainees. The photos and drawings can still be seen in American and Swiss archives.

As different as their experience was from that of typical Vichy prisoners, three things remained certain: they were separated from their families, their community, and their jobs; they had no idea what the charges

26. Prisoners in Saint-Paul d'Eyjeaux detention camp. André Trocmé, artist.

were, nor any legal counsel to refute them; and they lived in total ignorance of the final outcome of their experience. By this time, roundups and deportations were commonplace and deportees could expect the worst. As for the charges, there were none.

The best surprise came on March 15, when the commandant told them they were to be liberated, put on the 10:00 a.m. train, and sent home that very day. They had only to attend to some paperwork in the front office. They put their things together quickly—there wasn't much, only a blanket, a tin plate, and a tin cup—and reported to the commandant. How did this happen? The commandant said he had received an order from the office of Prime Minister Pierre Laval for their release. "Now just sign these papers and you can go." It was then that Theis discovered the clause requiring that they swear to obey the orders of the government and to pledge their personal support to Marshal Pétain. "But," they objected, "we cannot do that! It is a matter of conscience for us. Anyway, if we make that pledge and then break it, as we surely will, we make ourselves liars, and that is a violation of the ninth commandment. We are forbidden to bear false witness." The commandant's response was simple: "Don't be stupid, just sign them and go. Nobody will pay any attention to the papers." But Theis and Trocmé stood firm. Darcissac had no alternative but to sign. He was a teacher on the public payroll. If he refused to sign, he would lose his job and his only means of supporting his family. Darcissac left and Theis and Trocmé went back to the barracks, where their fellow prisoners were incredulous. Their reaction: it just proves that Christianity does not work when the chips are down. You refuse to tell the necessary lie and you lose your power to change your world.

Next morning, March 16, the commandant called the pastors in and told them to just leave. He was glad to get rid of them and their complicated moral convictions. They went back to the barracks to collect their things and say goodbye after all, a scene that ended with prisoners and pastors gathered around to sing the traditional song that the French used when friends must part: "Ce n'est qu'un au revoir. . . ." (It's only till we meet again), sung to the tune of "Auld Lang Syne."

Two developments complete the tale. For a long time, there was a question of where this initiative for release had come from. There were several instigators, as it turned out. Daniel Trocmé and Auguste Bohny tried to intervene, as did a delegation from Le Chambon. Pastor Boegner, the president of the church, also took an initiative. With the support of the Protestant pastor in Limoges, M. Chaudier, Boegner used his connections as a member of the National Advisory Committee to intervene with René Bousquet, Vichy's Secretary General of Police. He made the case that the detention of these men was totally unwarranted, and that keeping them locked up could severely damage the Vichy's diplomatic reputation abroad (386).

The other development was tragic. A few days after the three Chambonnais friends were liberated, the remaining prisoners of the camp, about 500 of them, were deported to Poland and Silesia. No one knows whether any returned alive.

13

Climax and Denouement
1943–1944

The Shadow of Arms: Spring 1943

Once liberated from the concentration camp, Trocmé and Theis went about their business in Le Chambon, more aware that they were being watched, but seemingly immune to the paralysis of fear. On the Sunday after their return, the two parsons and Darcissac told the congregation their story of Saint-Paul d'Eyjeaux. The pews were full and the atmosphere was a warm one. It was clear that all three men had earned the admiration of the parishioners. Unfortunately, however, LeForestier's assurance to Trocmé, Theis, and Darcissac that the duck would keep on walking automatically in their absence was a metaphor overtaken by circumstances.

As was the case throughout all of the Free Zone, groups of maquisards were becoming better organized and gaining more supporters, many of them young men of eighteen to twenty-one who never showed up for their term in the STO. That national program of obligatory labor had turned into a massive failure in the spring of 1943, when more and more young men discovered their obligatory labor would require being shipped to Germany for forced labor to replace Germans conscripted for military service on the Eastern Front. Increasing numbers of these young men sought a better alternative: they joined the new Résistance movements.

Inevitably, they lived openly in towns like Le Chambon. Their guns were now conspicuous on the street, which changed the tenor of life. That was the temper of the town when one of Le Chambon's greatest wartime tragedies took place, the roundup at La maison des Roches, a center for refugee students preparing for university studies.

27. Trocmé, Darcissac, and Theis are released. Unknown photographer.

The Story of Les Roches

Since refugees of every age were making their way to the safety of the mountains, a good preparatory program was needed for university students trying to keep up with their studies. In the fall of 1941, American Quakers had made it their task to find the place and the resources that would make such a Foyer Univérsitaire possible. They dispatched Burns

Chalmers' successor, Tracy Strong, Jr., an American volunteer working in the internment camps, to sort out the options, look at specific properties, and talk with municipal and departmental authorities to see what funds could be provided locally.

One of Tracy Strong's first stops was in Le Chambon-sur-Lignon, an obvious place to begin his search for a site. The Secours Suisse was already working very successfully there, and Strong had heard encouraging things about the community and the leadership of Theis and Trocmé. He arrived in Le Chambon in time to get to the Sunday service in the Temple, where he could get a sense of the community's involvement in the work of refuge, and where he could hear Theis preach and see Trocmé in action. It was clear that their call to create a "city of refuge" was working.

Sunday afternoon, Trocmé took Strong to see several properties that might be right for a Foyer Universitaire, the most inviting of them being the Hôtel des Roches, an old country house that had been remodeled into a hotel, with adequate furnishings already in place. It was no longer in use and could be rented for 500 francs a year, a manageable sum. The only question was finding the right person to supervise it.

Trocmé wrote to his young cousin Daniel, asking him to move from a Free Zone branch of L'École des Roches, an old and distinguished private school, and take on the job. At first Daniel demurred. He was committed for the rest of the academic year. But the story of what was happening in Le Chambon had another level of appeal to him. "It represents for me. . . . a place for a contribution to the reconstruction of our world . . . a vocation, an intimate calling, almost religious" (Bollon 2004, 4). In October, he decided he must accept André's invitation. He came to Le Chambon and took on the direction of the children's home known as Les Grillons, and by the following March he was ready and willing to take on the oversight of Les Roches as well.

During its first year of activity, the Foyer had admitted students from fifteen different nations around Europe, the largest number being German Jews. All of the students were under the titular authority of Chambon's municipal council, which had to keep track of the residents and comply with Vichy demands for information about them. The National Police

28. Hôtel des Roches. Postcard, unknown photographer.

Inspector, Leopold Praly, was charged with regulating the operation at Les Roches, even though virtually all the funding and teaching and support was coming from private sources. In practice, Praly's role expressed the Vichy government's need to keep track of Jews wherever they might be lodged or hidden. The Jewish students in these Chambon homes therefore had to have false papers and assumed names. So did some of the non-Jews who lacked proper identity papers.

The curriculum at Les Roches was rich and varied. In addition, students had learned all the street smarts necessary to keep the bureaucracy at arm's length. Whenever there was reason to expect a roundup, many of them moved temporarily into the homes of farmers and villagers. Before returning to a day's classes, they had to be warned of any threatening events at the Foyer itself. The way for students to avoid trouble on their way back to the morning's classes was simple. One window at the Foyer building became the signal station. If the shutters were closed, there was trouble. If they were open, that meant "all clear." One day that signal almost certainly saved the lives of Hans Solomon and two of his friends.

Alfred, Kurt and I slept on a farm, in the barn. In the early morning we would return to Les Roches. [That morning] we walked toward Les Roches and on the way two empty trucks passed us on the road. We looked at each other and did not say anything. From that point on, we could not see the special shutter in the special window. Carefully, we walked forward and kept very quiet. When we arrived at the point where we could see the shutter, we could see that it was closed. Something fishy was going on, but so far they could not catch us. We rushed back to the farmhouse and the farmer took us in and hid us in the hayloft. . . . Three or four nights later, through intensive work to organize and find shelter for all the Jewish boys, we . . . were put into the custody of French farmers . . . and I was welcomed by the family of Eugene Cotte. (Solomon 1989, 22–23)

Two weeks later Pastor Bettex, a minister colleague of Trocmé's from nearby Le Riou, near Mazet-St-Voy, visited Solomon and other Jewish boys in hiding and told them that efforts were under way to get them into Switzerland. Soon Mireille Philip had the arrangements made and a group of the boys got ready for the trek to Switzerland. Their brazen strategy was to dress as French Boy Scouts and march through the center of town in quasi-military formation, singing Boy Scout songs at the top of their lungs. At the edge of town, they kept on marching. Ten miles later they were housed for the night and then led on their way via one of the filières that would lead them into Switzerland.

Daniel Trocmé had not been long at his task when the first intrusion of German military authority happened at Les Roches. The Germans were aware that records of Jewish students were being kept by town authorities. From those records they picked out the name of Martin Ferber (Bolle 1992, 635). On the town record his name carried the notation *juif*, whereas virtually all the other Jewish students carried false papers that covered up their Jewish identity. Ferber was one student they could capture and send off to an internment camp. Two German military police officers made a discreet arrest of Ferber, but their discretion did not keep their action a secret, especially from other Jewish students, who were in a constant state of alert already. This only heightened their watchfulness.

29. Daniel Trocmé. Unknown photographer. Courtesy of United States Holocaust Memorial Museum.

Later the German forces came to do a major roundup. They arrived about six o'clock in the early morning of June 29, 1943. A team of German Gestapo officers and soldiers surrounded Les Roches and demanded to see the papers of everyone inside. This time they were after anyone whose papers were not in order, whether non-French Jews, Spaniards, refugee Germans, or French students avoiding their STO requirement. Two of the officers went up to Les Grillons to bring Daniel down to Les Roches and interrogate him as well. Daniel could have escaped out the back door of Les Grillons. His students urged him to do that when they told him the German Gestapo were at the front door, but he refused. These were his charges and this was a moment when they needed him most.

Immediately after he left, one of the Grillons' older students and a helper, Suzanne Heim, rushed downhill to the presbytère to share the frightening news with Magda Trocmé. Magda took a bicycle and set out for Les Roches at top speed. Her *Souvenirs* (234) includes a description of what followed.

> I went in but told Suzanne to return to Les Grillons. I don't know why the Germans let me into the house because the doctor had been turned away when he came to see the sick child of a servant and Pastor Poivre had also been kicked out. The doors were open and I entered. I had left my house in a hurry and was still wearing my kitchen apron. Did the Germans think I was an employee of the house? Perhaps . . . I walked through the kitchen and reached the large dining room. Three or four Gestapo men were sitting at a table on one side of the room and the house staff stood nearby; among them was the person in charge of accounting. The Germans were armed with sub-machine guns and the students were lined up against the wall, on the other side of the room. The last man in the line was Daniel Trocmé. Did the Gestapo know he was an important person?

Magda took advantage of the situation as best she could, moving in and out of the kitchen, bringing glasses of water or anything else that would give her an excuse for quick exchanges with Daniel and a few of his students. While doing that, she collected whatever messages or confidences she could from the students.

She left Les Roches to go down to the Lignon Hotel, where German officers and soldiers on leave were billeted. There she persuaded two of the officers to accompany her back to Les Roches. As they set out, Magda ran into two members of her church youth group riding their bicycles and quickly commandeered the bikes so that the Germans could bicycle back with her to Les Roches and save some precious time. They needed to speak up quickly on behalf of a Spanish boy, Luis Gausachs, who had saved one of their soldiers from drowning in the Lignon River. They reluctantly did so, and Gausachs was released when Daniel Trocmé and the students were taken to a prison in Le Puy, where they were booked.

A few of the eighteen students arrested that day were later released, but most went on to die in the concentration camps. Daniel Trocmé died on April 2, 1944, at Majdanek, a Nazi concentration/extermination camp on the outskirts of Lublin, Poland. Daniel's disappearance into the shadowy prison system was devastating to the Trocmés, and especially to André, who felt it was entirely his fault. He was the one who had invited Daniel to Le Chambon and later added the Les Roches post to his responsibilities. He wrote immediately to Daniel's parents and wrote again later expressing his anguish over Daniel's arrest. Their reply was "sublime," said André. They wrote, "You knew the uncertainty of the faith of our son who was still seeking his way. He gave his life and thus found what he was searching for" (Henry 2007, 45–63). In spite of this most compassionate letter André remained haunted by the ironic outcome of his request for the rest of his life.

The Pastors Move Offstage: July 1943–June 1944

Shortly after the tragedy at Les Roches, André received a visit from a strange maquisard, and a warning. Claiming to be a double agent, he told André that his name was on a Nazi list for assassination. The warning and its consequences came at a time when André felt a profound duty to stay where he was. The tragedy of Les Roches was still fresh in people's minds, and its consequences for the Trocmé family and for the parish were still being sorted out. It was a time when both he and Theis were needed more than ever. And he knew such a story could have been invented to get the pastors off the scene in order to have a wider span of influence for the maquisards. But when he learned that Theis had received a similar warning through Madeleine Barot, an impeccable source of such important information, he knew his visit from the maquisard was not a ruse to get him out of the way. He had to make immediate plans for exiting the Chambon scene.

The story of his going into hiding in Chateau de Perdyer has been told in the first chapter of this book. Both Theis and Trocmé entered the clandestine life in July of 1943, and neither had any idea how long it would last, except to know that only the end of the war would make it both safe and possible for them to return. There was no prospect that the Germans would give up their intent to have them both dead.

The time in hiding was a time of great uncertainty for André. It was hard to imagine that the whole parish would keep faith with his vision of a nonviolent City of Refuge. He knew that his congregation had not become hard-core pacifists. The bulk of the members were people who had their lives to live, and who would probably take recourse to violence if that were the only way to preserve their families, their farms, and their livelihoods. It was one thing to disobey nonviolently the authority of the Vichy government, whose collaboration with German policies had made that authority illicit, but by now resistance to that authority by force of arms had gained major momentum throughout the Free Zone.

Armed Resistance in a Center of Nonviolence

While Theis and Trocmé were in hiding, Police Inspector Leopold Praly was assassinated in broad daylight on the street in front of his lodgings in the Hôtel des Acacias. It happened on August 6, 1943, just over a month after the roundup at Les Roches. Two young maquisards took the action, presumably as revenge for Praly's spying on all sorts of people: village leaders, members of the Résistance, students, and others. The assassination may have satisfied their need for revenge, but it prompted a harder crackdown against the Jews on Praly's lists.

Praly was an intelligence officer who also had the power to order or make arrests. It was his primary task to keep track of Jews and the dissidents who might create trouble on the Plateau. It was a thankless job on all sides. The Vichy bureaucrats pressed for more names and more arrests, since they were in turn under pressure from the German forces to fill a quota of deportees every month. In addition to contributing to the quotas, Praly was expected to insure that civil order, as defined by the Vichy government, was kept in a town full of disguised refugees and both violent and nonviolent resisters.

As thankless a job as it was, Praly had his reputation to guard. It was that or lose his job and be exposed to the revenge of all those people whose hatred he had earned. He needed to be powerful and effective, but he couldn't always manage it. On more than one occasion he had made an arrest and then lost the prisoner.

While the people of the Plateau roundly despised Praly, no one took particular pleasure in his death, except perhaps his assassins. Everyone knew that reprisals would follow and would make things worse for the town and especially for the Jews being given refuge there. Praly had kept his lists carefully and filed them regularly with the departmental authorities. Now the Vichy regime had both the information and the provocation needed to take reprisals against this particularly troublesome town.

One consequence of Le Chambon's reputation was the appearance on the Plateau of increasing numbers of young men in search of a place where they could join one or another group of armed resisters and strike their own blow for freedom. The arrival of German forces in the Haute-Loire in December of 1942 had magnified that desire. Dozens of small resistance groups were already in existence, but now their numbers increased. They were training in secret for their moment of combat, and creating the threads that would weave the stronger fabric of small groups gradually coming under more and more centralized and experienced Résistance leadership.

Such leadership finally arrived on the Plateau in the person of Pierre Fayol, a Jew with experience in the resistance movement of his native Marseilles. When he came under close surveillance there, he was forced to move his family to the safety of mountains. He settled near Le Chambon and was soon well connected with the important Résistance leaders in the whole area. Fayol had kept his ties with other major Résistance groups in the Vichy-controlled areas and started the process of bringing scattered groups in touch with one another to create a more coherent set of strategies for dealing with the Germans as well as with the Pétain loyalists.

Among all the Résistance clusters in and around Le Chambon, one of the people Fayol was most eager to meet was Léon Eyraud. Eyraud and his wife were the owners of Les Ombrages, one of the boarding houses in Le Chambon; Eyraud was also one of the best-connected people in the town. Early in the history of the Résistance on the Plateau, he became a central figure by virtue of those connections. His Résistance pseudonym was Noël (Léon spelled backwards). He and his family were friends with the Trocmés, and Jacques Trocmé remembers to this day Mme. Eyraud's gâteaux de Savoie (sponge cakes) and her blueberry pies. Eyraud also commanded the respect of the Maquis, of key figures in the town, and of ministers of the twelve other parishes in the area (Bolle 1992, 232). He used those connections to see that functions did not become redundant, that skills were assessed and used wisely, and that the welfare of the town was properly served.

All this was going on throughout 1943. As much as he respected others' motives, André Trocmé was very worried that armed resistance would soon overshadow the grand experiment of nonviolent resistance to which he and Edouard Theis were so committed. His worry was well founded. When he and Theis were taken off to the internment camp at Saint-Paul d'Eyjeaux, the growth of armed resistance forces in the Plateau increased markedly. Larger political and military forces were at work now and would continue to be so whether or not the two pastors were in hiding. Between their arrest and internment in February and their disappearance into a clandestine life in July, both men were absent from the daily scene in Le Chambon for seven months of the year 1943. There was no longer a leading voice for nonviolent resistance in Le Chambon.

On one score, at least, André's commitment to nonviolence still had an effect on the thinking of his fellow Chambonnais. They made it clear that members of the Maquis were not welcome on the streets of Le Chambon if they were either in uniform or were carrying a weapon. That public attitude probably had two roots: a desire to avoid letting their children get the idea that guns were a desirable part of daily life, and a fear that parading guns or uniforms in brazen fashion would incite German retribution.

> When he returned from hiding in June of 1944, André found that the maquisards were everywhere in the town and its surrounding villages. Nonetheless, he quickly reconnected with friends and colleagues, many of whom had by now joined one form or another of the active Resistance. Léon Eyraud saw to it that he met Pierre Fayol, the new head of the organized Maquis. Despite his worry about the slide toward violence that had been happening during his absence, André developed relationships with the Resistance leaders that were clearly based on mutual trust and respect. In recalling that period many decades later, André wrote this assessment of things: Our old friend Léon Eyraud was at the center of a leftist resistance cell and I found this to be normal. He

was courageous and had long ago abandoned the Christian faith. Mr. André Bass, a.k.a. Monsieur André, a Jewish lawyer, had organized a Jewish maquis with more than one hundred men. This was all right, this was his role. Simone Mairesse, our courageous former parishioner in Maubeuge and close friend, had joined the "Service André" and we collaborated with them and others as long as they did not indulge in assassinations.

A strong concentration of "Armée Secrète" . . . was also in the Chambon and the surrounding area. Their leader, "Commandant Fayol," . . . whose character was filled with great nobility . . . tried to enlist me in the Secret Army and I refused for reasons of conscience. He remained our friend and often visited with us and we both of us felt our relationship was "natural." We both professed a moderate attitude. I felt it was insane to attack German units because it always resulted in bloody reprisals. He agreed with me and this probably protected Le Chambon from a destiny similar to that of Vassieux-en-Vercors. (A. Trocmé 1953, 323)

Early in 1944, many Résistance groups coalesced and became the FFI (Forces Françaises de l'Intérieur), a group strong enough to put great military pressure on the Germans in the occupied areas of France. The French population began to understand that German defeat was more than likely. Then came the June 6 D-Day landings in Normandy. French hopes rose higher, even though the Allied forces would meet stiff resistance every step of their way toward Paris. The liberation of the Free Zone began with an Allied landing in Provence on August 15. Pitched battles ensued, with the FFI and their allies confronting the better armed Germans more and more openly. The denouement was within sight.

The Paroxysms of Defeat: Three Tragedies

While the hallmark events of the war's slow end were playing out on larger fields, the small and remote populations of the Plateau felt the paroxysms of defeat in immediate and tragic events. Such was the case with three tragic deaths that happened in Le Chambon during July and August of 1944.

Manou Barraud, July 5, 1944[1]

Lesley Maber, a faculty member at the Collège Cévenol, described the atmosphere of Le Chambon during the weeks following D-Day as "indescribably feverish." Maquisards were harassing German troops wherever they could. The mayor had started calling for evacuation plans in anticipation of battles on the Plateau that would threaten civilians. Many of the children's homes were already vacant.

The Barraud family's pension, Beau Soleil, was almost vacant. Only three students were there, awaiting the results of their baccalaureate exams that would tell them whether they could have a university education. The other vacant rooms were already requisitioned by a group of maquisards recovering from a losing confrontation with the Germans.

On that Wednesday morning, the maquisards had gone to the village. Manou, Jean, her classmate and boyfriend at the Collège, and another student were idly looking around the vacant rooms when Jean opened a night table drawer and found a revolver that one of the maquisards had left behind. He carefully picked it up and examined it more closely. The cartridge clip was still in the gun, so he pulled it out and set it aside, for safety's sake. Then he handled the mechanisms, the safety catch, and the trigger. As he did so, the safety came unlocked and the trigger squeezed back in his hand.

It was all over in a flash. One cartridge was still in the barrel, and that one fired. To his horror, he saw Manou fall. The bullet had pierced her abdomen. Manou's older sister, Gaby, heard the commotion from downstairs and rushed into the room. She and Jean did what they could to make Manou comfortable. Gaby sent a student to fetch her mother while she ran to get Dr. LeForestier. The doctor drove Gaby back to the house as fast as he could, sensing that the wound was very serious. When they

---

1. For this account, I have relied principally on Lesley Maber's memoir, unpublished and now in revision, *Le Faisceau des Vivants, Le Fagot Chambonnais,* chapter 25, pages 2–6. Her recounting of the death of Manou Barraud is based in large part on her conversations with Manou's older sister, Gaby, who was in the house at the time of the accident, and on her conversation decades later with Manou's mother.

came into the room, Manou was barely conscious. LeForestier looked her over very carefully and said, simply, "She's lost." Jean fled the room in anguish as Manou's mother came in.

The bullet had severed an artery and the blood loss could not be contained. Manou's head was cradled in Gaby's arm when she drew her last breath and, in a weak voice, said, "Maman, I'm dying."

Her mother's shock was total, but she never lost her instinct as a mother. She said to Gaby, "I know there is nothing I can do for Manou. She is dead. But Jean, where is he? I know he must be crazy with grief. I hope he doesn't go and do something desperate" (Maber nd, chap. 25, 5). She went out and found Jean dissolved in tears; she embraced him, took him home to his house, and tried to console him, but his grief would be a long time resolving itself. Not surprisingly, the community as a whole took pity on him and the question of the event being anything but an accident was never raised.

Manou's death weighed heavily on the spirit of the Trocmé family, as it did on so many other families in the town. Mme. Barraud had been more than a parishioner. She was also a friend of André and Magda, just as her children were friends of one another, such close friends, in fact, that Manou was buried in the Trocmé family plot in the cemetery behind the Temple.

Jean-Pierre Trocmé, August 13, 1944

Jean-Pierre, the eldest of the three Trocmé sons, was a bright and conscientious student and a talented poet. It was his poetic turn of mind that helps us understand his accident. He had attended a memorable event the evening before in the meeting hall of the Temple: a nationally famous actor, Jean Deschamps, had come to Le Chambon to do a poetry reading. Among his selections was a poem by François Villon, a fifteenth-century lyric poet who had a penchant for the criminal life. After killing a priest in a barroom brawl, he had time to languish in jail and contemplate being sent to the gallows. Morbid as its title might seem, "The Ballad of the Hanged Men" was Villon's appeal for human brotherhood and understanding to stretch across all boundaries, even those that separate the righteous from the criminal and the living from the dead. Its first verse sets the tone:

Fellow humans who live after us,
Don't let your hearts be seared against us,
For if you pity us poor men,
God will have a greater mercy toward you.
You see here five or six of us hung up,
While our flesh, once well nourished,
Is rotted and devoured piece-by-piece,
And our bones have become ashes and powder.
Let no one laugh at our evil state;
But pray to God that all of us be forgiven.[2]

This *Ballade des Pendus* was studied in detail by students because it was on the program of the national baccalaureate exams. Jean-Pierre had memorized it and was fond of reciting portions of it on occasion. One especially compelling feature of the recitation that night was Deschamps' skill in capturing his audience by making his body go stiff, then swaying back and forth as the poem spoke graphically about corpses hanging in the wind, their rotting flesh being preyed on by the birds.

That Sunday afternoon, Nelly was off on a weekend camping trip with friends, and André and Magda had taken Jacques with them when they walked out to the Ferme École to help resolve a quarrel between the director and two of the Swiss nurses. Jean-Pierre had stayed at home doing his Greek translations for M. Hatzfeld.

On their return from their pastoral call, André left Magda and Jacques at the door of the presbytère and headed over to the Temple. Halfway there, he heard Jacques running toward him screaming, "Papa! Papa! Come quickly! Jean-Pierre is dead!" André rushed back in disbelief to find Jean-Pierre in the bathroom, his body stretched out on the floor with a loosely knotted cord around his neck.

Magda told André that she had walked in to find him hanging in a crouching position from the flushing lever on the high wall-mounted cast

---

2. Translation by the author. See the ancient French text in the Appendix.

30. Jean-Pierre Trocmé, August 1944. Unknown photographer.

iron toilet tank. She had lifted him down in hopes that he might still be alive. The family physician, Dr. Riou, arrived moments later, took one look and shook his head. He tried resuscitation nevertheless, but without success. Riou said the hanging injury had been accidental and Jean-Pierre's death was instant.[3]

Riou was required to call for a police inquiry before issuing a death certificate. The police chief came to the same conclusion as Dr. Riou's: it could not have been an intended suicide. The window was wide open and the door was also open, not locked, both of them circumstances atypical of suicides. He also noted that the cord used was not a stout rope but a piece of heavy mailing twine. Jean-Pierre had evidently lost his balance

---

3. This conclusion appears in the memoirs of both André and Magda Trocmé and was confirmed in my May 2002 interviews with two people present on the scene within a few minutes of the Trocmés' return: Olivier Hatzfeld and Simone Mairesse.

and fallen backward, pressing the cord sharply against his neck and causing a sudden and fatal trauma to the carotid artery.

In spite of the assurances of both the doctor and the police chief, André and Magda were both haunted by their own question: What would have motivated Jean-Pierre to put himself in such a position in the first place? He had never exhibited any signs of depression, and while the accidental death of his friend Manou had been a major emotional assault for him, as it had been for many of his friends, he had never shown any reaction that was other than appropriate grief.

Then it occurred to André: he had been reenacting Deschamps' recitation of the *Ballade des Pendus* of the evening before. The day might come that he would have to recite it in class, and if he did, what better way to display the power of the poem than to repeat Deschamps' dramatic imitation of the corpses hanging in the wind?

Jean-Pierre's death remained so painful for Magda that when she came to writing her memoir, she simply could not bear to recount the story. She left that for André to tell. He did so, and with the account of the happening, he also described his own inner turmoil:

> There is nothing positive . . . nothing and nothing. We are all toys of nothingness. . . . I lost my faith, at least my faith in a God who follows me and is supposed to protect me from evil. We are all thrown into an absurd world which is submitted to absurd and chaotic circumstances. . . . I could no longer pray because my prayer sometimes bounced against an angry God who told me: "It is because you went into hiding and because you have been afraid of death . . . that I took your son instead of taking you." At other times, my prayer simply got lost into nothingness and I stopped praying because I could not have a dialogue with a God who did not say anything, who was elsewhere, in another world which was so different from the world in which I struggled. . . . The scar of my wound has slowly grown thicker but it still bleeds inside. This wound will never heal. (A. Trocmé 1953, 439–40)

Jean-Pierre was laid to rest next to his friend Manou in the Trocmé family plot.

Dr. Roger LeForestier, August 20, 1944[4]

During the eight years LeForestier lived there, he became a major figure in Le Chambon-sur-Lignon, not only because of his medical practice, but also because of his gregarious nature and his irrepressible energy in adding a colorful dimension to life in Le Chambon.

When Theis and Trocmé were interned at the camp in Saint-Paul d'Eyjeaux, LeForestier was one of those who wrote to them to reassure them about the welfare of their parish. He also joined Daniel Trocmé on a trip to Vichy to try to persuade the Minister of the Interior to release the two pastors and M. Darcissac.

He made the Hippocratic Oath his moral gyroscope. When a German soldier asked for a diagnosis and was told he had a venereal disease, LeForestier did not report this (as he was required to do) to the soldier's superiors, for fear of harsh consequences for the young man. When young maquisards were injured, he took care of them without regard to any opinion he might have about their activity in the town. In short, he did not withhold either his concern or his skills from all persons in need of medical attention, and townspeople were very aware of that. It is what endeared the man to his village neighbors.

His extensive cooperation with the Résistance as their official physician put him at special risk, but one of the risks he willingly took occurred when two of his friends in the Maquis, Jean Mercy and Edmée Debray, had been held for three months in a prison in Le Puy. With the German forces coming under ever-greater pressure, there was a well-founded fear that these two people were in danger of being put to death.

On a Friday afternoon in early August, LeForestier left his house to drive down the western slope of the Plateau to Le Puy, hoping to make a case for the release of Mercy and Debray. He first asked Trocmé to

---

4. In recounting this story, I have depended on a wide range of references to LeForestier in Bolle 1992, a version of this story in A. Trocmé 1953, 419 et seq, and a well-documented article, "Roger LeForestier, Mon Père," written by his son, Jean-Phillipe, and published in Fabréguet 2005.

accompany him on the rescue mission, but Trocmé urged him not to go, warning him that German forces were as likely as not to fire on civilian cars about which they had the least suspicion. LeForestier argued that he would be safe because he would establish his medical credentials by draping a large Red Cross banner over the car. Trocmé insisted that he could not count on that strategy to protect his life.

LeForestier decided to go in spite of his wife's pleas and André's counsel. En route, he picked up two Maquisards who needed a ride to the city (but failed to check them for weapons). His "ambulance" soon rolled into the public square in Le Puy, the big Red Cross banner attracting some attention, but the timing could not have been worse. The local Maquis had just robbed a major Le Puy bank of several million francs. In a few minutes, the German military police surrounded the square, searching cars, looking for anything suspicious. They arrested several men and ransacked LeForestier's car. When LeForestier heard the commotion, he came back to the car and was immediately arrested himself.

The police blotter attested that two revolvers were discovered inside the car. LeForestier's passengers had disregarded his rule that no arms were ever to be carried in his "ambulance." As a result, his attempt to save two friends had come to a shocking and unanticipated end. The doctor remained in prison until he was brought before a military tribunal, which condemned him to death.

His wife, Danielle, made two attempts to visit her husband and, if possible, to intervene on his behalf with the head of the German command post in town, a Major Schmähling. Her first visit was to no avail. André Trocmé and Auguste Bohny accompanied Danielle on her second visit. This time she was received by Major Schmähling, who gave her to understand that her husband's death sentence had been commuted to deportation for medical work in the German war factories.

That is not, however, the way things turned out. LeForestier and others in the Le Puy jail were transferred to Lyon and confined in the notorious prison Fort Montluc, overseen by Klaus Barbie, the German officer who later earned the sobriquet "the butcher of Lyon."

On August 20, LeForestier was one of the 120 prisoners who were taken by a detachment of German guards from Montluc to Saint-Genis-Laval, a village outside Lyon. Under the command of Klaus Barbie, the group was herded, two by two, into a decrepit house on the grounds of an old fort outside the town. They were marched to the second floor of the house until that space was filled. The rest were crowded into the first floor. Once they were all inside, the prisoners were systematically machine-gunned until all were fallen. The German soldiers then set the house and its piled-up bodies ablaze, using gasoline and phosphorous to insure that there would be nothing left to identify either the victims or the killers.

The townspeople of Saint-Genis-Laval could not forget the incident. It was their firemen who dealt with the blaze for a full twenty-four hours, and it was their ambulances and hearses that removed the human wreckage. They developed a memorial park on the site of the horror and mounted in its center a stele engraved with the story and the names of those who died as heroes of the Résistance.

It was only after long and persistent research that Danielle could officially confirm her husband's death. It happened when she discovered in the town's collection of remnants from the fire a button which belonged to her husband's suit and a piece of cloth with the name of his tailor in Montpellier.

His death had happened only a week after Jean-Pierre's and a bare six weeks after Manou Barraud's fatal accident.

14

The Bridge from War to Peace

The Plateau Is Liberated

At age twenty, a young German-speaking Swiss by the name of Hans-Ruedi Weber was looking for a project, something that would help him sort out his future. He had heard about the work of the Secours Suisse aux Enfants in Le Chambon-sur-Lignon, and offered his services if they would have him. He was accepted and arrived in Le Chambon in January of 1944.

Hans kept a diary during the nine months of his service. His entry for June 14 notes the return of André Trocmé from his months in Château de Perdyer. He also records hearing the British airplanes that were on their way to one of the several sites close to Le Chambon where they could make nighttime parachute drops of arms and supplies to the Maquis (Bolle 1992, 460). His entry for August 31 speaks of attending a Bible study class on a portion of the Letter to the Hebrews, where St. Paul calls on Christians to have endurance in doing the will of God. That seemed very apt counsel for the work he was trying to do while furious and final encounters between the Maquis and the Germans were going on around Le Puy, the district capital.

On the way back to Faïdoli that day, he was surprised to see one lonely French tank at the side of the road. He stopped for a long conversation with the Alsatian tank commander, who told him of the battles that were going on south of the Ardèche. When Hans asked the commander where he was going next after Le Chambon-sur-Lignon, he did not know; but he knew that a plane would soon fly over and radio his travel instructions. It was a paradigm of the inchoate and rapidly unfolding events that signaled German defeat in the south.

Three days later, advance forces of Général de Lattre de Tassigny's army had arrived on the Plateau. As they drove from St. Agrève to Tence, they passed through the town square of Le Chambon, to the cheers and tears of the townspeople.

Preaching to the Enemy

In the course of those final days of the war in the Vichy zone, the last Germans remaining in Le Puy, about 120 of them, surrendered to the Maquis and were kept by the French police as prisoners of war. They were quartered in an old chateau at the Pont de Mars outside of the town, but still within the boundaries of the parish. Because they were within the town boundaries, André felt it his responsibility to serve as their chaplain. He paid a visit to the Pont de Mars chateau and found that the commandant was Major Julius Schmähling, the commandant of the Le Puy garrison who had presided at the trial of Roger LeForestier less than a month before, and was now a prisoner of war. In the course of their conversation, Schmähling told André that LeForestier had been sent to Germany, was still alive, and would return to his wife when the war was over.

Schmähling accepted André's offer to preach to the Pont de Mars prisoners, and suggested that services might begin the following Sunday. Being a Catholic, he would not be present, but his second in command would be there in his place. That next Sunday morning, André preached his sermon at the Temple and then, in the afternoon, went to lead Sunday worship for the German prisoners. Schmähling had given the orders and all the men were present and accounted for. It was clear they were there under orders and not necessarily by preference. André prevailed on a German officer, Captain Neunkirchen, to read the Lutheran liturgy. Neunkirchen was an officer in the military police, the Feldgendarmerie.

André's gesture of preaching to the enemy met with a divisive reception in the village. Revenge was the emotional order of the day in Le Chambon, as elsewhere in France. Reconciliation was still a long distance away from the conversations and concerns of most French men and women. But André's commitment to peace required reconciliation wherever possible, and he believed reconciliation was possible even with the very recent enemy.

It was his habit to preach essentially the same sermon to the prisoners of war as he had preached in the Temple that morning. In his memoir, he wrote, "My sermons have never been as scrutinized and discussed as they were at that time. My subjects were like a catechism that started with God's Commandments and ended with Justice, Truth and Non-Violence . . . My sermons, in fact, were a severe condemnation of all wars" (A. Trocmé 1953, 450).

He describes the German soldiers as being equally critical of his preaching nonviolence as his fellow Chambonnais were of his preaching to the enemy. The prisoners voiced their objection: "You should be preaching this to the Communists. They are the ones who preach the doctrine of violence throughout the world . . . Germans are honest people who believe in God and give their blood to save Europe and protect it from the 'red pest.' You will see the day when we are no longer here to protect you from Communism" (451).

Hans-Ruedi Weber was very aware that André was visiting the German prisoners in the name of the church and he was quick to respond when André asked for his assistance in preparing and conducting the services. The first two Sundays were daunting. His diary entries tell of André asking him, while they were on their way to Pont de Mars, to lead the liturgy that afternoon. He did his best, but it was his first ever experience in leading public worship. The next Sunday, André asked him to preach. After these surprise initiations into the role of the clergy, Weber accompanied André to Pont de Mars every other Sunday afternoon, sometimes preaching in André's place, sometimes translating a sermon for Trocmé to preach (Trocmé wanted to speak the soldiers' German).

It is not hard to imagine how difficult it must have been for a twenty-year-old theological student to step up to a makeshift pulpit and preach to a room full of prisoners of war, most of them older than he, and all of them compelled to be there. But he did so, for André needed the help of someone who knew something about conducting worship and was fluent in German, and there were no other people in Le Chambon who had both those skills.

Weber returned to Switzerland in September of 1944, and until the spring of 1946, André had no German-speaking preacher available for his sermons to the enemy. Meanwhile, he had to depend on Bohny or other German-speaking friends to edit his written text for sermons to be preached in German.

A Major Postwar Decision

While André was in the United States in the fall of 1945, Nevin Sayre, then the General Secretary of the IFOR, had asked him to serve half-time as the European Secretary of the Mouvement International de la Réconciliation (MIR). Its offices were in Paris, and even though much of the planning and correspondence could be done from home in Le Chambon, he would have to commute often to Paris, an eight-hour trip each way, and he would have extensive travel responsibilities to other countries in Europe.

When André returned from America, he and Magda discussed Nevin Sayre's request. Together they decided they should accept Sayre's proposal if the church council in Le Chambon would approve the proposal that he serve the Chambon church half-time at half salary. Before they did anything final, however, André would tell Edouard Theis of their decision, for his was one of the lives that would be most directly affected. He would still direct the Collège and have his half-time role in the pastorate, especially in the worship services. While he was a less demonstrative preacher than André, he was greatly appreciated for the quality of thinking that characterized his sermons and for the combination of determined Christian conviction and good common sense that came through in them.

The council agreed to André's half-time proposal and added a third, part-time minister to the team to cover some of Theis's activities. André Trocmé wrote to the American Congregational Christian Service Committee to ask if it would provide him an assistant to help with youth work in the Temple of Le Chambon-sur-Lignon. The Committee agreed and identified Howard Schomer for the job as a Fraternal Worker posted to Le Chambon. Schomer was an ordained minister and a conscientious objector who had refused a ministerial exemption from the draft. Instead of military service, he had spent the years from 1941 to 1945 in the Civilian

Public Service camps and hospitals, working with the American Friends Service Committee.

Howard and Elsie Schomer

Howard Schomer and his wife Elsie arrived in Le Chambon on the day before Easter Sunday of 1946, ready to accept whatever project Trocmé set before them. On Easter morning, Howard arrived at the church in an American-style Easter suit (bright pink, with a hat to match) and found that Trocmé had designs on his time that afternoon. Nearly fifty years later, he wrote this recollection of what happened that Sunday:

> As we left Easter worship in the packed Chambon church, we drove across the hills in [Trocmé's] little car to conduct the weekly services in the prisoner-of-war camps which he had initiated as soon as the rulers had become prisoners. Short as food was in the Chambon, at least the fruit was in season, so he threw a basket of fruit in the back of the car for the prisoners.
>
> We were just getting acquainted, for I had not yet been in Chambon twenty-four hours. "Schomer?" he said. "Isn't your name German?" he asked in French. "Yes," I answered. "Fine," he went on, "so you preach today," and he switched our conversation into German. Barely keeping up with him, I explained that my grandfather had come to the States at the age of nine, in 1861, that my father could not speak German, and that all I had was a bit of German from a course in school. His comment was crushing: "That's all right. Your grammar is awful but your German accent is better than your French. You will preach just fine."
>
> I protested that I had just gotten off a Swedish ship, was trying to refurbish my French, and had no sermon ready in any language. "You don't need to prepare," he responded. "You have been an interned conscientious objector in the U.S. throughout the war. None of these German POWs ever dreamed of objecting to their government's orders to do military service, or even for conscience sake to refuse to murder or even torture. There are S.S. men in this first camp. Just tell them what you believe, what you did about it, and how your government dealt with the American war resisters. It will blow their minds! It will be a wonderful Easter sermon!"

> So I did what my new boss asked me to do, with occasional help for a German word, and soon found myself replacing this overburdened pastor twice a week in various POW camps ... a ministry that surprised me by the depth of relationships that grew out of it ... with at least some young Germans who were becoming ex-Nazis and trying to find their bearings in a new era. (Schomer 1992, 2)

Trocmé had at last found another theologically trained, almost German-speaking preacher to replace Hans-Rudi Weber in preaching to the enemy.

Schomer was assigned another task as well: that of generating activities and meetings that would shore up postwar reconciliation in the town. All over France there were major political and cultural turnovers in progress. Liberation was not a moment but a process that went on from July of 1944 to April of 1945, as the German forces were slowly pushed out of control in one area after another. In many areas, communities and even whole cities were torn apart by the lingering sores of hate and revenge. Hundreds of people were seen as gross collaborators with the Germans. The women had their heads shaved but the men were often shot or hanged without trial.

Fortunately, the Plateau populations had been heavily involved in the protection of refugees and that created a different sense of things. The common instinct for revenge was under the constraint of conscience in Le Chambon, but there were a few outbreaks of angry revenge. Two young girls who had worked at one of the hotels housing German soldiers on leave had their heads shaved, a common way of shaming women perceived as collaborators. They were not collaborators, in fact, but rumors of their exchanging small talk with the soldiers were enough to prompt a few citizens to put them to public embarrassment. Many hot disagreements and accusations circulated in the town in the days immediately following liberation. That was probably unavoidable under the circumstances, but at least there were not the physical assaults and revenge killings so common elsewhere. Still, as long as there were groups with sharply contrasting attitudes about life under the occupation, there was always the possibility of those attitudes breaking into violence.

Trocmé asked Schomer to inaugurate a series of discussions among the leaders of groups that might be at odds with each other. He used the term

Groupe Contact. He had experienced great success with such conversational meetings, notably the kitchen meetings among miners and the mid-week Bible studies that served as information hubs for hiding refugees during the war years. It just might be a way to avoid escalating passions that could turn dangerous. Trocmé had a good reason for picking Schomer for this assignment. He was an outsider, an American; he was a recent arrival in the town, and a person who had not yet been labeled as a partisan.

Schomer made the contacts and got the key people together. In his "Icons and Mentors" essay, he wrote,

> On the national scene the Gaullists and the Communists seemed to be gearing for a civil war. In the mining town (St. Étienne) that was the gateway to our High Plateau shots were fired by the Gaullist national army, killing ten union workers engaged in a rowdy general strike. Many people were again climbing up to the Plateau for safety and for sure food sources. I convened a special meeting of Groupe Contact. We asked ourselves what could be our mission if it came to a dictatorship of either [the left or the right]. The chief communist of the region—a widely beloved peasant leader—was quick to respond: If it is our people who take over political power, I promise you I will insist on the peculiar vocation of the High Plateau as a nonviolent sanctuary for all who are refugees, and if any of your people—the Centrist Deputy Mayor was in our circle—should be arrested but have no blood on their hands, I'll do my best to get them freed. Soon those with quite different political affiliations responded in kind. Thank the Lord, the national situation calmed down and we did not have occasion to call in these pledges, but I believe they could have been counted on. André Trocmé had taught me that the church is called not only to resist absolute evil but to broker compromises between competing just causes. (4)

Partly as a consequence of the fruitful discussions in the Groupe Contact, Schomer went on to found an institution called L'Accueil Cévenol (A. Trocmé 1953, 489),[1] an international spiritual and intellectual conference

---

1. The name of the institute was later changed to "Accueil Fraternel."

center where overseas visitors to Collège Cévenol were received. Its president was Edouard Theis. Its purpose was to bring together similar diverse groups for discussion of on-going social problems that had the potential to break the postwar peace. Schomer had learned another lesson, this one from both Trocmé and Theis: that peace has to be created and re-created continually, and that it happens when persistent small gestures of inquiry, justice, and reconciliation are made before friction turns to violence, whether physical or social. After the Armistice, Schomer stayed on in Le Chambon, where he taught history in the Collège and served a number of administrative functions, often as a mediator when there were administrative conflicts. All his activities contributed materially to André Trocmé's ability to handle his IFOR tasks and his half-time obligations to the parish in the Temple.

Then in 1947 came an unanticipated turn of events. The regional Council stepped in with a major reorganization of the team ministry.

A Gradual Demotion

Le Chambon was the largest and most important assignment in the region, and the regional Council (Consistoire) felt it necessary to have some control over how its ministry would be structured if André were to be half-time. The head of the Consistoire, M. Rozier, told both André and his church council what was expected. The Consistoire had already decided on three things: there would need to be a full-time minister at the helm; that person would replace the Trocmé family as the occupant of the presbytère; and he would also replace André as the president of the church council. They had already settled on the person who would fill the role as senior minister: a recently widowed Parisian businessman, M. de Seynes, who had left a successful banking career to study for the ministry. Even though he had only four months of theological study behind him and was not yet ordained, it was determined somewhere in the church bureaucracy that he would be assigned the role of senior minister. It was also suggested that because of his business background, he could tidy up the administrative and financial records of the church. André did not think they needed tidying up, and wondered whether that was not part of a pretext for replacing him.

De Seynes' appointment began in April of 1948, but he was not scheduled to move into the presbytère until October. André and Magda had to find alternative housing for themselves and their family. They had no funds to buy property and a rental would have to be at their own expense. It was a period when finding any housing at all in Le Chambon was difficult enough. For someone on the penurious salary paid by the ÉRF it was impossible. There was only one appropriate option close to the center of town: a house owned by Mme. Schnerb, a Jewish woman in St. Étienne, who was very reluctant to rent it to anyone. It had been closed since before the war, but it had suffered from the vacancy. Normal decay from disuse was bad enough, and it been broken into and used by some maquisards in the last years of the war. Finally the President of the Jewish Community in St. Étienne intervened, reminding Mme. Schnerb how much the Trocmés had done for refugee Jews during the war years, and persuaded her to rent the house to the Trocmé family.

When de Seynes and his three children were ready to move in, the Trocmés had to make their move from the presbytère to the Schnerb house on a hill near the CFD[2] railroad station. It was all very painful and costly. Nonetheless, they made the move under Magda's unique management style. Always the practical person, she would stop friends (sometimes strangers as well) passing by and ask if they were walking in the direction of the railroad station. If so, would they mind taking along a valise or a box of things to leave at the new house? Granted that André and Magda were already feeling some disengagement from the Temple and its problems, these developments further loosened their emotional ties.

Soon it became clear that the de Seynes appointment was not working out well. After less than two years in Le Chambon, he was smoking heavily, he appeared exhausted and depressed, and he was often away in Paris, leaving essential tasks of a senior minister unattended. André tried

---

2. The narrow gauge railway system used in the mountains was known as the Chemin de Fer Départemental , CFD for short. Students quickly translated CFD another way and used it as the name of their school paper: *Ça File Doucement* ("it runs slowly").

31. The CFD railroad station. Unknown photographer. Courtesy of the Chambon Foundation.

to fend off parishioners' questions by telling them what he thought was true: that de Seynes was having serious health problems.

When de Seynes asked André to come and see him early in 1949, a different truth emerged: de Seynes was engaged to be married again, this time to a Catholic woman. Even though his ordination was already scheduled to take place in the Chambon church, high ranking clergy in Paris had told him he had to make a choice between the ordained ministry and the Catholic marriage, since it would be altogether unseemly for a Reformed Church parish minister to live in a Catholic marriage. He had now made his choice: he would leave the ministry and marry the Catholic woman.

Fortunately for André, a much happier development would follow the de Seynes chapter. In 1949, the Consistoire found an experienced minister who could fill the position of senior minister vacated by de Seynes. Christian Mazel was a totally different sort of person. He and his wife Solange became close friends and supporters of André and Magda. His view of André was simple and positive, and when postwar controversies swirled about him, Mazel expressed his distress vividly in a personal letter:

> I admired my Chambon colleague. He was the most eminent personality of Le Chambon, which owed him a lot: the Collège Cévenol, [and] a radiant worldwide reputation which made the town known throughout Europe and the United States. . . . His great stature, physical, moral and spiritual, casts a long shadow over Le Chambon and everywhere. . . . The Église Réformée de France did not know how nor did they really want to find a place for him. . . . I collaborated with him for two years in a paired ministry in the Temple, and we are bound by a great friendship.[3]

Mazel's letter goes on to list a further series of important contributions that André made to the town, some of them in tandem with Edouard Theis: his concern for the education of the children of the Plateau, the creation of a Protestant Family Association that was responsible for construction of a sports stadium, the organization of a farmer's cooperative and a cinema program that brought good films to town, and the Bar de la Croix Bleue, an alcohol-free café for young people. The friendship between the two men continued to flourish following Mazel's two years in Le Chambon, when he left to become pastor to the ÉRF's most prestigious parish, the Oratoire du Louvre in Paris.

The Collège Starts Flying: Carl and Florence Sangree

After peace returned to the Plateau, one of the most urgent tasks was to find a permanent home for the Collège Cévenol.[4] Howard Schomer was particularly well connected in American church and educational circles,

---

3. A personal letter to me from Mazel, written June 18, 1999.
4. The official name of the school was changed from École Nouvelle Cévenole to Collège Cévenol in February of 1944.

and he was able to provide many useful contacts that both Trocmé and Theis could explore in their difficult postwar search for funds to establish a campus, fund a faculty, and find an international student audience for its unique educational mission. With Schomer's help, André's appeals to the American Congregational, Methodist, and Presbyterian USA churches and the Riverside (Baptist) Church in New York provided funds enough to pay back the loans from Geneva and allow them to plan a campus for the Collège on the attractive Peybrousson pasture. That was at least a beginning, but there was still the question of renovating the old farmhouse, Luquet, to create the first Collège building.

Then in 1945, two other Americans, Carl and Florence Sangree, appeared on the scene. They would give twenty years or more of hard work and a significant part of their own money to insure the establishment of the Collège as a viable and functioning private school equipped to bring together an international student body under its banner of "An International Center for Peace."

32. Carl M. and Florence Sangree. Photographer, Gail Sangree. Courtesy of Gail Sangree.

It was on his first major fund-raising trip to the United States in the fall of 1945 that André met Carl and Florence Sangree. The circumstances were not auspicious. André was staying at the guest quarters of Union Theological Seminary in New York. He was exhausted at the end of this financially disappointing trip and was preparing to return to France the next day. Then the Sangrees appeared at his door. They inquired about coming to Chambon and helping with the young Collège, but André was not impressed by their language skills. They were about to leave disappointed when André changed his mind. As they were leaving, Florence turned and said,

> "We forgot to tell you that, during the war, we[5] opened a small house in West Cummington for Jewish refugees who had escaped from Nazism and we were particularly interested by your speech because of your work for refugees. We have developed a few methods of collecting money to feed these Jews, in which you may be interested. We organized small student committees in New England schools that we could perhaps revive to help Collège Cévenol."
>
> The great friendship that united Carl, Florence and me was born during the following hour and it is thanks to this friendship that the Collège Cévenol started flying. We decided I wouldn't take the boat the next morning and I stayed with the Sangrees for an entire month in order to set up a program for our school. (A. Trocmé 1953, 474)

The Sangrees went hard at the task immediately, working the phones as quickly as they could to enlist support for the Collège from people in all the schools and colleges where they had personal connections. Florence Sangree's own education and her professional educational career had brought her in touch with a wide array of people in schools and colleges throughout the American Northeast, and with others around the country

---

5. Trocmé's memory is inaccurate in one detail. The refugee house was opened by Carl and his wife, Elizabeth, who died soon thereafter. Florence joined the effort when she married the widowed Sangree. The quotation should have been attributed to Carl Sangree, not Florence.

who had church connections of consequence. Hers was a promising web of contacts.

They started a month-long tour for André to meet key people in these places, putting together the pieces as they went along. Before they were through, he had given innumerable talks, sermons, and classroom presentations, he had established personal connections with many educational leaders at both secondary and college levels, and he had tapped into the energies of a rising generation of American students.

The meetings with students were particularly rewarding. In the postwar years, and even well into the 1950s, American college students were very aware of the plight of refugees and deportees throughout Europe and Africa and of the desperate postwar economic circumstances in most European countries. It was an era that would produce the Marshall Plan, the Institute for International Education, and major efforts by national church bodies to organize service projects abroad. The student response to those opportunities was vigorous, and participation in service projects abroad was a lively option on many campuses.

Building a Campus

By the time André left for France, the Sangrees had laid out a plan for further fund-raising to get the Collège Cévenol campus built. They had also agreed to visit Le Chambon the following summer to get a better first-hand impression of the needs and priorities. As the project unfolded, Le Chambon became their summer home for the next fifteen years.

André had been in touch with the Swiss-based International Civil Service, the group that sponsored Hans-Ruedi Weber's work with refugee students. They urged him to find a way of organizing groups of volunteers to give their time and physical labor to building the campus, now that the Collège had the Luquet farm property. That was something in which the Sangrees were both enthusiastically interested. So in addition to finding funds for the Collège, they set to exploring the means for recruiting American students and other volunteers to contribute their manual labor. The work camps would tackle some of the drudgeries associated with putting up buildings and creating athletic fields: lots of digging, carrying, and painting, many wheelbarrows and rakes, and an abundance of sweat. The work camp idea caught on with remarkable speed.

The first work camp took place in the summer of 1946. A group of over 170 participants, the vast majority of them French students, was greeted on arrival by the Sangrees (Green 2004, 15). Among the handful of Americans joining this first group was Joseph Howell, a young Congregational minister from the staff of the Congregational Christian Service Committee. He became, for more than a decade, a legendary organizer and administrator of the American groups participating in this effort.

By the next summer, the work camp volunteers had grown in number to 270 or more. A majority were students, but there were many war veterans, particularly veteran conscientious objectors with their CPS camps and prison experiences. They finished work on the six Swedish barracks that had arrived the year before, dug endless trenches for water and electrical lines, began construction of two athletic fields, and remodeled the old granite farmhouse, Luquet, into a combination classroom, library, and administrative center.

33. The Luquet, 1961. Photograph by and courtesy of Richard Unsworth.

When the Luquet renovations were finally finished in the fall of 1947 there was a grand celebration, during which the abiding friendship and mutual regard between Theis and Trocmé were given voice. Jeanne, the eldest of the eight Theis daughters, wrote to a friend after the party, recalling that André "likened Daddy to a patient plowman, who, once he has planted his plow in the ground, walks straight ahead until he comes to the end of the row, then turns around and starts another row, and all the rest of us flutter around him, proposing this and that change, getting excited to no avail. Once he has decided something is to be done, his determination cannot be shaken."[6]

American veterans of these first two summers of manual labor for the Collège kept in close touch with one another. By the spring of 1948, and with the help of the Sangrees, they had organized the American Friends of the Collège Cévenol (AFCC), a group that recruits students for work camps, summer courses, and occasionally for enrollment in the academic year program, all the while gathering funds for the Collège's scholarship, maintenance and expansion projects.

Many of the overseas visitors to Le Chambon during those months shared strong impressions of both Theis and Trocmé. They saw both men as motivated by convictions of conscience that were larger than life, certainly larger than those of most people they knew. Both men had a story to tell about Le Chambon during the war years, and neither one spent much time talking about his own actions. Trocmé came across as an inspiring speaker and a moving force when he talked about what Christians must do to live up to their name in a world awash with both suffering and hope. Theis was seen as born with the same sort of conscience. One visitor described Theis as "chiseled out of the same granite as Trocmé" (Green 2004, 15).

The principal testimony to feelings about Theis and Trocmé and their mission for the school as a community with an international outlook was not what anyone said about the mission. The physical work these campers

---

6. The comment appears in a letter of Jeanne Theis to one of her work camp friends, written January 1, 1947.

were doing day by day made the purpose of the Collège Cévenol their own. It was common work for a common purpose. This was already an educational community with an international outlook and an international experience. That had been the case since refugee students became part of its reality when Spanish refugees joined the fledgling École Nouvelle Cévenole in 1939.

While the Sangrees kept in touch with both André Trocmé and Edouard Theis, Theis was their closest contact person in France, since he was the Directeur and was daily involved in the practical tasks required. As president of the board of trustees, Trocmé also stayed very close to the Collège Cévenol during its first years, even to scouting out some large prefabricated Swedish houses that would be ideal residences for faculty apartments and a dozen or so students in each one. What finally showed up on campus was a series of prefabricated barracks.

Both Carl and Florence were totally at home with the Plateau population and with Edouard and Mildred Theis. They were linked at a deep spiritual level to the Theises, to many of the people they met at Sunday services in the Temple, and to the simple, biblically rooted farm folk in

34. Work camp in action. Photograph by and courtesy of Richard Unsworth.

and around the town. They saw in them a group of people who held values that were not compromised by sophistication, either worldly or intellectual, and who would, in a pinch, do whatever they must to maintain the integrity of their beliefs and their lives. The correspondence between Theis and the Sangrees became voluminous over the following years. They discussed plans for buildings, architectural issues, cost estimates for the buildings, and plans for the summer work campers who would build the buildings and outdoor sports facilities.

Those personal relationships were later signified on campus when a new girls' dormitory was built and named Mil-Flor for Mildred Theis and Florence Sangree. The name is a deliberate pun on the thousand wild flowers (*mille fleurs*) growing in the fields outside the dormitory. Carl Sangree's name was honored when the Collège built proper clay tennis courts and named them Les courts Sangree. Two other classroom and administrative buildings would later be built and named for the Theises and the Trocmés.

The Sangrees' most active years with the Collège Cévenol ended with the retirement of Edouard Theis as Directeur in 1964. Their friendship, visits together, and correspondence continued for several more years.

The Bonds Unravel in Le Chambon

As much as André and Magda loved Le Chambon, André's 1947 demotion by the Consistoire had colored their feelings about working for the Temple parish. Then in 1949 another proposal came from Nevin Sayre. He wanted André to move his job as European Secretary for the IFOR from part-time to full-time beginning in 1950. It was a welcome resolution of the difficulties of his half-time ministry in the place both Magda and André had served for sixteen years. What neither one fully realized at the time was the scope of the change they would experience by this decision. The greatest challenge of the years in Le Chambon had been fending off the Nazi madness. Now the agenda would be initiatives aimed at building peace on the ashes of the war's destruction.

It was more than that, really. Given the parish turmoil of the last four years, André thought he would be able to close the gap he had often encountered between "the actual church and the real church." Looking back later, he wrote,

> My encounter with the Fellowship of Reconciliation had illuminated my soul because I thought I had discovered the real Church of Jesus Christ on earth, a church full of love, comprehension and forgiveness. The founders truly were exceptional, intelligent, generous and prophetic men and women. (A. Trocmé 1953, 526)

Ten years later, he would see things somewhat differently.

15

Versailles
The IFOR Years

The Trocmés' final four years in Le Chambon-sur-Lignon were also their first years of new and different responsibilities. Only a few of his parishioners shared Trocmés' understanding that the hard work of reconciliation was as important as the courage of resistance.

This was also a unique opportunity for Magda. She was clearly identified as a partner in this new ministry. The masthead of the MIR said "Secrétaires: André Trocmé et Magda Trocmé." And when Magda filled a speaking engagement, she was introduced as "co-director of the Maison de la Réconciliation." These were small but not petty acknowledgments that said to the outside world that Magda had her own set of responsibilities and the authority needed to carry them out.

The Pacifist's Core Realities

For a long time, André had wondered whether the MIR was not more like the real Christian church than was the average parish of any denomination. Under the leadership of his old friend Henri Roser, the movement had given new and richer meaning to the word and work of reconciliation. Roser made it clear that reconciliation was not only about healing wounds, it was about preventing wounds from happening in the first place.

The first principle of the MIR was faith in God through adherence to the teachings of Jesus, not adherence to an ecclesiastical creed. It was an understanding that Christian life is rooted as much in the heart and the hand as it is in the head, and is lived when the Christian addresses the problems on the street, where the practical conditions of peace are created. Both André's life and Magda's bore that out daily. It was one of the things that kept them so thoroughly bonded, in spite of their totally different assessments of Christian theology.

In his first article in *Cahiers de la Réconciliation,* André wrote a descriptive piece on the MIR in which he laid out the Christian foundations of the movement as well as the Christian motives of most of its members. There were others who found a place in the MIR, including the many who agreed with the strategy of nonviolent direct action, but came to that agreement through other channels than the Christian faith.

> The cross of Christ exempts us from striving for external success of our cause and thus of its defense by human means of violence and deceit. Because of Christ, accepting apparent failure has become for us the superior armament chosen by God for overcoming the power of evil. . . . Our faith in Christ presses us to open the doors wide to those who do not profess our convictions. Our Christ is the Christ of the total understanding of others, and not the Christ who rejects the unbelievers. So a great number of non-Christians are members of our movement and find themselves at home there. (A. Trocmé 1949, 1)

A second major tenet of the Christian faith, for both Roser and André, was the urgency of the claim of nonviolence. Roser put it plainly enough when he wrote in the MIR journal, "From the instant that [nonviolence] is a truth announced in the Gospel, it must be followed immediately and not only tomorrow when the law permits it, when the state will sanction that truth and it will no longer cost anything" (Roser 1983). That principle made conscientious objection a moral necessity, whether permitted by law or not. In France it would not be sanctioned by either the state or the ÉRF until December of 1963, when General de Gaulle pushed for a legal accommodation for COs.

Trocmé had no hesitation about making links with non-Christian groups with nonviolent philosophers at their core. There was only one group he would not admit into his Pantheon of the nonviolent, and that was the Communist Party's peace committees. Their roots were not in nonviolence at all, he said. Their peace protestations rose and fell, appeared and disappeared as the Soviet Union changed its policies.

In Roser's mind, as in André's, nonviolence could show the power of one person's witness. Probably the sharpest criticism of pacifism and conscientious objection at the time was the charge that it was a cowardly form of treason, that the conscientious objector was simply refusing to put himself at risk by defending the fatherland. The most active Christian pacifists, however, people like Roser, Vernier, Martin, Theis, and Trocmé, saw themselves as patriots who refused to join the rush to prove their patriotism by killing soldiers of another army. Those men in the gunsights were children of God, each one, and for that reason alone they deserved respect, "absolute respect," said Roser. When critics asked how one could claim to be a patriot and a pacifist at the same time, Roser's answer was very much like Trocmé's: if everyone caves in to the tides of war and accepts them as unavoidable, they compromise their own reason for living by giving death the upper hand. The true pacifist consistently strives for peace and reconciliation. It is slow and often lonely work, but it has a chance, at least, of turning those tides (Farrugia 1992, 288).

Never had André worked for an institution like the MIR. Its core values lined up precisely with his.

The Balm of Travel

During the four years André divided his time between Le Chambon and Versailles, MIR responsibilities were defined by the postwar realities. There was great need for someone to pull together the pacifist cells that had existed in Germany, Scandinavia, Britain, and elsewhere, and get them functioning, restoring past ties with each other, and finding ways to address the changed circumstances of a Europe no longer at war. André was handed that task, in part because of his language skills and in part because of connections he had forged in the years before the war. He began serious travel commitments immediately in 1946, sometimes with Magda, but usually alone.

As one of his first assignments, André took part in the first postwar gathering of IFOR representatives from throughout Europe. These 1946 meetings were held in Stockholm, a city that had escaped the Nazi occupations in Scandinavia.

The fact that Sweden had remained neutral meant that pacifist groups (and individuals) had not been compelled to operate entirely clandestinely. So when called upon to host this first postwar international conference of the IFOR, the Swedes were ready and willing. For André, it meant an opportunity to reconnect with many European pacifist leaders he had not seen since the war began.

Other groups in Europe had been sorely tried through the war years. In Germany that was especially true. Those who openly advocated conscientious objection to Hitler's war policies lived in danger of losing their place in society altogether, and even of losing their lives. Ministers had no exemption from the Nazi pursuit of pacifists. Many were imprisoned and one, Hermann Stöhr, was beheaded at the Plötzensee prison in June of 1940 for taking a firm position as a conscientious objector.

Because André was fluent in German, it fell to him and Magda, as co-secretaries of the MIR, to work with those decimated German pacifist groups. Their first extended trip to Germany involved traveling to thirty-five largely devastated cities from the Rhineland in the west to isolated Berlin in the heart of East Germany, with as many as four or five engagements in each, all in the space of the thirty days. His standard talk was titled "Is the Christian Faith Made Obsolete by the Revolutions of Our Time?" The word spread that this was a French speaker with ideas of interest to ex-Nazis and neo-Marxists as well as emerging democrats.

One of his stops was in Munich, where he had a chance to talk further with Major Julius Schmähling at his home there. He brought up the question of LeForestier's death with the major, whose response André described thus:

> Schmähling said, "I told the Court Martial I was convinced this man was not dangerous and I commuted his (death) penalty into voluntary work in Germany."
>
> "And then?"
>
> "Then," Schmähling tightened his fists and his eyes became cloudy, "then these *Schweinehunde*, (pig hunting dogs), of the Gestapo certainly

sent a message to their colleagues in Lyon." There LeForestier was removed from the group of people who were to be sent to Germany and thrown into the Montluc fortress. (A. Trocmé 1953, 456)

André had occasion to meet another German prisoner he knew from the chateau in Pont de Mars: Captain Neunkirchen. He learned that Neunkirchen had now become a member of the German Fellowship of Reconciliation and a conscientious objector.

A trip in August of 1948, this time for a week rather than a month, took him to Finland. The strains of travel in these years of split responsibilities are borne out by a comment on the Finland trip: "I came back from Finland one week, spent five long nights on trains and a ferry boat, to arrive in Le Chambon in time to climb into the pulpit on a Sunday, at 10:30 a.m. sharp" (501).

Conditions in Europe were still difficult enough that even ordinary trips could take excessively long times. For André, that applied especially to his frequent trips from Le Chambon-sur-Lignon to Paris for MIR meetings. They usually began when he left the presbytère at 4 a.m. and drove to St. Etienne for a train that arrived in Paris about noon. After several hours of meetings, he set out on the return journey, arriving home about 2:00 the next morning.

As tiring as such travels were, André found in them a certain inner quiet. "Traveling became the best medicine to cure the wounds left by the deaths in my family" (529). Doubtless it also provided some healing relief from the disappointments he was dealing with when back in Le Chambon he was now seen as the pastor who gave up his place as their senior minister. Home was still in Le Chambon-sur-Lignon, nevertheless, and it would remain so until they could move to new quarters in Versailles. Meanwhile, André did his best to get necessary MIR work done in his study in their new home, the Villa Schnerb.

André also tried to site any activities he could in or near Le Chambon. The only one that worked, finally, was a program of two "Consultations Fraternelles" on peace and peacemaking in July of 1947 and 1948. The name Fraternal Consultations was chosen to underscore the style of the meetings. They were open-ended exchanges among learned persons, seeking insights that built on one another and laid groundwork for ongoing inquiry into the issues of peace and reconciliation. The first had as its theme Education for Peace. The second was built around Violence and Nonviolence, with a focus on Lenin and Gandhi.

Someone described Le Chambon as "a Mecca for pacifists" and indeed it was for those participating in these two major consultations. Paul Ricoeur, André Phillipe, and many other pacifist leaders joined these analytical discussions, which were chaired by Ricoeur, now a professor of great repute at the Sorbonne. Albert Camus was living nearby at the time and attended at least one of these sessions, but as an observer, not as a contributor. André had been the organizing force behind these consultations and, predictably, they ceased after the Trocmés moved to Versailles. One can gather a sense of these consultations from André's report on the meetings.

The 1947 consultation on Education for Peace brought together leading pacifists from France, Sweden, Italy, Germany, and the United States. Le Chambon seemed the right place for such discussions, given three things: the long Huguenot history of resistance to tyranny, the recent experience of the Chambonnais living their beliefs in spite of Nazi policies and pressures, and the postwar re-launching of the Collège Cévenol as an "international center for peace."

The purpose of these consultations was research and analysis, not the construction of noble statements for public consumption. Those were all too prevalent in a postwar period of recovery. What was needed at this juncture was a body of critical thought that would lead to new ways to address the perennial issues of war and peace.

Those most committed to creating a new Europe rather than re-creating the old one needed to find ways to enable the next generation to contain power and stifle the growth of violence and the vengeance it invariably sanctifies. The problem was clear enough: as time passes, any society tends to forget war's grisly realities. As the memories and their nightmares fade, both the victors and the vanquished are motivated to construct the education of their rising generations around the last war's grievances and glories, while air-brushing its hideous scars. Education for peace means education that discloses the truth about violence. That was the agenda for the meetings of 1947.

The 1948 Consultation Fraternelle focused on a broadened understanding of violence itself: "an account of violence in all its forms—violence as one of the springs of history" (Roser 1948, 6).

The key to defining violence is knowing the end it seeks: the death of another. That stark definition might quickly be challenged. What about the violence of torture, designed to evoke confessions or critical information during wartime? Or better, what about the violence used to maintain order in society? Here the consultation began by distinguishing between the two poles of violence: violence as an end in itself (cruelty) and violence as a means to an end (juridical violence). That distinction was useful in understanding how a society could choose to build its power on attitudes of disrespect for another, as happened with the Nazis, or on respect for the individual, as Gandhi did in India.

The 1948 report on the two Consultations gave this summary of their findings: "One can define violence by its means: the subjection of one person's will to another. Whenever one's free will is bent into subjection, the process of violence is set in motion.... All imperialism over souls is violence." Violence is violence, whatever its shape or degree, and all violence fuels hatred as well as its major consequence: the distortion of truth.

While the two consultations achieved their stated goals, the plan for following-up on the consultations was dissipated when, in 1949, the Trocmés accepted Nevin Sayre's urgent invitation to move to Paris and give their full time to the International Secretariat of the MIR. By 1950 they were faced with a new and very demanding set of challenges.

Pacifism Overshadowed by Orthodoxy

In the public discussion of Christian theology, Trocmé's stance and that of the MIR had lost much of its influence by the postwar years. Protestant mainline churches had moved away from pacifism and nonintervention and embraced theologians who provided a rationale for the military violence needed to answer Nazism in Europe and Japanese aggression in the Pacific Rim countries. By the end of the war, the work of Swiss theologian Karl Barth in Europe and Reinhold Niebuhr in America had taken deep root among Protestant theologians.

Barth perceived the pacifist as a person who attempts to achieve salvation by his own good works, rather than by faith. Trocmé objected vigorously, saying, "If and when the church proclaims that goodness is impossible, faith necessarily wanders outside the church into 'World Citizenship,' Communism, and 'Moral Rearmament'" (A. Trocmé 1953, 138).

At the same time, Reinhold Niebuhr, an ardent pacifist for some years, added his great weight to discrediting pacifism in the name of "Christian realism."

In France there were others who filled a comparable role by insisting on "political realism" as a necessary component of Christian theology. The best known and most influential such figure in the Église Réformée was the Protestant theologian Pierre Maury, a friend of Karl Barth and a translator of many of his works. Since Maury was also a personal friend of church president Marc Boegner and shared with him the pastorate of a church in Paris, he had great influence on the policies of the ÉRF. Maury held fast to the Barthian dismissal of pacifism and gave it angry expression, saying, "If I drop bombs while beating my chest, I am in God's grace, but if you refuse to kill [in order] to have clean hands, your vainglorious pride separates you irremediably from God's grace" (292).

Now that the war was over, André knew that pacifism's voice would not be heard unless its community of followers could be invigorated and its activities given new prominence. To manage that, the infrastructure of the MIR needed a great deal of attention. During the war years, its leaders, including men like Henri Roser and Philippe Vernier, had repeatedly been given long prison sentences for their conscientious refusal to serve in the military. They were acting out their convictions with inspiring courage, but no one was "minding the store" in their absence.

When Roser was released from prison, he resumed his work as president of the MIR, and André became the European Secretary of the parent IFOR. In that role, he had to digest the fact that the potential membership support for IFOR activities would depend on someone stirring the conversation between pacifism and mainstream church thinking. The dialogue needed voices like his own and that of people like the German pastor Martin Niemöller, a survivor of the concentration camp at Dachau who later became a president of the World Council of Churches.

Letters from India

In the months before their move to Versailles, Magda was invited to be one of four French delegates to the World Pacifist Congress in India, scheduled for the month of December 1949. American Quakers and some of Gandhi's closest associates had organized it. The Congress brought together some fifty delegates from throughout the world to learn in greater depth the thought, the heritage, and the peace strategies that enabled Gandhi to lead Indians to freedom from their British colonists.

Presiding over the conference were two of the best known of Gandhi's colleagues, both in India and in the wider world: Rajendra Prasad, who would be elected in 1950 as the first president of the new Republic of India, and the poet Rabindranath Tagore, India's Nobel Laureate in literature. The congress, originally to be headed by Gandhi, now marked the anniversary of his assassination.

Most of the delegates arrived three weeks early to have a thorough immersion course in Indian culture. The flavor of their experience comes through in a recording Magda made for broadcast back home. She speaks of travels from Agra and the foothills of the Himalayas in the north to bathing in the Ganges River at Haridwar in the east, and of visiting the famous Elephanta caves on an island off Bombay (Mumbai) in the south. In addition to the cities and the famous sites like the Taj Mahal, Magda made sure she saw life in small villages with thatch-roofed mud houses, watched snake charmers in the streets of Benares, and visited one of the Gandhian ashrams on the back of an elephant. This indefatigable woman soaked up the life around her and listened carefully for the spiritual center of the people.

In the course of the congress, she met and spent time with C. Rajagopalachari, the last Governor-General of India, and Indira Gandhi, then Minister of the Interior in the new Indian government and from 1966, President of India. That visit marked the beginning of a lasting friendship between the two. While the Trocmés were in their Geneva parish in the 1960s, Mme. Gandhi often came to international meetings there and invariably got in touch with Magda, and, when possible, came to their house in Petit Lancy for tea.

35. Indira Gandhi, C. Rajagopalachari, and Magda Trocmé, 1949. Unknown photographer.

Magda wrote frequent and thorough reports of those weeks, some in letters to the children, Nelly and Jacques, and more formal ones in her summary reports to the IFOR. One entry in her "Journal of a Chambonnaise in India" (M. Trocmé 1950), recounts the days spent at Sevagram, the ashram that Gandhi established as his home village and the place from which he would direct the freedom movement. She arrived in time to celebrate Christmas Eve with the villagers, to hear Rajendra Prasad's Christmas message of peace spoken from Gandhi's hut in the center of the village, and to see a scroll unrolled displaying the Nativity scene at Bethlehem with Indian figures in local costumes. Returning to her hut, she saw the village children gathered around a Christmas tree decorated with snowflakes made of cotton balls, a lovely star at its top, and light from candles on the ground. It was hardly what she might have expected, but she did remember seeing Hindu holy men in a temple chanting the many names of God, including Jesus and Buddha. The Christmas tree did not seem so strange after all.

As much as Magda admired Gandhi and his followers, she was not blind to the faults that threaded through that era. She was convinced that Gandhi's nonviolence was sincere and integral to his whole philosophy of Satyagraha. That philosophy required of all its followers resistance to evil and search for truth marked at every level by the inner disciplines of peace and nonviolence. At the same time she knew that the Indian capitalist bourgeoisie supported Gandhi at every turn because his successful tactics of resistance served their own ends. The result was continuing interest in Gandhi's personality and history, but little popular desire to practice his personal and social disciplines.

In a November 1949 letter home, she contrasts the open spiritual attitudes of the Indian followers of Gandhi with cultural attitudes too common in the West: "We have contempt for other countries, for people of other races or other religions, for people who speak other languages, especially when they challenge us in the name of other ideals. The sincere and truthful people among us must open their eyes to their own behavior and see it as it is, without finding excuses, without hiding it in a moral or religious shell. We will be answerable for our acts of violence before God and men."

For Magda as for Gandhi, nonviolence was never simply a tactic. It was a comprehensive way of life and thought.

The Mill of Peace

The move to the full-time position in Versailles in 1950 meant that André and Magda would have to find and fund an appropriate place to live and carry on their new work. That task was made considerably more complicated by their own grand expansion of the job definition. They decided that the program should include hospitality for youth groups, church groups, and others who had an interest in knowing more about pacifism, as well as regular conferences for IFOR member groups across Europe. They would also bring together groups whose languages or ideologies would ordinarily make them strangers to one another, all in the name of building the personal foundations of reconciliation.

They found just the place on the rue du Général Pershing, about two kilometers from the center of town. It was an old mill tower with added living quarters built in the 1780s by Louis XVI's young Queen, Marie Antoinette, for the express purpose of grinding more wheat flour for the poor.

The architecture of this abandoned mill was designed to reflect a royal origin. The entry was recessed in a large crenellated stone tower that looked over the rue Général Pershing and thus resembled a mini-chateau more than a grain mill. It had been put to many varied uses since the Revolution: most recently it was a financially unsuccessful boarding house.

Any old house is a black hole that swallows money, but this old house with its ambitious mission swallowed more than usual. Next, they had to settle on a rental fee for the use of the building and a purchase price for the business good will and the house furnishings. When the cost had been driven down far enough, André signed the papers, and the work of rehabilitation began. There was an enormous amount to be done, outside and inside, from cleaning out the overgrown and unkempt grounds to repairing floors and furnishing a kitchen capable of serving forty or fifty people occasionally and smaller groups frequently.

Magda and the tireless Jispa set to those tasks with little money and much muscle. For example, the floor of the living room had many rotten boards. The previous inhabitants of the building had bought a rug big enough to cover the unsightly damage. Magda and Jispa rolled back the rug, found some discarded large tins, cut and flattened them, and nailed the pieces into place. Then they rolled the rug back into place. Nobody was the wiser and nobody dropped a foot through a hole in the floor: an essential for a meeting center for international guests.

As for meeting the cost of preparing their mini-chateau to become an international conference center, the only answer they could see was to spend their entire retirement savings, and then borrow whatever they could from interested benefactors and from banks that would make loans at lower than standard rates. André laid out the painful details of their financial situation in a March 1951 letter to his daughter Nelly.

36. "The Tower," Maison de la Réconciliation, 1954. Drawing, Sigmund Vivaloy, artist.

In the battle between purpose and prudence, purpose won out, but the black hole was still there and had to be fed. Once restored, the building had to be maintained and its conferences staffed. To this end, they retained a couple, M. and Mme. Quétier, to take that responsibility in return for the rent-free use of the gatehouse on the property.

They named their "Mill of Peace" the Maison de la Réconciliation. In those early postwar years, revenge was only slowly giving way to reconciliation, and the Mill's unusual functions carried its reputation far beyond Versailles. It attracted pacifist and church groups from around Europe and the United States. The first was an American group of ministers, lay people, and professors led by Max Adams, the Chaplain at Macalester College in Minnesota. The groups themselves often illustrated the theme of reconciliation: a group from the Catholic Worker-Priest movement, a weekend dialogue between Communist and non-Communist pacifists, and other groups with provocative possibilities for crossing ideological borders. They were often favored with speakers of great renown in the pacifist world.

A Healing Serenade

The first European group was a German young people's choir and their conductor. Their visit provided them a shocking eye-opener to the policies and behavior of the Gestapo and the S.S. Troops. André welcomed the group and the encounter with truth on both sides. It meshed closely with his enduring commitment to reconciliation as an outcome of nonviolence. Here is his account of the visit:

> The Quétier family finally arrived [as cook and caretaker]. . . . Our first encounter with Mme. Quétier was dramatic. The first busload of guests to arrive was a German singchor [choir] from the Weser valley, with their music director. Mme. Quétier refused to cook for them because her brother, a maquisard, had been tortured and murdered by the Germans. She simply could not cater to Germans. . . . [So] Jispa and Magda improvised a very simple meal and explained to the youngsters what was going on. The boys and girls were stunned, because they had

never heard of the suffering inflicted on defenseless populations by the Gestapo in occupied countries. This revelation literally crushed them and they kept repeating to us and to themselves that they had not participated and that they could not believe such things had happened. These youngsters were sincere.

When the group departed, the choir director came up with a moving idea. He organized his choir in a half circle around Mme. Quétier's house, where they softly sang some well-chosen songs. A face appeared behind the upstairs window, then two or three more . . . and the windows opened.

The choir director made a little speech in French and expressed the sorrow and remorse his pupils felt for what had happened during the war. He then exhibited a bouquet of white flowers and said, "In respect, remembrance and homage to your brother."

Madame Quétier came downstairs, opened the door and accepted the flowers. She was understandably very moved, and we no longer had to ask for her permission to welcome such and such a group. (A. Trocmé 1953, 510)

The Parson and the Pope

Magda took the lead in developing the IFOR's Italian constituency. Italy had very few pacifists, the only organized group being a small gathering of Quakers in Rome. Magda quickly searched out and made connections with the principal Italian peace activists and leaders in nonviolent social change: Tullio Vinay, Aldo Capitini, Danilo Dolci, Lanza del Vasto, and others. Among this group, Vinay, a Waldensian minister, was the sole Protestant. The others were prominent Catholic social activists and anti-fascists.

This was Magda's cup of tea: a group more interested in direct action than in theological discussion. She had very soon organized an Italian chapter of the IFOR. It had a vigorous life that led to formation of a pacifist women's organization that Magda organized and shepherded. Subsequent years saw the Trocmés in Italy more frequently. With much help from his wife, André was even able to deliver some of his speeches in Italian.

On one of their early visits to Italy in November 1948, André Trocmé and his friend l'Abbé Pierre[1] were received at the Vatican for an audience with Pope Pius XII, along with a number of representatives of labor unions in France. They had come to urge papal recognition and support for the worker-priest movement in France. It was natural enough, then, for l'Abbé Pierre, a partisan of the homeless and later the founder of the Emmaus Movement, to seek out papal support for the recognition of the worker-priests.

It was a long shot. Pius XII was not known for championing the cause of the poor, the working classes, or racial minorities. In June of 1944, as Allied forces were about to liberate Rome, the Pontiff contacted General Mark Clark with a firm entreaty to see that no black soldiers would be among those occupying the city. General Clark disregarded the demand (Weinberg 1994, 448; see also Bess 2006, 38).

Pius XII gave his visitors every assurance that the papacy was working diligently to sustain peace in a perilous time. Since his visitors were from many European countries, he added his earnest desire to see Europe united. While nothing of value came from that visit, Pius XII's reassurances at least permitted André and l'Abbé Pierre to return to the lesser Catholic authorities and press the case of the worker-priests. They were, after all, forging new bonds with the union movements in a period when working-class French Catholic families were skipping Mass in increasing numbers. For more and more French workers, the Catholic Church was simply unconnected to the daily struggles of working people and others who lived at the unnoticed margin of the poor of France.

Trocmé and Abbé Pierre returned to France and discovered that a new papal nuncio had just been installed. His predecessor, Valerio Valeri, had been all too close to key figures in the Vichy government. By December 1944, with World War II nearly over, he had become a most unpopular Catholic leader. His successor was Angelo Roncalli, a man who had a proven record of care and protection of Jews and others during his term

---

1. Born Henri Antoine Groués, Abbé Pierre was a French Catholic priest who was active in the Résistance.

as papal nuncio in Istanbul. Here was a Catholic leader who might understand the need to regularize the status of the worker-priests. But while Monsignor Roncalli was cordial and understanding, he could offer them no satisfaction. Pope Pius XII was adamant about not giving official standing to the worker-priests. Too many of them were aligning themselves with left-wing labor causes.

Through an unusual circumstance, the connection between Monsignor Roncalli and the Trocmé family emerged. Oscar Grilli di Cortona, Magda's father, had converted from unobservant Anglicanism to equally unobservant Catholicism, largely to insure that he could be buried beside his second and Catholic wife. When he told the family he was going to visit with Magda's family in France, there was unease about the fact that he might be lured back into Protestantism and spoil the carefully crafted plans for his burial.

When Grilli assured his Catholic mentor, the Cardinal Archbishop of Florence, that he would do no such thing, the Archbishop gave the planned visit his support on condition that he would go to confession weekly with Monsignor Roncalli at the Nunciatura in Paris. Jacques Trocmé was assigned to drive his maternal grandfather to these weekly meetings, but he noticed that Grilli and Roncalli were much more interested in their chess games than in the formalities of confession. At least Grilli had made the visits and had firmed up a familial connection between his mentor Roncalli and his son-in-law Trocmé.

After nine years in Paris, Nuncio Roncalli was elevated to the rank of Archbishop and appointed Patriarch of Venice. Five years into that appointment he was, to his own great surprise, elevated to the papacy in 1958, taking the name of John XXIII. Soon l'Abbé Pierre asked Trocmé whether they might go once again to the Vatican, in hopes that they might find a more sympathetic hearing for their concern about the worker-priests. They did get an audience with their friend the Pope. While their visit was again unproductive, their reception was most cordial. This is Jacques Trocmé's recollection of his father's account of that visit:

> Something very funny happened during the closing papal benediction offered by the Pope to the people he had met that day. The people

were lined up in two rows and, after hesitating, Pastor Trocmé decided to join them to be diplomatically polite, [but] he decided to discreetly stand at the end of the second row. The Pope inched his way down the first row. He was followed by a priest who held a red velvet cushion on which blessed medals with the Pope's effigy were displayed. The people knelt, kissed the papal ring and received a quick benediction along with a blessed souvenir medal. André Trocmé observed the ceremony with great attention and decided that, as a Protestant minister, he could not kneel nor kiss the ring nor accept a blessed medal. The Pope came closer. André counted and re-counted the medals on the pillow. He was greatly relieved to see that there was not one for him. "What an intelligent man," he thought.

The Pope finally stood in front of the Parson, shook his hand, and took a medal from the pocket of his vestment, saying, "I have not blessed this one, and it is especially for you, dear colleague."

The gesture was not lost on André. It was consistent with the way Pope John XXIII opened doors to ecumenical understanding among Christians and reconciliation with the Jewish community.

16

Versailles
Rebuilding Peace

Return to America

The Italian visits were, like those in Germany, a return to familiar nations and networks, and the Trocmés had a handle at least on what had happened there during the decade from 1935 to 1945. America was another story. Both Trocmés had done their graduate studies there. Both felt at ease in the United States and in the English language, but they were not nearly as familiar with what had transpired in America during the two decades since their single year as foreign students there.

Although an ecclesiastical pariah in France, André found himself something of a celebrity in American churches and peace movement groups. By 1954 he had given the Robert Treat lectures at Boston University, published under the title *The Politics of Repentance*. André took a great many speaking engagements, as did Magda, who often made three or more presentations a day to differing groups. Both of them used their fees to meet their meager expenses and turned the rest over to Nevin Sayre to repay the IFOR for the advances it had made to restore the Mill of Peace for its new role.

The story of Le Chambon had been heard in America, and many church congregations, particularly those in the Northeast, welcomed André's presence. The celebrity role made him very uncomfortable, however, especially since he knew it was based in part on false assumptions. During those "heroic years" in Le Chambon, he had been a leader but not a star. Star status was something peculiar to America and reflected wide public approval, something a pacifist did not get in France.

André and Magda were most interested in the issue of peace, of course, whatever the literary appetite of their hearers. The audience might be eager to hear of wartime adventures, but the Trocmés were interested in stirring fresh thought on the church's role in keeping the peace and building the social environment that would allow a peace to survive the vagaries of political rationales for war.

André's most disquieting confrontation with the change in attitudes toward pacifism came on a fund-raising trip to New York. Once again, he stayed in Union Seminary's guest apartment, the Prophet's Chamber, where he learned the practical meaning of Jesus' words: "A prophet is not without honor, save in his own country, and in his own house." As a pacifist, he found himself representing a position that prevailing theological trends no longer recognized. Even his long-time friend, the president of the seminary Henry "Pit" Van Dusen, did not invite him to speak to the student body or preach in the seminary's chapel services. He was only allowed to post an invitation to conversation on the bulletin board. A handful of students showed up for those conversations, and most of them had never heard of the IFOR.

As he renewed connections with American Christian pacifist groups, he also began to understand why they had become marginalized. When speaking to pacifist groups, he often found it difficult to know how to respond to their questions. They were naive in the extreme. A Quaker might ask, "Couldn't you go and speak to these Nazis and awaken within them that little voice, which is present or dormant in every man? . . . You had to tell them the truth, all the truth, with love, just like Christ and Gandhi did. . . . You should not have lied to them by giving false identities to the Jews and to yourselves" (A. Trocmé 1953, 470). The best he could do in response was to draw a more vivid picture of the reality of Nazi policy and behavior.

Magda ran into the same naiveté when she was giving talks in the United States. She was always well received, but there were invariably a few innocent souls to deal with. She did the best she could, but she was less patient than André. When she read the dialogue about the ethics of lying to save a life, going on in the IFOR's American journal *Fellowship*, her impatience took the form of an article of her own: "There Was a Jew at the Door." It was a plainspoken rebuke to the disquieting naiveté of some American pacifists:

> I was very much interested to read the opinions of readers of *Fellowship* on the question of lying to save a life. . . . When we started our work of saving the Jews in occupied France, we had no time to sit down and discuss ethical problems. There was a Jew at our door. If you opened the door you realized that the Jew was hungry and . . . needed clothes and shelter. . . . When I read some of your statements, I feel that if all Christians behaved as you think they should, and if I was persecuted as the Jews were, I would avoid knocking at the door of a Christian. (*Fellowship*, Jan. 1955, pages 10–12)

There was one huge anomaly in her experience with American churches, one she saw clearly and was never able to accept. It summed up her experience in speaking at Sunday services in churches around the country:

> It was a moving experience speaking in a church, processing in a robe behind the choir, stepping up into the pulpit, and later going out in a formal recessional, knowing that churches everywhere were full of congregants Sunday after Sunday. But such Christians!! What a surprise for me, who came from a mostly dechristianized nation, to be in a rich and powerful nation that was mostly Christian. But how was it that they could fill their temples and churches every Sunday, and prepare for war on the weekdays? (M. Trocmé 1988, 388)

A Last Look at Russia

Four years later, Magda had an opportunity for a new look at Russia. Her last impressions dated from 1914, when World War I broke out. Now, as a mature woman, it helped that she was Russian by her maternal lineage. She was at least able to put Western stereotypes of Russian society in clearer context. Instead of judging everything she saw against the measuring stick of social progress in Western societies, she insisted that the only way to get a true and balanced understanding of Russia in the late 1950s was by measuring what she saw against her own family's experience in 1914, when her Russian grandfather left his illiterate gardener to spend the night sleeping on the hard dirt floor of a shack in the garden.

By 1958, Russia had nearly eliminated illiteracy, and free education was available on the basis of merit, not as a privilege reserved to the nobility. Living conditions for many peasants, although still meager, were at least a long step away from pre-revolutionary feudalism. But Magda was no more persuaded by Russian propaganda about the classless society than she was by the moral arrogance of Western nations. Being the firm peacemaker and peace-seeker, she stretched to see some possibility for Russian and Western populations to appreciate each other's humanity and with it, the possibility of a peace that the Cold War era did not hold out. It was clear once again that the biggest stakeholders in building peace were the ordinary citizens, while their leaders were often the biggest stakeholders in war.

The Clarity of Christ

The years in Versailles were a struggle in many ways. Clergy who were followers of Karl Barth further stiffened the already stiff back of the Église Réformée on the questions of conscientious objection and pacifism in general. At a personal level, André was not able to form professional friendships with more than a very few clergy, and even those were measured in their contacts with him. Their reception and the reception of their mission were more than disappointing. The Trocmés simply had to find new arguments for the necessity of pacifism and nonviolence. André and Magda both put themselves to that task in their speaking and their acts of witness, and for André at least, in his prolific writing during the period.

During his first year on site in Versailles, he wrote an article for *Réconciliation* in which he addressed the question of conscientious objection by citing Origen, the third-century Greek patriarch who wrote, "We no longer draw the sword against the nations, having become children of Peace because of Jesus Christ our leader" (Origen 3rd century, *Contra Celsius*). Trocmé also quoted St. Paul on reconciliation, the flip side of conscientious objection to killing: "God was in Christ reconciling the world to Himself," and "He has given us the ministry of reconciliation" (2 Corinthians, 5:19). It was that ministry of reconciliation that had driven André to act as unofficial chaplain to the German prisoners at Château du Pont de Mars.

As examples of the work of reconciliation, André did not cite the truce agreements or international treaties, but the practical activities that would lead to mutual international and cross-cultural understanding. A case in point was Switzerland's founding of the International Civil Service immediately after the First World War. The organization was still an active source of help to Le Chambon during World War II. It was, for example, the agency that provided Hans-Ruedi Weber his opportunity to live and work in the Swiss homes for refugee children in Le Chambon. During the war years, peace-building had gone on apace as hundreds of volunteers joined the American Friends Service Committee's efforts to relieve the suffering of refugees, and continued after the Nazi demise when other hundreds came to Europe to help repair the horrendous war damage.

All these actions are rooted in deep but often shrouded human instincts. For André, it was the clarity of Christ's teaching and example that still put the spotlight on those instincts, as it had in Origen's early church, with its mandate that Christians were never to take up the sword.

André never accepted the idea of the just war. Violence was violence, however it might be rationalized by the person using it. When a tyrant appeared, the Christian's resistance could only be nonviolent. In this, he departed from the position of his own ÉRF, as he did from the teachings of Jean Calvin, the founding figure of the Reformed Tradition.

Calvin recognized the necessity of war under certain defined limits, saying, "The magistrate's exercise of force is compatible with piety."[1] He had even allowed for the possibility that a Christian might, in good conscience, take part in the assassination of a harsh and unrepentant tyrant. It was a position that Trocmé had flirted with briefly, as Hitler's forces threatened France.

For a long time, André had maintained that the MIR and its parent organization should hold their focus on a Christian membership, and not

---

1. *The Institutes of the Christian Religion,* chapter 20, section 10 et seq.

offer membership status to other religious or secular pacifists. However, when the American parent organization moved toward accepting members whose motives were entirely secular, he was deeply distressed. He read its newly crafted statement of purpose and found the IFOR described as "an international, spiritually-based movement of people who, from the basis of a belief in the power of love and truth to create justice and restore community, commit themselves to active nonviolence as a way of life and as a means of transformation—personal, social, economic and political." Almost everything was there except God. He felt that the Christian foundations of the MIR had been hijacked in a misguided effort to offend no one in order to keep its numbers growing.

Later in the 1950s, his extensive international pacifist contacts made him realize that such a breadth of membership was, at some level, very desirable. That was clear as the Italian chapter of the IFOR came into being under Magda's leadership, and he knew her practical approach to peacemaking was valid. He accepted her view that religious integrity trumps doctrine.

The MIR's energies were stimulated by a common and sustained commitment to build the social structures that would make peace the norm among nations. That was especially important in the postwar years when a new Cold War was taking shape and the shadow of atomic disaster was afflicting the emerging generation. So was the shadow of colonial wars in Africa. Nonviolent approaches to those social problems were necessary, but the context for building them was new, and the models of nonviolent resistance that pacifists had known during World War II did not necessarily fit these new challenges to peace.

Peace Projects in Algeria

While the Trocmés, like most French citizens, had paid scant attention to the situation in North Africa during the years immediately after 1945, the rising tensions in Algeria during the 1950s called for a thorough review of the issues by the MIR. In 1953, André was asked to do an on-site two-month study about French and Muslim relations in Morocco, Tunisia, and Algeria, since demand for independence was escalating in all three.

That study led in 1954 to his participation in a groundbreaking dialogue between Christian and Muslim theologians in Beirut, where they set out to develop the best means of bringing about reconciliation between their two communities throughout Africa and the Middle East.

In the spring of 1955, André and Magda set out for a six-week experiment in Algeria. They wanted to find out how volunteers from these two religious communities could undertake serious discussion and share the practical work that makes for peace. They put their focus on literacy, a problem with wide effect and enduring consequences for the Arab population. Given the illiteracy rate among lower-class Arabic Algerians, the task of increasing literacy and opening educational opportunity was an urgent one, and one in which few Pieds Noirs showed any interest.

At every turn, André was struck by the class divisions between the two populations. The French traveled in Tourist Class or First Class, the Arabs in Steerage. The French commanded; the Arabs obeyed. Arabs were expected to know enough French to understand what was being demanded of them, but the French felt little inclination to learn how to communicate in Arabic.

Most French dismissed the desire for Algerian independence as futile and foolish. They regarded the Arabs as by nature incapable of managing their own affairs. The list of their faults and weaknesses was long, and should independence be won, the certainty of chaos was deep and axiomatic. By contrast, André and Magda made every effort to reach out to ordinary Arabs and found their attempts welcomed. They lived very simply, in what André described as a slum, "but a clean slum," with the bare minimum of furniture: two beds, four chairs, a couple of wooden tables, and a few cooking implements. They made that choice because they wanted to avoid being characterized as prosperous French tourists.

Establishing that kind of image with the local people gave their efforts a distinct edge. It was clear in the literacy effort. There were some outcomes they did not anticipate. They hung a sign by the door of their apartment saying "Free Tutoring." A neighboring butcher came in one day to ask, "Why are you doing this?" He went on to say that if he sold eight 150 gram steaks, for instance, he had to write down the price eight times and then add up the list. "You French," he said, "write down only two numbers and get the same result. How do you do that?" André answered by introducing him to multiplication, and writing down the whole multiplication table for him to take back to the shop and show others how it worked.

They saw this kind of learning as a two-way street. If they were able to gather together a teaching team, the volunteers would have to make a considerable effort at learning Arabic. But first they had to know whether there would be any volunteers. With terror and assassination a feature of everyday life, it would be difficult to persuade French or other Western volunteers to come into such a high-risk situation.

They prepared 1,400 copies of a brochure titled "A French-Algerian Bridge of Good Will," printed it on eye-catching red paper, and sent copies to the ÉRF ministers in France, asking that their parishes send volunteers to help address a problem that some, at least, would see as urgent and close to home. Brochures also went to their long list of friends and acquaintances elsewhere in the world. The results were mixed. A few volunteers came from Holland, Belgium, Germany, and the United States. From France, there was total postal silence.

The Trocmés thought it would be equally difficult to persuade Algerian Muslims to come into the open by participating in direct discussion with Christian volunteers. They would surely be seen as collaborators with the enemy and therefore as fair game for assassination by the FLN (Front Libération National). One of the Trocmés' Arab friends, a M. Kebaili, had that experience himself: he had seen one of his closest friends assassinated by a terrorist while the two of them were talking in the street.

But here again the results were positive and surprising. The Arabs' response was immediate and enthusiastic. About fifty young students showed up at the outset and many more followed soon thereafter. Soon parents were asking for a similar opportunity and were accommodated with a schedule of evening classes.

The strongest institutional response came from local churches with French names and Algerian congregations. Before the Trocmés returned to France, the local people had established a study center that would continue the program throughout the year. It seems that the thing most needed was a demonstration that something could be done about illiteracy, and done without the imprimatur of the colonial government.

Magda's record of these developments illustrates her perennial concerns as a social worker. She visited her tutorial students in their homes and found unimaginable living conditions. In one large house, each room contained an entire family, often with ten or a dozen members.

She gathered stories of the real cost of illiteracy from many of the women, most of whom had shared one common experience. It concerned the husbands who had left Algeria to go elsewhere to find work, some even to Metropolitan France. When they sent a check home to the family, the wife would have to appear in person at the post office to redeem the check. Most often, the clerk would cash the check, set aside a very large tip for himself, and hand the rest to the wife. Being unable to read the message or even the numbers on the check, she would have no way to know that she had been cheated.

Magda, the Civil Rights Movement, and Dr. King

In 1956, Magda went to Tallahassee, Florida, for a Christmas visit with her youngest son, Daniel. She took great interest in the bus boycott the black community there had established after two young African-American girls sat down next to a white and were arrested for doing so. She was eager to see nonviolent activism, American style, in action. The Sunday evening before Christmas, she met the Rev. J. Metz Rollins, the founding pastor of Tallahassee's first African-American Presbyterian Church and a leader of the coalition that led the 1956 bus boycott. Rollins took Magda to an evening mass meeting in one of the black churches. The agenda for the meeting was preparing for an imminent direct action. The leadership planned to bring an end to the boycott that week by asking members of the African-American community to return to using the buses, but in a democratic and non-segregated fashion.

Magda was seated on the dais with the several leading figures guiding the boycott. Aside from reporters and cameramen, she and Daniel were the only whites in the church. Her description of the mass meeting rings true to anyone who has experienced one of these gatherings:

That evening, I understood the Negro spiritual and jazz, the mystical hymns, the hope of souls to rise to a higher world where justice reigns, a world far from the suffering of this world, a world close to the Almighty God. Slow and moving hymns alternated with hymns full of rhythm that transformed, little by little, into shouts of joy accompanied by clapping hands and stamping feet, bodies swaying in rhythm and voices rising to remarkable pitch. The prayers were punctuated by "Amens" to the preachers' words and invocations calling on God as their witness.

God was there. How could he resist this crowd, determined to gain justice by love and non-violence? (M. Trocmé 1957)

When the talks about strategy and keeping nonviolent disciplines were over, Reverend Rollins announced that Magda would preach the sermon the next Sunday at the largest black church in Tallahassee. The attendees were eager to hear about her experience of nonviolent direct action in France during the war.

That week, the local papers carried a headline "a white woman will speak to the blacks." The next Sunday, the church was packed and the response of the congregation was vocal and active as Magda described how much alike were the two experiences of nonviolent direct action: Le Chambon in 1942, when the town refused to hand over to the Nazi-backed government the Jews living hidden in Le Chambon-sur-Lignon, and the Tallahassee African-American community in 1956, insisting with nonviolent resolve that public facilities must be open to all the public, not just its white members.

White friends had told her that the whole venture would be very dangerous for her, but Magda wrote instead, "It was not dangerous. It was one of the most beautiful experiences of my life. Never in my life had I been able to 'measure the temperature' of my talk as I could that time." (M. Trocmé 1957)

Not long after her Christmas in Tallahassee, Magda spent an evening in Alabama, visiting with Martin Luther King Jr. at his home in Montgomery. She could not help comparing him with the leaders of nonviolence she had met in India.

He was not an ascetic. He did not have the air of a saint or a prophet. His suit was clean, his face was shaven; he wore a felt hat and had a good-natured smile. He was lively, athletic, and he did not play the role of "the great man." He is a modern saint. Not only does he use the mundane human discoveries—the airplane, the car, the radio and television, he moves in this modern world like a fish moves in water. He lives in the world but he does not accept it as it is, and he works to make it better.

In our conversation, he said, "We who live in the Twentieth Century are very privileged because we live in one of the most important periods in human history, when we are present at the birth of a new social order; but there is no birth without suffering. . . . There are about 2.4 billion people on the earth, and the great majority, about 1.6 billion, are people of color. Twenty-five years ago most of them lived under oppression by whites . . . Now more than 1.3 billion men and women of color have gotten their freedom. [But] in the United States, the Black person is still an object to be used, not a person who has a right to be respected. A sort of peace had been found in segregation, but it is a negative peace: the absence of conflict, confusion and war. Positive peace is the presence of justice, good will and brotherhood. We must learn how to live together or we will be forced to die together. Now we face a new problem: we have to realize our spiritual unity." (M. Trocmé 1957)

Magda saw in Martin Luther King Jr. a "modern saint," but she was also talking with a man who could interrupt their lofty conversation to adjust the television set so he would not miss the end of the wrestling match!

EIRENE in Morocco

In 1957, while the French-Algerian war was still in full motion, André and Magda took a second trip to North Africa, this time to Morocco. With the Algerian conflict becoming an ever-increasing burden, France wanted to reduce its North African holdings and only a few months earlier had granted independence to both Tunisia and Morocco. Each of them, like Algeria, had vigorous independence movements, and both were causing France no little distress.

Morocco was a place that André remembered from his brief military adventure at the end of World War I. It was there that he became an unarmed soldier trying to serve both his country and his conscience. While he was not in Morocco for long, the experience left him sensitized to the plight of these territories that were so systematically stripped of their resources by his own France. If the IFOR had any call to service, it was certainly in places like these, where there was an opportunity to participate in peace building while the new nations were immersed in their nation building.

In Algeria, it had made the most sense to focus on teaching French to the Arab and Berber populations, since their future was so tightly bound to France. In Morocco, however, the Trocmés focused on more elemental things. The newly anointed king, Mohammed V, had embarked on an extensive reform program, touching everything from education to farming. It all needed attention and money. André and Magda asked themselves the activist question: "Why not us?" They could not move to Morocco, but they could get something started that would outlast their presence. Once again following on the work camp model in use at the Collège Cévenol and in the International Civil Service groups, they set about organizing a group of volunteers who would help the local population develop new and more effective means for organizing the persons and talents needed to deal with their most urgent development needs.

During their several postwar trips to the United States, André and Magda had strengthened their ties with the traditional peace churches. Now, a decade later, the Trocmés were able to enlist the help of Mennonite and Brethren Churches in recruiting volunteers and finding support for their new project in Morocco. It began with a strong pacifist identity. André was one of the founders of the original project, which, in 1957, brought the IFOR together with the Mennonite Church and the Church of the Brethren, both historic peace churches. The founders gave the project the name EIRENE, after the ancient Greek goddess of peace.

This first EIRENE project drew five young volunteers from Europe and America for two-year terms of development work in Oulmès, a small town at the edge of the desert in western Morocco. They developed a modern facility for poultry husbandry, an essential for the local farmers, introduced new and productive methods of vegetable gardening, and taught the illiterate how to read and write. They also succeeded in getting a doctor who would provide medical services for the remote town. When they arrived, the nearest doctor was sixty kilometers away and available to the people of Oulmès only once a week. As an illustration of the Trocmés' thorough approach to such problems, they had already gotten an agreement from the Moroccan Minister of Health to have the government provide the doctor's salary.[2] True to their intent, the Moroccan project continued to exist after they left. EIRENE still describes itself as an International Christian Service for Peace. Now headquartered not in Switzerland but in Neuwied, Germany, it sends out a hundred or more volunteers for shorter or longer terms of service wherever needed.

Wars Both Hot and Cold

During their ten years in Versailles, the Trocmés had "peace business" in at least sixteen countries, from the United States to Japan and from Sweden to North Africa, visiting some of them several times. Some of the visits lasted days, others weeks. It was a grueling schedule, and one that always required extensive preparation and follow-up and almost always required more fund-raising. The correspondence and financial accounting alone were enough to test their resolve.

One item on the "peace business" agenda of those years was Vietnam. It was the decade during which French Indochina collapsed when, in May of 1954, the French army surrendered to the Viet Minh army at Dien Bien Phu. In that battle, Ho Chih Minh's army had put an end to the French colonialism that had controlled the Vietnamese people for nearly a century, but now the struggle for independence would have to face down American forces that were in Vietnam with a different mission: to keep it from becoming a communist power.

The day after the French surrender, an International Peace Conference was gathered in Geneva, where the decision was made to divide Vietnam

---

2. These details found in an attachment to a letter from Magda Trocmé to the Moderator of the Waldensian (Protestant) Church in Italy, dated June 14, 1958.

at the Seventeenth Parallel, with North Vietnam ceded to the communist regime and South Vietnam to a western style republic, yet to be formed.

A year later, while real peace was still very far away, Trocmé traveled to Vietnam and Cambodia as part of a European pacifist group trying to persuade Ho Chih Minh to enter peace negotiations with his South Vietnamese and American adversaries. But at that juncture, there seemed no avenue for them to propose negotiation instead of bloodshed.

The question would arise again ten years later, when in the summer of 1965 a team of Trocmé, Howard Schomer, Martin Niemoller, and others went to North Vietnam, once again seeking an audience with Ho Chih Minh. They did have that meeting, in the midst of an American bombing attack on Hanoi. Again their objective was to persuade Ho Chih Minh to enter into a negotiated peace with the Americans and the regime in South Vietnam. They found Ho Chih Minh open to the discussion but very determined in his commitment to the political independence of Vietnam. Niemoller's participation in this effort brought an angry response from American Foreign Service quarters, especially because Niemoller was a world-renowned anti-Nazi Christian leader. While their visit did not stop the war, it at least opened a channel of communication.

An earlier major trip to the Far East had occurred in the summer of 1958, when the Berlin Crisis had brought Russian-Western tensions to a high point. The Cold War was at one of its most perilous periods. André was invited by the Japanese Committee Against the Atom Bomb and Hydrogen Bomb to join them and other pacifist organizations from around the world for the Fourth Annual International Conference Against the Atom and Hydrogen Bombs.

André quickly found out that the delegates included a large number of young Marxists, some from the Far East, and others from Eastern Europe and the Soviet Union. They were of one voice on almost everything, including votes taken on commission decisions and policies. Here are his reflections on the International Conference floor discussions: "A sort of unexpressed convention dominated the Conference. If an American or English or French or Japanese delegate got up and said 'My government was wrong,' loud applause would break out. But if anyone suggested that perhaps Russia has a part in the general fault of developing nuclear

37. André Trocmé and Kozo Tanaka Kokutai, Hiroshima, 1958. Unknown photographer.

weapons, a dead silence would fall over the assembly, as if one had criticized the Pope while in the Cathedral. No one responded to the criticism, but its author was left ignored and under public reproach."[3]

If ever André needed proof that pacifism could be a political instrument, the International Conference was a convincing case in point. Indeed,

---

3. Trocmé's report to the MIR on his trip to Japan from July 31 to August 30, 1958.

a young woman from East Germany took time to explain to André that it was a matter of faith among the Marxists that only capitalism and its competitive systems create wars.

During these Cold War years, both André and Magda felt the urgency of the growing nuclear power race among the western nations, and especially the growing commitment of France to become one of the leading forces in producing nuclear energy and nuclear bombs.

On April 11, 1958, two related things happened: the out-going French Prime Minister, Felix Gaillard, signed an official order for the manufacture and testing of a nuclear device; and eighty-two pacifists, under the leadership of André and Magda Trocmé, Lanza del Vasto, and Robert Barratt, paid a visit to Marcoule, one of France's first nuclear power plants, where they conducted a nonviolent demonstration against the production of atomic bombs.

They managed to get past the gates and asked for an interview with the plant's director and some of his employees. When they were turned down, they sat down in the plant yard outside the director's office and made it clear that they would stay as long as it took to make their case against the production of nuclear weapons. The predictable things happened: the police were called; the demonstrators stayed where they sat; the police said they would carry them away by force. André made a practical point, telling the police captain, "I weigh 230 pounds. It will take four men and a corporal to move me!" He got the four men but not the corporal and was carried into the assembly room outside the director's office.

The demonstrators kept a civil conversation going with the police, who finally understood that they had no criminal intent. The conversations between them became more understanding, in a few cases even cordial. The elderly female demonstrators were given a courteous carry into the building. Meanwhile, the workers on the day shift walked through the scene, having some of their own conversations with the demonstrators.

Finally, about 9 p.m., they decided they had made their point, and got back in the bus that had brought them (and whose driver waited an extra three hours to accommodate them) and went on their way. The next day's press was full of reports, accurate and inaccurate, about the event. It was, at least, a public demonstration of nonviolent direct action.

Versailles: Rebuilding Peace ✣ 267

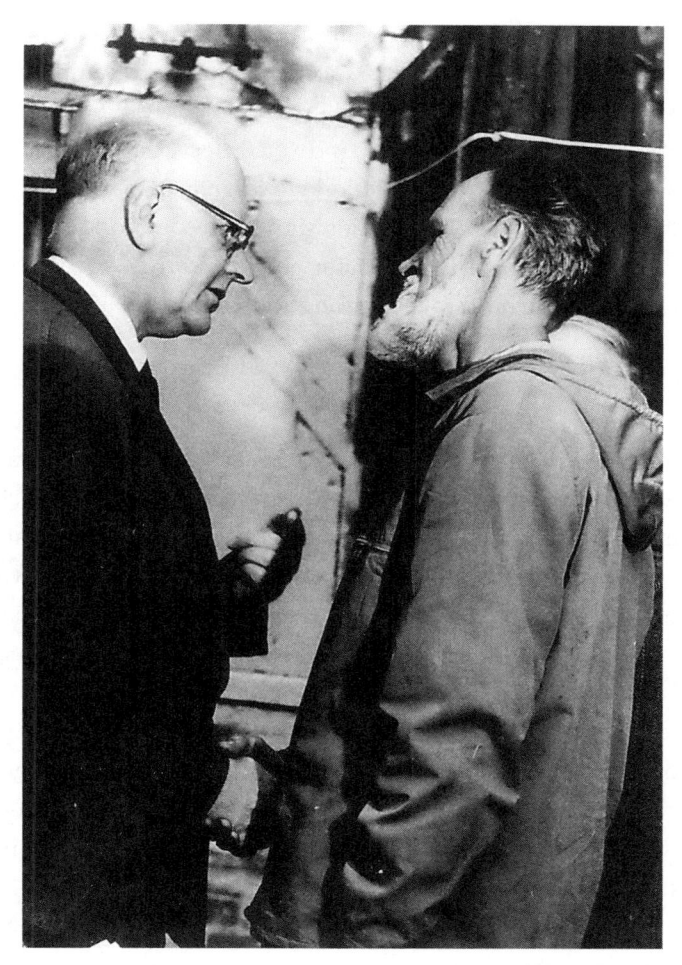

38. André Trocmé and Lanza del Vasto, Marcoule, 1958.
Unknown photographer.

A month after the Marcoule demonstration, Charles de Gaulle was restored to power as President of the French Republic. His first act was to begin building a French nuclear "strike force." His decision gathered increasing attention throughout France, but also throughout Europe and the "Nuclear Club" nations.

The following June, between trips throughout Europe and the United States, André, together with Alfred Kastler, a French physicist with a

Nobel laureate, created another organization designed to dampen down France's role in the nuclear arms race: the French Federation Against Atomic Arms. The fact that de Gaulle was still charging ahead with his own nuclear ambitions prompted André to prepare a long letter to the president, describing why this would be a terrible idea. The better to get de Gaulle's attention, he and Kastler signed the letter as co-presidents of the Federation. It was his last major gesture of the sort. Within a few weeks, the Trocmés would take a different turn in their life.

Clouds Gather over Versailles

By the end of the 1950s, André and Magda had both begun to realize that their time in Versailles was limited. Now approaching their sixtieth birthdays, they were exhausted by the incessant travel, however interesting and stimulating it might be. In his final issue of *Cahiers de la Reconciliation*, André wrote that it was time for a younger person to take over the responsibilities he and Magda had shouldered throughout the decade. He had said as much privately to others as well, and it was one reason he cited prominently in his letter to Edouard Theis about the forthcoming move. Both André and Magda also realized that they were approaching retirement age with only the most meager resources to bring to those non-salaried years ahead. They would need to accumulate some savings, and the IFOR was not the place to do it.

There was another stream running in this part of their lives, one mentioned in André's memoir but never publicly cited as having anything to do with leaving the position of European Secretary. His position was a rank below that of the IFOR General Secretary, whose scope was worldwide. Until 1938, the General Secretary had been his good friend and contemporary at the Faculté de Théologie, Henri Roser. By the time André arrived in Versailles, however, another person had moved into that role: an English pacifist named Percy Bartlett. They did not cross each other's line of vision until after the war when, in the 1950s, Bartlett began traveling in Europe to meet with IFOR groups there. André held him in low esteem, chiefly because he lacked "intellectual culture" (Bartlett had no university training) and he spoke no other language than English.

They ran afoul of one another in Italy when Bartlett came to meet with the small group of English-speaking Quakers in Rome. He seemed totally unaware of the most prominent Italian pacifists: people like Aldo Capitini, Danilo Dolci, Lanza del Vasto, and others. Because these were not Protestant Christians, but "culture Catholics" who did not identify with the church, Bartlett routinely dismissed their interest in becoming members of the IFOR.

Magda had worked hard to get a wider pacifist momentum in Italy by bringing the most influential pacifist figures into the game. Her extensive correspondence with her Italian contacts shows that clearly, and Bartlett's bureaucratic response to the membership question was a severe rebuke. Her answer to the problem was to treat her Italian cohort as members anyway and organize as much Italian FOR activity around them as possible.

About that time, André was in the United States, speaking and raising money. He wrote a letter to Nelly from Cambridge, Massachusetts, in which he reveals unease about continuing the IFOR work in France: "Two days ago at Yale, I was asked whether I wanted to stay in the U.S. I was offered a wonderful job as a chaplain in a New England College, with a decent salary.[4] And here I am, totally upset, far from Magda. My heart says Yes, Yes, Yes we must see our grandchildren grow up. My reason says Yes, Yes, Yes, for with the intensity of Mother's activities, she will die soon and it will be my doing. My conscience says No, No, No. Your duty is with the incarcerated conscientious objectors, and with the North Africans. One doesn't have the right to be a deserter. Ah, this miserable conscience. . . . And I already know my answer will be No, No. In fact I have already said No."

On October 24, 1959, while still on his American tour, Trocmé wrote to his friend and colleague, Edouard Theis, about the opportunity in Geneva and the decision he and Magda had made to accept the post. His letter outlined the reasons he felt that it was time to go: a large fundraising effort would be required to bring the Maison de la Réconciliation

---

4. The institution was Mount Holyoke College in South Hadley, Massachusetts. The letter of October 16, 1957, is in Nelly Trocmé Hewett's possession.

up to par; he and Magda and Jispa were all experiencing extreme fatigue from the relentless demands of travel and fund-raising; and there was always in the background the difficulty of arousing any interest in the MIR and its mission within the Église Réformée. In addition he had become increasingly impatient with the sluggish response of the IFOR headquarters in the United States to the agenda of its European members. There was no prospect that any of these things were likely to change. It was not a bright future.

It was the accumulation of all those things that convinced the Trocmés that they should move on at the end of their tenth year working full time with the IFOR. They set to exploring other options, hoping to find another parish in the ÉRF. They ran into the old familiar obstacles to finding a parish in France. The official church was still a long way from recognizing the legitimacy of André's pacifism, and the reluctance to offer a parish to a pacifist was still alive.

Much to Do, but Time to Go

Early in the fall of 1959, the main Protestant church of Geneva, the Temple St. Gervais, had been given André's name as a candidate for a vacancy in the team of ministers there. It would be a unique opportunity to be a pastor of a church in his own tradition, but one that actually had room for a practicing pacifist. He had been elected to the post with the enthusiastic support of the majority of the church council and all three of the other clergy of St Gervais. For both Magda and André, the choice was clear, and they accepted the election.

Now that the die had been cast, he delighted in the irony that he would be only the second French minister to hold a post in a Reformed church in Geneva, the first being Jean Calvin in the sixteenth century, and Calvin had only lasted two years before the Geneva magistrates expelled him from the city! André's tenure would last a decade and end not in expulsion but in honorable retirement.

17

Geneva and Beyond

Landing on Their Feet

In May of 1960, André and Magda left Versailles and made the move to Petit-Lancy, a small suburb on a hill just southwest of Geneva. A generous Quaker had rented them a house there at a reasonable price. The move turned out to be just the right one, both for the St. Gervais parish and for the Trocmés.

The Swiss Reformed church had no anti-pacifist policy concerning its clergy, nor did it forbid its ministers to speak of public and political issues when interpreting the Gospel for today's world. Further, at the time André joined the other clergy at St. Gervais, the church was well accustomed to sponsoring social service projects among its parishioners. That openness reflected Swiss attitudes toward the church's role in peace making, and the influence of the World Council of Churches, the ecumenical council that has been in Geneva since 1938.

Nonetheless, there were constraints on his appointment. A cautionary note threaded through the text of his official installation ceremony on May 8, 1960. In his welcome to André and Magda, the president of the church council, Ernest Schwab, rehearsed the events and discussions that led to his election. He said, "You certainly have a message to bring, not only to our parish, but to the whole Church of Geneva," but then made reference to an apprehension that some of the council members had expressed.

> It is quite possible that, after a ministry as vast as the one you exercised during your many years as European Secretary of the International Fellowship of Reconciliation, you might feel a little stifled (in a single parish).
>
> We know you and Mme. Trocmé have been pleased to find that your housing will likely be an apartment on the trolley line that leads out to

the World Council of Churches headquarters; but we hope that, when the trolley passes by St. Gervais, you will remember to get off here. . . . Your place is here at St. Gervais and we hope you will give your time and energy to St. Gervais above anything else.

Ten years later that air of caution had dispelled altogether. André had, in fact, traveled a good deal and had mounted major service projects abroad. But now M. Rouiller, the current president of the church council, took the occasion of his own retirement to cite how much the Trocmés' ministry had changed the life and spirit of St. Gervais for the better. He recalled that brief note of caution in his welcoming speech, that "some feared that he might find a parish a bit stifling." It had turned out that he had proved to be "just what the heart of the parish needed. Those who feared he might find the parish stifling were very quickly reassured: our pastor was a leader, both by opening one window after another on the wider world and by preaching inspired sermons, where a great prophetic wind quickly freshened the air and shook up our lazy spirit."

The rest of the farewell message was an impressive list of contributions the Trocmés made to the quality of church life.

> He established a twin-church relationship with the Reformed Church in St. Étienne, and teams from the twin churches visited each other's services and meetings twice a month. Then the horizon broadened when he established the Association for Technical Aid that brought St. Gervais into active work with the parish in Philippeville, Algeria, and with others in America. There were also the "Great Conferences of St. Gervais" that brought us a series of personalities of the first order for group discussions on the major problems of our time. Then he inaugurated a program of "hospitality" in the church, with members welcoming people at the door as they came to services, brief newsletters on church activities left in every pew, and a coffee hour after services.

The list went on, and the celebration ended with heartfelt wishes for long years of happiness and tranquility ahead. Thirteen months later, André died and Magda began her ordeal of living twenty-five years without him.

For André the move to Geneva had meant the opportunity both to preach regularly and to launch other activist projects, such as the Association St. Gervais-Philippeville. He was still being called on to travel on behalf of the peace movement, and this with the encouragement of his colleagues in the St. Gervais ministry. None of those things were likely to have been tolerated in the much more conservative ÉRF.

For Magda, the move had meant a new teaching career, part of it at the University of Geneva School of Interpreters, teaching budding translators serving the many international organizations headquartered there, and part of it at a French lycée just over the border in Annemasse. There, she had quickly become an honored member of the faculty.

For Jispa, it was a new and pleasant home to keep in order for two hyper-productive people. It was also the place she would associate with her first birthday celebration in a foreign country. When she turned sixty-seven in October of 1960, the family took her at her word and prepared three practical gifts, which André accompanied with this citation:

> Little Jispa, your three wishes now have been fulfilled. Here are
> - a towel rack to dry the tears we have made you shed while you wait for heaven, where God will dry your tears;
> - a grocery cart on wheels so you may spoil your children (with chocolate) while you wait for heaven, where God will take his turn to spoil you,
> - and a stepladder to compensate for your diminutive size while you wait for Jacob's ladder to climb up to heaven, where God will give you a body as big as your heart. (A. Trocmé 1953, 260)

Yet Another Tragedy

They had been in Geneva barely a year when their family was diminished again by an untimely death. Their youngest son, Daniel, took his own life.

Daniel had more than his share of emotional burdens to carry. As the youngest child in an active, outspoken family with a demanding agenda, he was more than a little shy, even secretive, a youngster who must have felt much more pain about himself and his performance than any of his family would have intended him to feel. But children early develop their own private ways of dealing with the stresses they face, and some can be damaging and uncomfortable.

Later, when he was on his own, it was a great sadness for Magda and André that he sought solace, as did so many in his generation, in drugs and then in alcohol. He was married early to a Swedish girl and finally finished his educational career with a diploma in restaurant management from the University of Florida. He found a job managing a food service for Montgomery Ward in Chicago, and then another in Denver. Things went well for a while, but the alcohol problem did not go away. Almost from the outset, his marriage had reflected the impact of his addiction. The summer of his death, his wife took their two children to visit with their Swedish family. Given the turmoil in the family, she sought professional counsel and finally decided not to return directly to the United States. Daniel was then living alone in Denver and having limited contact with his children. He ultimately became severely depressed and committed suicide.

Jean-Pierre's tragic accident sixteen years earlier had been a shattering event for both André and Magda, one to which neither of them would ever become reconciled. Daniel's death was different only in that it was nested in a troubled history, which both of them knew well but never entirely understood. Nonetheless, they had to accept his death because it had happened and because it was the outcome of circumstances that were beyond the control of anyone, including Daniel himself. With all of that, Daniel was still their own child and now the second of the four to die before they did. This too was an irreconcilable loss that would scar their remaining years.

Preaching the Fundamentals

André's preaching in St. Gervais was memorable. Radio-Genève Suisse Romande, a radio service that reached virtually all of the French-speaking Swiss population, carried many of his sermons. Throughout his preaching, the theme of peace is never far from the center of his thought, a notion of peace that leans heavily on its biblical source, that links intimately with ordinary life experience for his hearers, and that is always predicated on the ultimate reconciliation with God for which all humans wait and which all humans fear. Reconciliation has both those characteristics of desire and fear, desire to be rid of violence, war, and uncalled-for suffering, and fear of the cost of daring to live one's life toward that reconciliation.

There were also personal qualities that made André's preaching memorable. Some of them were not necessarily talents, just physical facts. Everything about him was outsized. He towered above the average Frenchman, his big frame, head and hands radiating both physical strength and strength of will. There was also his very powerful voice, a voice with a deep resonance that required no amplification in public speaking. His speaking style registered a confidence in what he was saying and an underlying certainty about the matter at hand, but it was also the preaching of a man who had weathered daunting dangers and monumental tragedies. Students in his confirmation classes were quick to point out the fact that he simply commanded attention not by asking for it but by putting his rich and colorful mind to work in their presence.[1]

As a preacher he also had a talent for bringing the meaning of his sermon close to the ordinary experience of his hearers. One of these sermons, "Destiny raps four times at your door"("Les Quatre Coups du Destin," Nov. 11, 1962), begins with a hypothetical preacher citing an automobile accident, an example that immediately recalls André's own bitter experience when his mother was killed because his father misjudged his new car's speed and the road conditions.

> "I do not refer to the natural catastrophes that overtake us," says the preacher, "but to the murderous brutality that lies in the hand of man. The example might be one among us. He drives a car, everyone drives a car these days; he goes a little too fast, or he is distracted, or he makes an error of judgment. He thinks he can pass the other car and he is not able to do it. He hesitates. A split-second later there is an accident. And in that accident, his responsibility is involved. He realizes it, and he reacts often with remorse, especially if there are victims."

Then he moves the question to another plane. Only two weeks had passed since the Cuban missile crisis. The fear was worldwide that the

---

1. This impression came out in many interviews in Le Chambon, Geneva, and elsewhere.

standoff between Kennedy and Khrushchev would trigger a nuclear exchange that would wipe out a third of the human race. Then Khrushchev took a step back.

> It was as if the pale horse of the Apocalypse had passed very near us and then moved away. Our feelings were first of gratitude that the accident had been avoided, and then of thanking God that we were still alive.

But then, André points out what everyone there knew all too well. When tragedy moves away from center stage, we go back to normal life, life that keeps a distance between us and the God of love and reconciliation. We go about our work with the same intensity and preoccupation as before, keeping our distance from the underlying question.

> "What is this destiny whose wing has brushed against us? What are these raps that I heard at my door, at the same time both menacing and seductive? Is there catastrophe behind that door? Is there death?"

It seemed always to be André's goal to "move the question" first, and only then to preach the sermon. Typically, André did not start his sermons with "proofs" of the Christian faith, but with insights into the human condition, insights designed to touch all his hearers. Only then did he present the Christian faith as a resource for addressing those insights with intelligence and reflection, and for understanding the meaning of living one's life in the presence of the God of love and reconciliation.

Themes appear in others of his sermons that show yet another characteristic of his preaching: he was not predictable. One sees his struggle with the tragedies of losing Jean-Pierre and Daniel lingering in the background. In the sermon "Destiny raps at your door four times" the struggle is only barely concealed. The same is true of his Easter sermon four years later.

In the 1965 Easter morning sermon, he addresses the struggle between suffering and faith. He begins by identifying himself as a companion to all those who are unable to resign themselves to the loss of a loved one. The substance of his message is not "Here is how to resign yourself to the loss" but "Don't do it!" It is one thing to accept your own death, but you must not be resigned to the death of others, as he was never resigned to the loss of Jean-Pierre and Daniel, and as he was never resigned to the death of soldiers in wartime or to the death of malnourished populations who starve while the wealthy prosper. Refusing such resignation is to conform to the will of God. The significance of Easter is God's relentless affirmation of life, in the hardest situation, against all the odds. You too must learn to affirm life in the hardest of circumstances. Yes, Easter is joyous; it is also demanding.

Some of his sermons are shaped more by the need to teach than by the need to persuade. He did a long series of sermons on the Ten Commandments, each one as clarifying as the last. In these and other "teaching" sermons he resorted to a formal structure of "thesis, antithesis, synthesis, and consequences," headings that even appear in the printed transcription of the sermons. When André wanted to explain something, all the force of his well-ordered mind came to the fore, and his hearers went away with a well-structured argument that stuck in their memories.

Thanks to his rigorous classical French education, his inherent love of language, and his voracious reading habits, André Trocmé's sermons were on topics that had meaning for his congregation and were delivered with rich imagery and eloquent command of the French language. And when he appealed to his congregation to take a public stand on a matter of peace and Christian integrity, as he did in the famous "City of Refuge" sermon in Le Chambon in 1939, his congregation was more than likely to respond with conviction.

The Diesel School in Algeria

Some members of St. Gervais were already aware of EIRENE, André's IFOR volunteer work project in Morocco, so it came as no surprise to his colleagues or his parishioners when André proposed a similar volunteer project for Algeria, this one with a narrower and more precise objective.

André had a major talent for organizing volunteer projects that captured the imagination and enriched the spirit of those who participated in them. It was a talent that had been evident all through his career in the ministry, from his early assignment in the mining town of Sous-le-Bois to his efforts to make Le Chambon into the "City of Refuge" that saved the lives of innumerable Jews and other refugees from deportation and death. Now he exhibited the same talent for the Temple St. Gervais.

In Geneva, the St. Gervais-Philippeville Project, as it became known, was designed to bring a Swiss bourgeois church into face-to-face contact with the changing Third World. A newly independent Algeria faced huge economic, professional, and social needs. Independence had drained the country of many specialized talents, with devastating effects and a mountain of needs. Most of the Pieds Noirs had fled, leaving behind them a shriveled infrastructure, clear-cut forests, and farmland turning to desert. André had seen the evidence. The deforestation led to lack of rain, and the lack of rain left farmers with a dust bowl.

On a Sunday in 1963, André preached a sermon on the story of four men who carried their paralyzed friend to Jesus in hopes that he would be healed (Mark, ch. 2). Jesus was meeting and healing people in the little fishing village of Capernaum. The house was already jammed, and the four men could not get near Jesus. Determined as they were, they dug a hole in the adobe ceiling and lowered the paralytic into the room on a mat. Jesus told him his sins were forgiven and he could take up his mat and walk home.

In the course of the sermon, André brought up the situation in arid Algeria. Throughout the farming regions, Algerian farmers were working the soil as they had before becoming part of France: using hand tools and what animal labor they could find. The diesel trucks and tractors, brought in by the Pieds Noirs years before to make farming more efficient and productive, were sitting in the fields rusting. There was now almost no one who knew how to service or repair them. Why couldn't the parish of St. Gervais get something going to fix that problem?

At the end of the sermon he made an appeal to the congregation: "If there is someone in the congregation who is an engineer and could take two years' leave from his work to head a new Diesel maintenance school in Philippeville, I hope that person will come to the coffee hour after the service and introduce himself to me."

One church member, a watchmaker named Willy Engel, was present that morning with his wife. He recalled André saying that the message of the story was simply "open up your homes and let the breath of God flow through them. You will see how your lives will change." He wondered whether he and his wife could make a go of it in Algeria for a couple of years. He could work for the Diesel project and she, a hairdresser, could certainly find a market for her skills.

It was André's practice to gather anyone interested in talking about the sermon for a cup of coffee at a café across the street. That Sunday Willy Engel introduced himself and opened discussion of the Diesel school. He and his wife asked a string of questions about the details, and finally told André that, if no one else came forward for the post, he would do so, even though he was not an engineer.

Before he knew it, he was sent off to Stuttgart for a four-month intensive course in Diesel engineering and maintenance. The Bosch Company became so interested in the project that they offered to sell the project a group of second-hand Diesel repair benches and ship them, free of charge, to Philippeville. Now trained, Engel went off to Algeria to set the project in motion. Others followed and the organization blossomed. They were given access to a 2,100-square-foot unused garage as their workshop. A sector of the Algerian Ministry of Agriculture provided some funding; the Swiss government matched the funds raised by several Geneva churches; a permanent organization, an Algerian government agency engaged in professional training for adults, provided the umbrella sponsorship.[2]

Experienced engineers showed up from Holland, Switzerland, France, Germany, and America for terms of service of a few weeks to two years. They were given the mission of "teaching the teachers" so that the whole enterprise would ultimately be handed off to Algerian nationals. That finally happened at a ceremony in which the key to the workshop was handed over to the mayor of Philippeville. The project turned into an engineering version of Frank Laubach's "each one teach one" method of

---

2. An account of the whole Philippeville venture appeared as an article in Geneva's Protestant newspaper, *La Vie Protestante,* April 14, 1967. Additional details were provided in a May 2001 interview with Jean Pierre Marchand, one of the project's principal volunteers, an engineer, and a member of the St. Gervais Church Council.

attacking illiteracy. It was a new kind of mission for the Geneva church, but the work-camp model had worked in building a permanent campus for the Collège Cévenol; it had worked in Morocco when the EIRENE project was founded. Certainly it would work to the benefit of Algerian farmers as well. It did, but not for long.

The frailty of momentous projects like this one is legendary. Some last for long periods, adjusting to the changes in cultures around them; others ossify and become fixed in time even when time leaves them behind; still others collapse as later generations mismanage the money or forget the founding principles or watch the original need disappear. The projects that André and Magda had launched were cases in point. The Collège Cévenol still provides an international education to young people; the EIRENE project continues to fulfill its original purpose but in changing places and circumstances; but the Algerian Diesel school collapsed under the fiscal mismanagement of its Philippeville directors.

Magda and André responded differently to the various fates of their projects. André was more inclined to see the shadow of his own failure in the projects that changed radically or disappeared altogether. Magda's inclination was much more matter of fact. She seemed to understand that only a few footprints are preserved in rock. Most are left to disappear in the sand.

Flight and the Family

In January of 1968, André was called back to St. Gobain for the funeral of his eldest brother, Francis. The visit to the place brought back layer after layer of recollection and reflection on his experience with his father and his large family and a sober reassessment of the world-view it represented. He describes the family's long-time summer estate, le Fringolet, in January as

> grey, wintry, and silent as the landscape you see in a dream.... A house like an Advent calendar, with many windows that a child opens to find some surprises, but a house without great style, without any "future" for its "past," a house where you close the windows one by one with each

passing death—the shutters closed on Papa (27 years already), the shutters closed on Jean-Pierre 24 years ago, they closed on Daniel 3 years ago and now the last shutters close on Francis-and-Rose, for I think I have attended the last act of the saga of le Fringolet, since Francis—the last of the family who still loved le Fringolet—has died.[3]

That was a difficult moment for André. Francis, enough older to be his parent, had been remarkably understanding of André's unusual career decisions. He was one member of the family who had developed a deep respect, even admiration, for André's preaching, however much it might be fixed on the issues of pacifism. Francis wrote of that admiration to another brother, Robert, right after visiting Le Chambon and attending a service at which André was the preacher. He described the event in almost awesome tones in his letter.

All the comments about Francis offered in André's letter to Nelly are said without rancor, for André still regarded Francis as a kind of totem figure, on whom the spiritual history of the family was carved.

> Francis remained to the end the Family incarnated, whose devastating ironies were but a screen behind which was hidden a timid, tender, hesitant man trapped to the end in the life style inherited from Papa.... (But) with Papa, faith was so strong that there was no need for a "credo" to be a Christian, and with Francis, faith was so feeble that there was left only an austere moral tradition to be loyal to until the end.

The death of Francis was the death of le Fringolet, thought André. The others of his generation had left that Protestant culture of 1900, and the next generation had altogether different notions of relaxation and retreat, as did the grandchildren. Granted, everyone needs to take flight from the family nest, but for his family, the question was still open: did they have some other "promised land" where they would seek a purpose and a fulfillment for their lives?

---

3. From a letter to his daughter Nelly, written in Petit-Lancy on February 1, 1968.

The Garden at Petit-Lancy

By the time of his retirement, André was increasingly grateful to have the house in Petit-Lancy. It was far enough from the city center to be quiet, to have a long view, and to seem protected from the noise and hustle of downtown Geneva. He and Magda had begun planning for the use of this house well before his retirement date, with one main focus on the gardens as an aesthetic and practical bonus. As he aged, André had become increasingly captured by the thought of having a manageable and quiet house, especially one that would be simple enough for him to take care of, in spite of the life-long back pain that was steadily worsening and limiting his mobility.

Whenever a window of time was open, André and Magda planned for changes that would be required in the house. André would need some device for getting around the grounds without lengthy standing or bending over. Their garden was a lovely array of trees and shrubs that they had far too little time to enjoy, so gardening became a major part of his retirement plan. It would provide a change from incessant travel, and it would be spiritually calming.

The nurture of his spiritual life was often on his mind as retirement approached, for it had been too often preempted by the rigors of his work. He made a revealing comment about this to his long-time friend Howard Schomer, who was often in Geneva with his international responsibilities in the World Council of Churches. He confided to Schomer that he was truly looking forward to a quieter life, for it was time to reckon with the meaning of his physical limits. At this point in his life, he simply wanted to get to know Jesus better and cultivate that relationship without constant interruption.[4]

He was no less concerned about his life-long war against war, but he was realistic enough to know that he could not go off to North Africa to set up a new service project, nor could he join the demonstrations at an atomic energy facility, as he had in the past. But he could still write,

---

4. I learned of Trocmé's comment in a conversation with Schomer in 1999.

and he could manage a brief trip now and again. In fact, he was already preparing a speech he had been invited to give at the Collège Cévenol to celebrate the opening of the new gymnasium.

He could carry on his legendary and literate correspondence and finish writing his memoirs. Perhaps he could even come to terms with some of the personal and spiritual uncertainties that had been with him all his life. A good garden would help all that.

André, Magda, and the Age of Recognition

Many people who have lived active and prominent lives find that retirement is, among other things, a time of recognition. The awards that hang on the wall, the legendary gold watch, the appreciative articles—even books—are all symbols of a useful past, not calls to a promising future.

In the postwar years, the American Friends Service Committee nominated André for the Nobel Peace Prize on two occasions, in 1949 and again in 1955. While he appreciated the sentiments, the whole effort made him uncomfortable. In general, he did not like "decorations." They reminded him of the portraits of family members who had earned distinction in military service. These were portraits that always had to be at least full upper body paintings, since extra room was needed to display the array of ribbons and medals that hung on full dress military jackets. This was different, however. The Nobel nomination was, after all, a singular honor that would add to the recognition of the worldwide peace movement in general. The nomination remained just that, however, and nothing further came of it.

Later he found himself in an awkward position. Another effort was under way that would hang a decoration around his neck. He first learned about it from an old friend, Amy Latour. Then came a note from André Chouraqui, a Jewish refugee who had been sheltered near Le Chambon during the war and worked with a Jewish service organization in France: the Organisation de Secours aux Enfants (Organization for the Relief of Children). The note informed André that there was a movement afoot in Jerusalem to nominate him for the "Medal of the Just," a recognition accorded to non-Jews who had distinguished themselves in the effort to save Jews from the Holocaust. Chouraqui had become the Vice Mayor of Jerusalem and was the one who would forward the nomination to the Yad Vashem. (The name derives from Isaiah, chapter 56, verse 5: "And to them will I give in my house and within my walls a memorial and a name that shall not be cut off.")

When the letter announcing the honor came to Petit-Lancy, it proposed that there be a gathering in Bern, at which the Israeli Ambassador to Switzerland would present the medal. André wrote back that he was complimented by the proposal, but he would decline the honor all the same. If there were to be any such recognition it ought to go to the villagers in Le Chambon and its surrounding villages, and André had made that proposal to the Israelis.

To Amy Latour, he wrote,

> Since I am opposed to decorations, I would have to refuse such a decoration. Why me? Why not the throngs of humble peasants of the Haute-Loire, who did as much and more than me? Why not my wife, whose conduct was much more heroic than mine? Why not my colleague Edouard Theis, with whom I shared everything and all the responsibilities? I would not be able to accept the Medal of the Just except in the name of all those who were "anchors" for their unjustly persecuted brothers and sisters, even to the death. . . . Could you intervene with the Yad Vashem so that Le Chambon might be the place for doing this?[5]

Ultimately, that is just what happened; the Yad Vashem did make the policy exception that the award would be presented to the population of Le Chambon and its surrounding villages. The ceremony was scheduled to take place in the Town Hall on Pentecost Sunday, May 31, but André could not attend. He was confined to the Cantonal Hospital in Geneva, where he would die five days later. The award was handed to Magda in the Temple of Le Chambon immediately after the funeral service for André.

The award to André and Le Chambon was one of a series of recognitions of people from the Plateau who had participated in the rescue of

---

5. Letter to Mme. Latour, written from Petit-Lancy March 8, 1971.

Jews during the Nazi regime. The number was already 3,158 for all of France and about eighty for the Plateau. Soon thereafter, Edouard and Mildred Theis were so honored, then the public school director, Roger Darcissac, and Simone Mairesse, who had been a helper to the Trocmés in Sin-le-Noble and now lived in nearby Le Mazet, where she had been active in a predominantly Jewish resistance group, known simply as "Monsieur André." Another friend honored by the Yad Vashem was Roland Leenhardt, a minister in nearby Tence and later Director of the Collège Cévenol. In 1986, Magda Trocmé was added to the roll of the Righteous Among the Nations at a ceremony at the Israeli embassy in Paris.

Both Magda and Mildred Theis were also honored by honorary degrees for their work on behalf of dispossessed refugees who were cared for in Le Chambon. Mildred's Doctor of Laws degree was conferred by her alma mater, The College of Wooster, in Ohio. Her citation was an apt comment on her personality and her hospitality during the hardest years of the war and after, noting that she "did so much with so little and kept a great heart in a small house."

A disproportionately large number of those "Righteous" are from the Ardèche and the Haute-Loire. Considering that the seventeen towns and villages of the Plateau had, in 1936, a total population of only 24,000 (Bolle 1992, 132), and fewer than 30,000 during the war years, the numbers of those recognized by Yad Vashem are remarkably high. It was no wonder that the Yad Vashem thought it appropriate to recognize the whole village.

In addition to those cited by name, the Yad Vashem erected a stone stele near the entry to the "Garden of the Righteous" inscribed in Hebrew and French "To the inhabitants of Le Chambon-sur-Lignon and the neighboring villages who saved the lives of countless Jews."

Although the award is worded as André and Magda wanted it, their two names are still associated with that stele in the minds of many who visit the Garden. In 1996, Richard Deats, of the IFOR, visited the Yad Vashem and took pictures. He found that previous visitors had followed the Jewish custom and brought a stone as a symbol of their remembrance of Magda and André. Deats found, tucked in by one of the stones, a note in English, saying "Dear God, bless this woman. . . . Clasp her to your lovely bosom. She gave the world so much of your light and love." Under the stone next to the note the writer had left a package of marigold seeds. Then Deats left his own note of thanks and a stone.

In recent times, other honors have come to the Trocmés and the people of the Plateau for their rescue efforts during the war. In 1987, a Canadian scholar, Ben Sokoloff, established an endowment at the Martin Buber Institute of Hebrew University in the names of the Trocmés and the people of Le Chambon.

More recently still, in July of 2004, President Jacques Chirac selected Le Chambon as the place to give an inaugural speech for his program on "the values of the Republic," a program to get France past a newer outbreak of anti-Semitism. In it, he pointed to Le Chambon as "a place (where) the soul of the nation manifested itself. Here was the embodiment of our country's conscience."

In January 2007, President Chirac delivered another speech, this one in the Panthéon in Paris. The occasion was a ceremony to honor all French rescuers, those cited by the Yad Vashem and the many others not known by name. In the course of pointing out the chain of ordinary citizens who participated in the saving of Jews and other refugees, President Chirac cited André Trocmé and the village of Le Chambon, "whose name" he says, "still resonates in our hearts today."[6] A delegation from Le Chambon was present to hear these honors.

Much other recognition came to the Trocmés in the years following André's death, including the Médaille de la Résistance avec rosette. The medal was created by General de Gaulle in 1966 and as of 2007 had been conferred on some 64,000 resisters. The addition of the rosette is reserved to those resisters (now 4,253 of them) considered by the governing commission to have made the most distinguished contributions to the French Résistance. André Trocmé is among that smaller group.

It may be, however, that the recognition of his life and work is best underscored by the number of times his name still appears in books,

---

6. Allocution de M. Jacques Chirac, Président de la République, à l'occasion de la cérémonie nationale en l'honneur *des Justes de France,* January 19, 2007, made available to me by the office of the President of the Republic.

articles, films, and plays about Le Chambon and resistance in the 1940s. Another measure of recognition in this electronic age is the number of "hits" that occur on the worldwide web when his name is typed in. In 2010, it exceeded 87,000.

In a great many cases, it is André's name that appears in the recognitions, although Magda had a goodly share of her own. Yet when called upon to accept the honorary Ph.D. from Haverford College, it was she who set the condition that she could only do so on behalf of the whole network of communities around Le Chambon, just as André had accepted the honor of the Yad Vashem only on condition that it be given to the village and not to him alone.[7] Neither André nor Magda hungered for such recognition, and both saw those honors in a larger historical framework. Such awards held up values to be acknowledged and strengthened. They both saw the honoree as an instrument to that end.

Magda shared the honors that day with the villagers of the Plateau, and with Rosa Parks, whose famous decision not to move to the back of the bus earned her the nickname "Mother of the Civil Rights Movement."

After her death another honor came Magda's way from the city of Annemasse, where she had taught through the 1960s. The city, along with the Department of the Haute-Savoie, had decided that their lycée had to be given major renovation and expansion. The renovated middle school would be named "Lycée des Glières d'Annemasse." The new name deliberately recalls a famous battle between the Maquis of the area and a combined force of Vichy militia and German troops in March of 1944, a battle that galvanized resistance in the whole Rhône-Alpes area of southeastern France.

In mapping the building, the authorities decided to name the most important academic spaces in honor of four outstanding Résistance figures: Tom Morel, the young commander of the Résistance forces in the Haute-Savoie; Jean Moulin, the iconic leader of the Résistance, who consolidated scattered Maquis cells and brought French Résistance forces under the sway of General Charles de Gaulle; Albert Camus, author of *The*

---

7. The full text of the Haverford Doctoral citation is in the Appendix.

Plague and editor of *Combat,* the newspaper of the French Résistance; and Magda Trocmé.

Outside the Magda Trocmé Faculty Lounge hangs a plaque that cites her nonviolent resistance to the Vichy and the German forces, her work in receiving, protecting, and saving the lives of Jewish and other refugees, and her avid work on behalf of Third-World populations in North Africa.

39. Trocmé plaque in the Avenue of the Righteous of the Nations, Yad Vashem, Jerusalem. Photograph by and courtesy of Douglas Guthrie.

Life after André

Magda kept to her plan of retiring from Annemasse in 1965, but she took on another assignment in a high school called "Le Cycle d'Orientation," near Petit-Lancy, and continued her part-time work at the Geneva School of Interpreters. It was only after her third retirement in 1971 that she focused on the beginning of a different and more private life together. With André's untimely death, however, she now had to build that life alone. She and Jispa lived on in Petit-Lancy for another six years until, in 1977, they gave up the house in Petit-Lancy and moved back to France. Magda was only 76, but Jispa was already 84, and it seemed to make more sense to settle in Paris where they could be closer to Jacques and his family. Both Jacques and his wife Leslyn were now able to give them closer attention in their advanced years.

Magda and Jispa remained inseparable, for Jispa was the only remaining family of Magda's generation. After almost thirty years of sharing a home where professional life came first, they established a different kind of life together in a comfortable apartment on the Avenue Parmentier in Paris. But threads from the patterns of the past still held in place. Jispa was still "the little mother," and she made it her business to see that Magda was well cared for in daily life. Magda, for her part, remained habituated to leaning on Jispa for dealing with the practical details that kept life organized, including dealing with the massive collection of André's papers.

Throughout her 70s, Magda remained as active as ever, traveling often and writing incessantly. A lot of her travel was to family in the United States and elsewhere in Europe. She traveled with Jacques to see Greek cousins in Corfu, where Magda pleaded for a chance to go parasailing! Those letters reveal her continued focus on world affairs in the light of her passion for nonviolence. They also reveal her relationship to Jesus, still not as God Incarnate but as one of the clearest windows on God in history. In a long and discursive 1974 letter to her Nelly, she wrote,

> Jesus spent his time demystifying what the Pharisees and many others were saying. And now despite the reforms made within the church,

Jesus has been locked in a tabernacle sitting on the altar. Watch out if Jesus comes down from his tabernacle! Watch out for whips that fall on merchants in the temples; watch out for labels such as "race of vipers," watch out for revolutions! Watch out for the Holy Spirit if it takes hold of the souls of our leaders, the Nixons, the Giscards, and the Mitterands, the Russians and the Chinese, the Arabs and those who sit on oil fields, and those who don't have any oil. If the Holy Spirit conquers the souls of simple people, watch out for the love and the equality of all the people who would claim their rights. What a mess it would be!!

The Wakening Memory

When André died in 1971, the French memory of the war years was still a clouded one. So many things had divided the French population during the war that the postwar period was fraught with divisions and with the desire to keep them out of sight and out of mind. There were French survivors of the Holocaust, French Résistance figures, French institutions for saving refugees on the one side, and on the other were former members of the *Milice,* the official Vichy paramilitary police force, the private and public collaborationists who understandably wanted to keep a very low profile, and the government officials who had served the German cause by providing it some of the bureaucratic support it needed.

There had been flare-ups of revenge in many areas of France, but that was tamped down in a relatively short time and the desire to return to normal held sway again. Although slow in coming, the need to resolve sleeping conflicts would not be restrained. Among the things that stirred the memory and the need for resolution was the publication of two books in the 1970s: the scholarly treatment of the Vichy years by Robert Paxton (1972), and the ethical inquiry in Phillip Hallie's book of 1978, *Lest Innocent Blood Be Shed.* But it was the trial of Klaus Barbie, "the Butcher of Lyon," in 1987 that really lanced the boil. From that point on, scholars, politicians, and others began to engage in a dialogue that searched for understanding of what had happened in France and to France during those years from 1940 to 1944. The dialogue still goes on, and it is one that drew Magda into activities that continued the search for understanding, not only of the events that occurred in Nazi-occupied Europe, but of war as a major affliction of the human race.

Magda remained as interested as ever in the issues of justice and peace, but she could no longer muster the focus and energy to continue the kind of activism for peace that had been the hallmark of her life with André. The activist's "fire in the belly" had gone out. But another kind of fire would burn more brightly: her passion for unpretentious truth in human affairs.

That fire was nothing new. It appears clearly in many earlier accounts of her travels for peace representing the MIR: the long weeks in India for the World Pacifist Meeting during the winter of 1949–50; the tour of "Quaker Institutes" (brief study conferences) in America in 1954; the trip to Russia in the summer of 1958.

Now in her late seventies and eighties, she remained clear-eyed about national and cultural pretensions on all sides, and just as committed as ever to her own and her husband's mission, so she still tried to respond to speaking invitations that came her way. She could at least speak the truth to those pretensions. A number of such invitations did come to her in her late seventies and into her eighties, but the reservoir of energy was running dry.

Magda knew that wars are too easily forgotten and new wars too easily kindled when the sordid facts of war are put out of one generation's memory or withheld from the next. It was with that in mind that she added to her own memoir and continued editing Andre's. She did not want the grandchildren to be unaware of their grandparents' lifelong commitment.

André was an inveterate documenter of his life and work. The private files were extensive and by dint of long concentration and effort, Magda faced up to the daunting task of putting his handwritten pages into order and reducing them to a typed manuscript of 584 pages. Fortunately she had good help through her last years, which gave her time to carry on her prolific correspondence with old friends who throughout those years had remained in close touch. The last letter she wrote was to James Lowenson, a German Jew who had survived the Holocaust, had come to America, and was always ready to serve as her personal chauffeur. She had met

40. Magda in her late eighties. Unknown photographer.

him while visiting her daughter in Minnesota. Lowenson had already responded to that final letter, but his reply arrived in her mail just days after her death.

The job of ordering André's papers must have seemed endless. His capacity to recall details of events long past was far beyond the ordinary, but the details did not always match her own recollection of the events she shared. Being Magda, she did not hesitate to add the marginal comment now and again, just to set the record straight.

Both of her children, Jacques and Nelly, were adamant about the importance of her doing this work, and equally adamant about finishing her own memories of a lifetime. She had begun making notes of this sort as early as 1942, but it had been a task she set aside repeatedly in deference to her lifetime need to be useful to people who needed her.

For Magda, the task of actually gathering the memories and documents that would make up her own *Souvenirs* was even more daunting. She had many of the same qualities of mind as André, and certainly the same squirrelly habits about her own papers and mementos. The children persisted, and she once again took pen to paper and set down more thoughts and memories about her life. Neither André nor Magda completed these tasks. Magda could not carry the narration past the years in Le Chambon, and André's memoir papers ended with the move to Geneva in 1960. In addition to the task of the memoirs, Magda prepared collections of letters and papers for her children, documents that would give them a livelier understanding of the lives their parents had led.

She was at a loss to find the right place to deposit them. After a visit in Paris with Mennonite scholar John Yoder, and on his suggestion, she was invited to place them with the Peace Collection in the library of Swarthmore College, a college with a strong Quaker heritage. She accepted the invitation quickly, packed the many boxes of papers, and sent them to Swarthmore, where the Director of the Peace Archive got a grant sufficient to have the papers properly identified and prepared for access.

The Trocmé archive at Swarthmore is a large and well-managed one, but there was need for a second archive of family papers that came to light after her death, when her son Jacques began going through his own collection. In order to make the Trocmé materials more available to European scholars, a new collection has been established in the archive of the World Council of Churches in Geneva.

In her final years, Jispa's role was still focused on seeing to the well-being of her dear friend, Magda. While she never asked for relief from that role, she was glad when it came from time to time, especially as her strength and resilience waned. In 1989, Jispa died at the age of ninety-six, while at home with Jacques and Leslyn. She had spent forty-three years as an essential and steadying spiritual gyroscope for Magda and as an undemanding and affectionate presence to the rest of the family.

Magda lived until October of 1996, just short of her ninety-fifth birthday. She had always dreaded death. It was a shadow cast from childhood over her long life, and she sensed death could not be far away. It became a topic of conversation between her and her daughter-in-law, Leslyn. Leslyn tried consoling her about death as a state of the human experience. She had always believed that there was something beyond the line of death that sustained the human experience. She did not pretend to know more than that, but she took comfort herself in the fact (as she saw it) that death was a passage, not an empty hole.

"Do you really believe that?" asked Magda. It was as if she admired Leslyn's faith in the matter but could only yearn for it herself. She could never realize comfort in the face of death. At ninety-five, she was as much haunted by the prospect as she had been at five. What had happened to her mother? Where was that lovely woman in the portrait on the wall? The echoes were still with her.

Years before, she had written her own brief and very personal statement of faith. After she died, the children found among her papers a series of envelopes, each one addressed to a child or grandchild, and each one containing a handwritten copy of that testament. At the core of her beliefs, she wrote, "Two ideas seem fundamental to me. We wouldn't have, deeply rooted in us, a sense of ideals and hope, a need for justice, truth and love, no matter what our religion or degree of civilization, if there were not somewhere a well-spring of hope, justice, truth and love, and it is that well-spring that I call God."[8]

There this story ends, but storytellers will continue returning to it for as long as the human quest for peace remains unfulfilled; and when they do, they will have to deal continuously with two critical questions raised by the Trocmés' friend, philosopher Paul Ricoeur: "Of what are there memories? and Whose memory is it?" (Ricoeur 2004, 3). Biographers are beset by those questions at every turn, for they demand of the writer both appreciation and objectivity, empathy and accuracy. As long as those questions are open, no biography will ever tell the sole and final story.

---

8. Translated from the French by her daughter, Nelly Trocmé Hewett.

APPENDIX

CHRONOLOGY

SUGGESTED READING

REFERENCES

INDEX

Appendix

Appended to Chapter 5

Presented here is a more detailed picture of Magda Trocmé's Decembrist ancestry from an unpublished essay, "Magda Elisa Larissa Grilli di Cortona: Poggio Russian Ancestry," written by Jacques P. Trocmé, and from a book, *A.V. Poggio Notes and Letters*, prepared by N. P. Matkhanova for publication by East-Siberia Publishing House, 1989, in Irkutsk, Vostock-Siberia.

From Jacques P. Trocmé:

> Alexander Poggio and his brother Osip-Giuseppe or Joseph were both officers in the Tsar's Imperial Guard. They were close friends of Prince Sergeï Volkonsky and objected to Tsar Nicholas 1st dictatorial and absolutist ideas and behavior. They were Decembrists or Dekabrists and led an unsuccessful uprising on December 14 (Dec. 26 new calendar) 1825.
>
> They provided a source of inspiration to succeeding generations of Russian dissidents through their martyrdom and exile to Siberia. Their objective was social justice and the abolishment of serfdom. They were primarily members of the nobility and the upper class who had military backgrounds; some had participated in the Russian occupation of France after the Napoleonic Wars or served elsewhere in Europe. A few had been Freemasons and some were members of the secret patriotic societies of Russia. The two Poggio brothers fought in the battle of Moscow against Napoleon in 1812 and I, Jacques Trocmé, have an oil portrait of one of them in uniform, hanging over my bed in Perpignan.
>
> Following the death of Tsar Alexander I, they staged their uprising and convinced some of the troops in Saint Petersburg to refuse to take the oath to Nicholas I and to demand instead the accession of his brother

Constantine. The rebellion was poorly organized and easily suppressed. 289 Decembrists were arrested, 5 were executed, 31 imprisoned including Joseph Poggio and the rest were banished to Siberia, among them Alexander Poggio and Prince Sergei Volkonsky.

Magda's grandmother, Varia Alexandrovna Poggio referred to as Grand-Maman Wissotzky in Magda's story, was born in Siberia. . . . They were eventually liberated and first came to Geneva, Switzerland, then moved to Florence where Varia's daughter Nelly married Oscar Grilli di Cortona.

From N. P. Matkhanova:

In the city of Nicolaev, district of Novorossia, "On May 6, 1798, the senior priest . . . baptized baby Alexander, the son of local parishioners, born on April 14, 1798. . . . In 1850, A.V. Poggio married Larissa Andrevna Smirnova, a class supervisor at the Irkutsk Institute for Girls. . . . After his marriage and his daughter Varia's birth on October 22, 1854, Poggio's life was changed and filled with new meaning. . . . On May 2, 1859, Poggio finally left Irkutsk with his family . . . and settled in Znamenskoe in the province of Pskov, where his nephew owned property. . . . [Poggio had relentless financial problems until] on May 30, 1862, A. V. Poggio went from Moscow to Voronky, the . . . last shelter of the Decembrist family in Russia. In 1863, he went abroad for medical treatment in Switzerland and finally in 1870 the Poggio family went to Florence, Italy, where Hans von Bulow, the famous musician, gave lessons to Varia. In December 1872, he [Poggio] became very sick, and in the spring of 1873 he was brought back to Voronky . . . where he died on June 6, 1873, a month before Varia's wedding day. He was buried in the chapel next to Prince Sergei Volkonsky (pp 6–53).

Appended to Chapter 13

The ancient French text of the opening portion of François Villon's *Ballade des Pendus*, published in 1489 by Antoine Vérard.

Frères humains qui apres nous vivez
N'ayez les cœurs contre nous endurciz,

Car, se pitié de nous povres avez,
Dieu en aura plus tost de vous merci.
Vous nous voyez ci-attachez cinq, six
Quant de la chair, que trop avons nourrie,
Elle est pieça devoree et pourrie,
Et nous les os, devenons cendre et pouldre.
De nostre mal personne ne s'en rie:
Mais priez Dieu que tous nous vueille absouldre!

Appended to Chapter 17

The full text of the honorary degree given by Haverford College to Magda Trocmé and the citizens of Le Chambon-sur-Lignon and presented by President Robert Stevens on May 18, 1981:

> I have the honor to present Magda Trocmé for the degree of Doctor of Laws, *honoris causa*, to be awarded to her in the name of all the inhabitants of Le Chambon-sur-Lignon.
>
> Impelled by a single man, their pastor André Trocmé, upheld in his efforts by his colleague Edouard Theis, the village of Le Chambon-sur-Lignon gave its name to a great victory. Unarmed and unassuming, quietly and selflessly this community said no to hatred. It made itself into a refuge for the Jews hounded by Nazi persecution. Men, women, and children placed their lives in jeopardy, braving the injustice of the laws as well as the rage of the oppressors. They opened their hearts to the persecuted when all who stood by looked away.
>
> Magda Trocmé shared their pastor's resolve with all her strength, with all the clear-eyed goodness of her heart, with all her courage. None are more worthy to bear witness before that community to the immensity of our gratitude. For we owe them no less than a faith still unimpaired in our own humanity.

A Partial Chronology of the Trocmés' Lives and Events

1901	André born April 7, Magda born November 2, Magda's mother dies November 29.
1910	Magda's father remarries.
1911	André's mother dies in auto accident.
1914	German army occupies St. Quentin.
1916	André confirmed, joins the Christian Union.
1917	St. Quentin evacuated. Trocmés become refugees in Belgium.
1919	Trocmés move to Paris. André begins theological studies.
1921–23	André does required military service.
1921	Magda admitted to Istituto Superiore de Magistero.
1925–26	Magda and André meet in New York, become engaged, and return to France where they marry.
1927	André begins his ministry in Sous-le-Bois; first child Nelly is born.
1928–34	Family moves to Sin-le-Noble. Three sons born: Jean-Pierre (1930), Jacques (1931), Daniel (1933).
1934	André begins ministry in Le Chambon-sur-Lignon.
1938	Trocmés and Theis open l'Ecole Nouvelle de Cévenole.
1940	German forces invade France, create the Vichy "Free Zone."
1942	Round-up of 7,000 Paris Jews. Deportation begins.
1943	Alice Reynier (Jispa) joins the family.
1944	Death of Jean-Pierre. Le Chambon-sur-Lignon liberated.
1945	V.E. Day ends the war in Europe.
1946	André begins service as European Secretary of the IFOR.
1949	Magda a delegate to World Pacifist Congress in India.

1950	The Trocmés establish Maison de la Réconciliation.
1952	André studies French-Muslim relations in North Africa.
1957	André co-founds EIRENE in Morocco.
1958	André attends Japan's fourth International Conference Against Atom and Hydrogen Bombs. Both Magda and André join antinuclear protests at Marcoule power plant.
1959	André co-founds French Federation Against Atomic Weapons
1960	André joins the ministry at St. Gervais Parish, Geneva
1961	The Trocmés' youngest child, Daniel, dies. Magda begins teaching in Geneva and in Annemasse, France.
1963–64	Trocmés establish a French language school for Algerian Arabs and another school for Arab diesel technicians to restore abandoned farm machinery.
1965	André joins a delegation of religious leaders visiting Vietnam and Cambodia to contain the escalation of war.
1971	André retires from St. Gervais, becomes ill and dies on June 5. He is presented posthumously the Medal of the Just by Yad Vashem.
1981	The village of Le Chambon is awarded the honorary Doctor of Laws by Haverford College.
1984	Magda is awarded the Medal of the Just at the Israeli Embassy in Paris.
1989	Jispa dies at the age of 96.
1996	Magda dies at the age of 96.
2001	French *Lycée des Glières* honors Magda, Albert Camus, Tom Morel, and Jean Moulin naming rooms for them in a new facility.

Suggested Reading

Trocmé, André. 1988. *Angels and Donkeys*. English edition translated by Nelly Trocmé Hewett. Intercourse, PA: Good Books.

Trocmé introduces the tales thus: "May the readers remember that several of these stories were written during the occupation of France by Hitler, and that the gospel of the birth, the death, and the resurrection of Christ was the only valid answer to the diabolical horrors perpetrated by the princes of this world."

Trocmé, André. 1961. *Jésus-Christ et la Révolution non violente*. Genève: Labor et Fides. The English translation, *Jesus Christ and the Non-violent Revolution*, has been republished in a new edition by Orbis Books, 2003.

Trocmé wrote this book during the 1960s, when he served as the International Secretary of the International Fellowship of Reconciliation. His account of Jesus' nonviolent revolution is rooted in the concept of the Jubilee Year, when accumulated human disorders of injustice, greed and self-centeredness are set to rights, and God's people have a chance to begin anew with a clean slate.

Batten, Alicia J. 2010. "Reading the Bible in Occupied France: André Trocmé and Le Chambon." *Harvard Theological Review* 103.

This excellent article should be available through any good academic library, and it can be purchased through Cambridge Journals online.

Bess, Michael. 2006. *Choices Under Fire: Moral Dimensions of World War II*. New York: Vintage Books.

Historian Bess has brought together a catalogue of stories of the choices men made while serving their countries, some of them remarkably courageous and patriotic, and others cold-hearted and egocentric. In the course of retelling these choices, he invites us to look without blinking at the many moral dimensions of choice that faced military personnel.

Boismorand, Pierre. 2008. *Magda et André Trocmé, Figures de résistance, textes choisis et présentés par Pierre Boismorand*. Paris: Edition du Cerf.

Boismorand's collection of the writings of Magda and André Trocmé covers all of their careers and includes a rich array of letters, sermons, reports on travels, portions of their memoirs, reports on public protests against war, and portions of articles they have written: a beautifully organized and presented book.

Brock, Peter, and Nigel Young. 1999. *Pacifism in the Twentieth Century*. Printed by Toronto University Press, Inc. and distributed by Syracuse University Press, Syracuse, New York.

This remarkable book begins with forty-seven pages of photographs of major pacifism figures and events, beginning with Leo Tolstoy and his wife. The authors have covered the varieties of pacifism at the opening of the century. They go on to describe the changes and developments of conscientious objection and war resistance through the periods of World War I and World War II, the cold war years, and the outreach of pacifism to the date of the book's publication.

DeSaix, Deborah Durland, and Karen Gray Ruelle. 2006. *Hidden on the Mountain, Stories of Children Sheltered from the Nazis in Le Chambon*. New York: Holiday House.

As the tales in *Angels and Donkeys* were spoken to children but informed everyone present, so *Hidden on the Mountain* is written about young people who were living as refugees in and around Le Chambon-sur-Lignon, while providing adult readers poignant interviews and stories as well as a timeline of events and a good bibliography.

Fry, Varian. *Surrender on Demand*. 1945. New York: Random House, and republished in 1997 by Johnson Books, Boulder, CO, in cooperation with the United States Holocaust Memorial Museum.

Fry's brief thirteen months in Marseilles as the agent of the Emergency Rescue Committee were aimed at rescuing as many as possible of the Committee's list of "invaluable European intellectuals" the Nazis were determined to destroy. Among them were painter Marc Chagall, sculptor Jacques Lipchitz, harpsichordist Wanda Landowska, and political scientist Hannah Arendt. In fact, his small group rescued about 1,500 refugees. The story makes riveting and important reading.

Hallie, Phillip. 1979. *Lest Innocent Blood Be Shed: The Story of the Village of Le Chambon-sur-Lignon and How Goodness Happened There.* New York: Harper and Row. Now in paperback by Harper Perennial 1994.

    Hallie's book stands with Robert Paxton's book on Vichy France as one of the few books that awakened the English-speaking world to what had happened during the Vichy years. It is still in print and should you look it up on the Internet, you will find it is regarded as influential still by many groups of students, scholars, and inquirers. It is a very good read.

Henry, Patrick Gerard. 2007. *We Only Know Men, the Rescue of Jews during the Holocaust.* Washington, DC: Catholic University of America Press.

    Henry's fine book begins with a chapter on what moved people to become rescuers, followed by three chapters in which he tracks closely three very different rescuers: Daniel Trocmé, Madeline Dreyfus, and Albert Camus. Their three stories help us greatly to understand war, resistance, and rescue.

Sutherland, Christine. 1984. *The Princess of Siberia: The Story of Maria Volkonsky and the Decembrist Exiles.* New York: Farrar, Straus and Giroux.

    The Decembrist exiles figured large in Magda Trocmé's heritage. In this excellent book, you will be introduced to a different world and to the 30-year saga of these 1825 Russian revolutionaries. You will also meet Magda's grandmother, Varia Alexandrova Poggio Wissotsky, a child when a new Tsar gave amnesty to the long-punished exiles, but a child who never forgot the ideals harbored by these young officers of the Tsar's Imperial Guard.

References

Bastide, Samuel. 1965. *Pages D'Histoire Protestante. Les Camisards.* VENNES-s/-LAUSANNE (Suisse): AUGUR, Editeur.

Bess, Michael. 2006. *Choices Under Fire: Moral Dimensions of World War II.* New York: Vintage Books.

Boegner, Phillipe. 1992. *Carnets du Pasteur Boegner: 1940–1945.* Paris: Editions Fayard.

Boismorand, Pierre. 2008. *Magda et André Trocmé, Figures de résistance, textes choisis et présentés par Pierre Boismorand.* Paris: Edition du Cerf.

Bolle, Pierre. 1992. *Le Plateau Vivarais-Lignon: Accueil et Résistance 1939–1944.* Le Chambon-sur-Lignon, France: Société d'Histoire de la Montagne.

Bollon, Gérard. 2004. *Les Villages sur la Montagne: Entre Ardèche et Haute-Loire, le Plateau, Terre d'Accueil et de Refuge.* Le Cheylard, France: Editions Dolmazon.

Brock, Peter, ed. and translator from the Slovak. 2002. *Life in an Austro-Hungarian Military Prison: The Slovak Tolstoyan Dr. Albert S. Škarvan's Story.* Toronto: Printed by the University of Toronto Press and distributed by Syracuse University Press.

——— and Thomas P. Socknat, editors. 1999. *Challenge to Mars: Essays on Pacifism from 1918 to 1945.* Toronto: University of Toronto Press.

——— and Nigel Young. 1999. *Pacifism in the Twentieth Century.* Syracuse NY. Toronto: University of Toronto Press, distributed by Syracuse University Press.

Fabréguet, Michel (ed.). 2005. *Les Résistance sur le Plateau Vivarais-Lignon, 1938–1945.* Polignac, France: Editions du Roure.

Farrugia, Peter. 1992. "French Resistance to War, 1919–1934: The Contribution of Henri Roser and Marc Sangnier" in *French History* 6(3). Oxford: Oxford University Press.

Fayol, Pierre. 1989. "Le Chambon in 1943–44." Société d'Histoire de la Montagne. Le Chambon-sur-Ligon, France: S.H.M.

Green, Raymond B. 2004. *Les Camps du Travail au Collège Cévenol*. Unpublished collection of papers assembled by a member of the 1947 work camp.

Hallie, Phillip. 1979. *Lest Innocent Blood Be Shed: The Story of the Village of Le Chambon-sur-Lignon and How Goodness Happened There*. New York: Harper and Row.

Hatzfeld, Olivier. 1989. *Le Collège Cévenol a Cinquante Ans, petite histoire d'une grande aventure*. Le Chambon-sur-Lignon, 43 Haute-Loire, France: Collège Cévenol.

Henry, Patrick Gerard. 2007. *We Only Know Men, the Rescue of Jews in France during the Holocaust*. Washington, DC: Catholic University of America Press.

Hoffman, Hans. 1989. *A Personal Story: The Holocaust Years 1940–1942*. Washington, DC: The United States Holocaust Museum.

Horesnyi, Vanessa. 1997. *Les Maisons d'Enfants du Secours Suisse au Chambon-sur-Lignon: 1939–1945*. M.A. thesis. Lyon, France: Univérsité Jean Moulin.

Jackson, Julian. 2001. *France: The Dark Years 1940–1944*. New York: Oxford University Press.

Jaulmes, Antoine. 1991. *De Génération en Génération: Histoire des Trocmé*. Paris: Article déposé à la Société d'Histoire du Protestantisme Français.

Kershner, Howard. 1941. *The American Friends Service Committee in France*. Published report on activities from July 1940 to May 1941. Philadelphia: AFSC.

Kotek, Joel, and Pierre Rigoulet. 2000. *Le Siècle des Camps*. Paris: L.C. Lattès.

Maber, G. Lesley. *Le Faisceau des Vivants, Le Fagot Chambonnais*. An unpublished early draft manuscript, now in revision by her literary executor, Richard G. Maber.

Maillebouis, Christian. 2004. *Influences du Christianisme Social au Mazet-Saint-Voy, 1920–1940*. Le Chambon-sur-Ligon, France: Société d'Histoire de la Montagne.

Marrus, Michael R., and Robert O. Paxton. 1995. *Vichy France and the Jews*. Stanford CA: Stanford University Press.

Matkhanova, N. P. 1989. *A. V. Poggio Notes and Letters*. Vostok, Siberia: Irkutsk, East-Siberia Publishing House. Portions translated by Nadia Oparistaya and edited by Nelly Trocmé Hewett.

Origen. 3rd century common era. *Contra Celsius. Book 5. Chapter XXXIII*. Internet: www.earlychristianwritings.com/text/origen165.html.

Paxton, Robert O. 1972. *Vichy France, Old Guard and New Order, 1940–1944*. New York: Columbia University Press.

Poznanski, Renée. 1997. *Les Juifs en France pendant la Deuxieme Guerre Mondiale*. Paris: Hachette. Translated by Nathan Bracher. 2001. *Jews in France During World War II*. Waltham, MA: Brandeis University Press.

Rasson, Luc. 1997. *Ecrire contre la guerre: littérature et pacifismes, 1916–1938*. Paris: L'Harmattan.

Ricoeur, Paul. 2004. *Memory, History, Forgetting*. Chicago: University of Chicago Press.

Rolland, Romain. 1915. *Au-dessu de la Melée*. Paris: Ollendorff.

Rockefeller, David. 2003. *Memoirs*. New York and Toronto: Random House, Inc.

Rose, Peter. 2004. *The Dispossessed*. Amherst, MA: University of Massachusetts Press, published in association with the Kahn Liberal Arts Institute at Smith College, Northampton, MA.

Roser, Henri. 1948. Consultation Fraternelle. *Cahiers de la Réconciliation*. Paris: Mouvement de la Réconciliation.

———. 1983. "Lettres ouvertes à mes deux amis." *Cahiers de la Réconciliation* 50(1).

Sauvage, Pierre. 1989. *Weapons of the Spirit*. Documentary film with interview of the filmmaker by Bill Moyers. Los Angeles, CA: Chambon Foundation.

Schomer, Howard. 1992. "In Homage to My Icons and Mentors." February 20, 1992, Howard Schomer Papers, bMS 551, Andover-Harvard Theological Library, Harvard Divinity School, Cambridge, Massachusetts.

Solomon, Hans. 1989. *A Personal Story: The Holocaust Years—1940 to 1942*. Washington, DC: the United States Holocaust Memorial Museum.

Strong Jr., Tracy. 1942. Unpublished diary of a year with the Quaker relief program in 1941–1942. A copy of Strong's handwritten pages was provided by the Chambon Foundation. Los Angeles, CA: Chambon Foundation.

Trocmé, André. 1926. *Alexandre Vinet, A Champion of Individual Socialism in the Early Nineteenth Century*. Thesis for the Master of Theology. New York: Union Theology Seminary.

———.1927. *Une experience de Christianisme Social: Les Eglises et la Prohibition de l'alcool aux Etats-Unis*. Thèse soumis au Faculté de Théologie Protestante de Paris.

———. 1944. *Oser Croire*. Unpublished manuscript. Swarthmore, PA: The Peace Collection, Swarthmore College library.

———. 1949. *Le Mouvement International de la Réconciliation, ses principes*. Brochure printed by the MIR. Versailles.

———. 1952. *The Politics of Repentance*. The Robert Treat Payne Foundation lectures for 1951; translated from the French by John Clark. New York: Fellowship Publications.42.

———. 1953. *Mémoires*. Unpublished manuscript, now in the Swarthmore College Library Peace Archive.

———. 1971. *Visage de Dieu sur la Terre, écrit d'une malade à un autre*. (The Face of God on Earth, written from one sick person to another). Privately published in Geneva.

Trocmé, Magda. 1946. *Souvenirs Autobiographique de Magda Trocmé Grilli di Cortona, fille d'Oscar Grilli di Cortona et de Nelly Grilli Wissotsky*. Swarthmore, PA: The Peace Collection, Swarthmore College library.

———. 1950. "Parmi les Disciples de Gandhi, Journal d'une Chambonnaise aux Indes." Circulars 1–4, October 1949–February 1950. Unpublished.

———. 1955. "There Was a Jew at the Dorr." *Fellowship* (January), 10–12. Nyack, NY: International Fellowship of Reconciliation.

———. 1957. "La Lutte non-violente des noirs aux États-Unis." *Cité Nouvelle* (journal of Christianisme Social), April 4, 1957.

Trocmé, Magda, Madeleine Barot, Pierre Fayol, and O. Rosowsky. 1988. "Le Mythe de commandant SS protecteur des Juifs." *Le Monde Juif* (April–June).

Vinet, A. 1841. *Nouveaux Discours sur quelques sujets religieux*. Paris: L. R. Delay, successeur de J. J. Risler. Republished 2010. Paris: Nabu Public Domain Press.

Weinberg, Gerhard. 1944. *A World at Arms: A Global History of World War II*. Cambridge: Cambridge University Press.

Von Klemperer, Klemens. 2001. *German Incertitudes, 1914–1945*. Westport Connecticut and London: Praeger Publishers.

Weber, Hans-Ruedi. 1993. *A Way: Remembrances for the Family*. Unpublished book.

Zasloff, Tela. 2003. *A Rescuer's Story*. Madison, WI: University of Wisconsin Press.

Index

Above the Fray (Rolland), 92
Absolutists, 11
Adams, Max, 246
African-American Presbyterian Church (Tallahassee, FL), 259–60
agricultural co-ops, Darbyist, 141
alcohol consumption: abstention from, 44–45, 78; impact on poor and working classes, 120, 129
Algeria: conversations between Christians and Muslims, 258–59; deforestation, 278; literacy project, 256–58; needs following independence, 278; position of Arabs, 257
Alsatian Lycée (Paris), 77
American Congregational Christian Service Committee, 217
American Friends of the Collège Cévenol (AFCC), 229
American Friends Service Committee. *See* Quakers
American Protestant Church, 225, 253
American Quakers. *See* Quakers
American Red Cross, 159
Angels and Donkeys (A. Trocmé), 47, 303
Annemasse, France, 273, 287–88
Ardèche, France, 143, 285
Arendt, Hannah, 164, 305
aristocrats, 52, 55–56
Armée de Salut (Salvation Army), 140

"Armée Secrète," 203–5
Armistice Day, WWI, 69–70, 75, 85
Auschwitz, Poland, death camp, 170, 184

Bach, M., 183
bachot (baccalaureate) exams, 75–76
Ballade des Pendus ("Ballad of the Hanged Man," Villon), 207–8, 210, 298–99
baptism, conditional, 63
Barbie, Klaus, 212–13, 290
Barbusse, Henri, 92
Barmen Declaration (Barth), 132
Barot, Madeleine, 201
Barratt, Robert, 266
Barraud family, 206–7
Barth, Karl, 85, 132, 239–40, 254
Bass, André, 205
BCWSR (Blue Collar Workers and Soldiers Republic), 70, 72
Beigbeder, Jean, 182
Belgium, Trocmé family relocation to, 38–39, 66–68
beneficial funds, Darbyist, 141
Berthe (refugee), 175
Bess, Michael, 303–4
Bettex, Pastor, 198
Bettini, Cesare, 52, 54–55
Bible: André's study groups, 139, 214, 220; critical reading of, 84–85, 93;

Bible (*cont.*)
Darbyist view, 141; as rationale for protecting Jews, 6; study of at Christian Union meetings, 34–35
Blue Collar Workers and Soldiers Republic (BCWSR), 70, 72
Blue Cross (Le Croix Bleue), xxv, 44–45, 120
Boegner, Marc: André's letter of resignation to, 158; efforts to rescue A. Trocmé and Theis, 192–93; French Protestant Federation leadership, 50–51, 140; friendship with Maury, 240; open letter to Schwartz, 164; protest of Yellow Star mandate, 177; relationship with Pétain, 163–64, 174; role in convincing André to hide, 4–5
Bohny, Auguste: on atmosphere in Le Chambon, 180; children's homes run by, 169–70; description of internment camps, 165; efforts to rescue Roger, 212; efforts to rescue A. Trocmé and Theis, 192; marriage to Reiter, 171; photo of, 172; during roundups of Jews, 178–79; Yad Vashem recognition of, 171
Booth, William, 140–41
Bosch Company, Philippeville diesel maintenance school, 278–80
Boston University, Robert Trent Lectures, 251
bourgeois values: and André's military career, 86; in Brussels, 68–69; and class divides, 86, 120; conflicts about, 38–39, 83, 102; and education, 120; Église Réformée Évangélique, 129; Protestant haute-bourgeoisie, 56; rejection of, 106, 109, 115, 136; Trocmé family, St. Quentin, 42–43, 67
Bousquet, René, 192–93
Brémond, Arnold, 80, 97–98, 112

Bridge, Evelyn, engraving of Temple Sanctuary, Le Chambon, 147
Brown, Robert MacAfee, 22–23
Brown Shirts, Hitler's, 127
Brueghel the Elder, Pieter, 67
Brunet, M., 10
Brussels, Belgium, Trocmé family in, 66–70
Bulletin de l'Église Réformée, "The Diaspora" section, 73
bullying, André's response to, 32

Cahiers de la Réconciliation, 95, 234, 268
Calvin, Jean, 255, 270
Cambodia, visit to by pacifist clergy, 22
Cameroun, LeForestier clinic in, 176
Camisards ("White Shirts"), 6, 139–40
Camus, Albert, 238, 287, 305
Cantonal Hospital (Geneva), 1–2, 15, 284
cartoons, André's, 48–49
Casalis, Roger, 134
Catholicism, Catholic Church: dominance of in Sin-le-Noble, 125; Magda's exposure to, 56–57, 62–64, 103, 105; as voice of state, 129
Centre de Séjour Surveillé de Saint-Paul d'Eyjeaux, 189–193
Cévennes region, Christian separatist groups in, 139–40
Chagall, Marc, 164, 305
Chalmers, Burns, 164–66
Château de Perdyer, 10
Château de Rochebonne, 143
Chaudier, M., 192
Chemin de Fer Départemental (CFD), railway station, 222, 223
children's stories, André's, 47
Chirac, Jacques, 286
Chouraqui, André, 283–84

Christianisme Social, xxv, 128–29, 139
Christians, early, 93
Christian Student Federation (Paris), 76–77
Christian Union, 33–35, 67–68, 78, 83–84, 94
Church Dogmatics (Barth), 85
Church of the Brethren, work in Morocco, 262
Church of the North. *See* Église Réformée Évangelique (Église du Nord, Evangelical Reformed Churches of the North)
CIMADE (Commission Inter-Mouvements Auprès des Évacués), xxv, 164
cinema/movies: in Le Chambon, 224; in Paris, 109; Protestant proscriptions against, 45
City of Refuge: as biblical concept, 167; Le Chambon as, 99, 154–55, 166–67, 196; nonviolence, 202; organization and management, 167–68. *See also* Le Chambon-sur-Lignon, France
"City of Refuge" sermon (A. Trocmé), 277
Civilian Public Service camps, xxiii
Civil Rights movement (U.S.), Magda's experience of, 259–60
Clamart, France, 80–82, 131–32
Clamart Team, 81, 84
Clark, Mark, 248
class struggle: André's lessons about, 28–30, 36–37, 69–70, 83–84, 94, 107–8; and education, 120
Clifton Springs, New York, spa, 113–14
coal mining, Sin-le-Noble, France, 125–26
Colin, M., 175
collaborators: Algerian Arab fears of appearing, 258; treatment of following liberation, 219
Collège Cévenol: creation of permanent home for, 224–28; endurance of, 280; honoring of Sagrees at, 231; as "international center for peace," 154, 225, 238; Theis's role in building, 230; volunteer work crews, 227–30. *See also* École Nouvelle Cévenol, Le Chambon; Theis, Edouard

Collège Lucie Berger, 151
Comité de Nîmes, 164–65
Commission Inter-Mouvements Auprès des Évacués (CIMADE), xxv, 164
Commission on Jewish Questions, 186
communion, first, 63–64
Communist Party: anti-war position, 93, 234–35, 265–66; in social action movements, 139
communists: efforts to negotiate with, 263–64; establishment of, 145–46; in France, 28, 125, 128–29, 200; roundups and arrests, 172, 189–90; view of among German POWs, 216
Compagnons de France, Les, 180–81
compromise: absolutism versus, 11; conscience and, 83, 97–98, 126, 156, 235; necessary, 78, 99. *See also* pacifism; Vichy France
Comte, Louis, 166
conditional baptism, 63
conformity: as price of privilege, 83; and submission to Christian life, 116
Congregational Christian Service Committee, 225–27
conscience, and refusal to compromise, 126, 156, 235. *See also* pacifism
conscientious objectors. *See* COs (conscientious objectors)
conscription/military service: André's, 86–87; and conscientious objectors, xxiii–xxiv; *Service de Travail Obligatoire* (STO), xxvi; soldier without a gun, 35–36, 86; student deferments, 85–86;

conscription/military service (*cont.*)
Theis's, 96. *See also* COs (conscientious objectors); pacifists
Consistoire (regional council), Le Chambon, 221, 223, 231
"Consultations Fraternelles" (Fraternal Consultations) (Le Chambon, 1947–48), 237–39
Cortona, Magda Elisa Larissa Grilli di. *See* Trocmé, Magda
COs (conscientious objectors): arguments to support, 254–55; Darbyist fund for, 141; de Gaulle's legal accommodation for, 234; in Église Réformée, 79; in Europe, xxiii–xxiv, 132; peace churches, xxi; refusal to serve, 85, 95, 98, 217–18; in United States and Great Britain, xxiii–xxiv; in WWII Germany, 236. *See also* conscription/military service; pacifists
Cotte, Eugene, 198
Crépin (solder), 87, 88
"Crimes Against Humanity," 21
Croix Bleue, Le (Blue Cross), xxv, 44–45, 120
Cuban missile crisis, 275–76
"Cycle d'Orientation" high school (Geneva area), 289

dancing, abstention from, 45
Darbyists, 141
Darcissac, Marco, 179, 190
Darcissac, Roger: arrest and detention, 188–89, 192; honoring of by Yad Vashem, 285; photo showing, 195; role in refugees' escape, 7–8, 186–87
D-Day landings, WWII, 205–6
Deats, Richard, 285–86
Débacle (French surrender to Nazis), 154

Debray, Edmée, 211
Decemberist revolt (1815), 52–53, 297–98, 305
deforestation, in Algeria, 278
de Gaulle, Charles: legal accommodation for COs, xxiv, 234; Médaille de la Résistance avec rosette, 286; nuclear buildup, 267–68
de Lattre de Tassigny, Jean, 214
Delroche, Mme., 10
Demulder family (Belgium), 38–39, 67–68
Deschamps, Jean, 210
de Seynes, M., 221–24
de St-Affrique, M., 73
detention center, Saint-Paul d'Eyjeaux, 189–93
"The Diaspora," 73
Dictionnaire de la langue français, definition of "pacifism," 97
Die, France, hiding place in, 10
Diény, Jacques, 76–77, 79–81, 84
Diesel maintenance school (Philippeville, Algeria), 278–80
Drancy internment camp, 160, 175, 177
Dreyfus, Madeline, 305
Durand-Gasselin, Pierre, 131
Durkheim, Emile, 85
duty: French Protestant views of, 44–46; as price of privilege, 83; as Trocmé family value, 43–45, 68

Echo de la Montagne (newsletter), 144
École des Roches, 196
École Nouvelle Cévenol, Le Chambon: co-directors, 151; commitment to, 145–48, 154; educational characteristics, 150–52; establishment of, 136, 149–51; founding, 144; funding, 151, 187; honor system/co-education, 151;

international perspective, 151, 154; Magda's courses about, 145–46; name change, 224; refugee students at, 230; resistance at, 162, 183, 189. *See also* Collège Cévenol; Theis, Edouard

Edict of Nantes, 139–40

Education for Peace Consultation (Le Chambon, 1947), 238

Église du Nord. *See* Église Réformée Évangélique (Église du Nord, Evangelical Reformed Churches of the North)

Église Réformée de France. *See* ÉRF (Église Réformée de France, French Reformed Church)

Église Réformée Évangélique (Église du Nord, Evangelical Reformed Churches of the North): André's career with, 103, 123, 131, 140; André's commitment to, 68–69, 115, 224, 270; emphasis on obedience, 115, 129; establishment of, 50–51; merger with Église Réformée, xxv, 50–51, 140; minister salaries, 115; pastors of (photo), 121; rejection of pacifism, 240, 255; P. Trocmé's involvement with, 51

EIRENE project, 262–63, 280

Elementary Forms of Religious Life, The (Durkheim), 85

Emergency Relief Center, 164

Emergency Rescue Committee, 304–5

Emmaus Movement, 248

Engel, Willy, 278–79

ÉRF (Église Réformée de France, French Reformed Church): André's conflicts with, 51, 95, 181–82, 270; *Bulletin de l'Église Réformée*, 73; conservative values, 129, 273; engagement in peace-building activities in Algeria, 258; expectations of ministers, 115–16; Fédération Protestante, 150–51; function in keeping communities together/recovering from past, 73; merger with Église du Nord, xxv, 50–51, 140; minister salaries, 222; origins of authority, 116; Paris Regional Council, 131; rejection of pacifism/COs, 69, 79, 234, 240, 254–55; support for André's decision to hide, 4–5; support for Vichy regime, 174, 181–82; Swiss Church, Florence, 57, 61–62, 271–72

escapes from Le Chambon, process of, 186–88

Estoppey, M., 7–8

European Secretary, Mouvement International de la Réconciliation (MIR), 217, 230, 235–36

European Union, conscription in, xxiv

Evangelical Reformed Churches of the North. *See* Église Réformée Évangélique (Église du Nord, Evangelical Reformed Churches of the North)

Eyraud, Léon, 204

Eyraud, Mme., 203

"Face of God on Earth: one sick person speaks to another" (A. Trocmé), 1–2

Faguet, Emile, 97

Faïdoli children's home (Le Chambon), 171

"Faith in Humankind" symposium, 22–23

Falkenberg, John, 103, 105

Fayol, Pierre, 203–4

Fédération Protestante de France (FPF), xxv, 50, 140, 150–51

Fellowship (IFOR journal), 252–53

Ferber, Martin, 198

Ferme École (school farm) (Le Chambon), 170

FFI (Forces Françaises de l'Intérieur), 205
Fifty-fourth Infantry Regiment, First Company, disciplinary platoon, 86
Finet, Pastor, 131
Finland, trip to, 237
Fort Montluc (Lyon, France), 212
Foyer Univérsitaire (residence hall) (Le Chambon), 195–96
FPF (Fédération Protestante de France), xxv, 50, 140, 150–51
France: armistice with Nazi Germany, 99, 147, 159, 163, 168; conscription, 79; impact of WWI, 30–31, 91; rationalist tradition, 128; resistance to pacifism in, 240; responses to Yellow Star mandate, 177; revenge activities following liberation, 219, 289; surrender to Nazi Germany, 154; treatment of colonies, 262. *See also* Vichy France
Free French Forces (North Africa), 179
Free Zone (Unoccupied Zone), France: implementation of "Final Solution" in, 178; liberation of by Allied forces, 205; Pétain's focus on youth, 180; pressure to increase anti-Semitic actions, 177; registration of Jews in, 162–63; round-ups and deportations of Jews, 175. *See also* Maquis (French armed resistance); Vichy France
"French-Algerian Bridge of Good Will, A," 256–58
French Federation Against Atomic Arms, 268
French Indochina, 263
French-Muslim relations, efforts to improve, 256–57
French Protestant Federation (FPF), 50, 140
French Protestants: culture, 117; as majority in Le Chambon, 137; role in business after Revolution, 56; strict morality of, 44–46; temples, xxvi; tradition of courage, 6; views on pacifism, 132
French Reformed Church. *See* ÉRF (Église Réformée de France, French Reformed Church)
French Resistance, 179, 287–88. *See also* Maquis (French armed resistance)
French Revolution, 56
Freud, Sigmund, 128
Fringolet, le (Trocmé family summer estate), 280–81
Fry, Varian, 164, 304–5

Gandhi, Indira, 242
Gandhi, Mohandas: assassination, 241; Magda's views on, 242; as model for nonviolence, xxii; poverty of, 109; visit to, 80, 97, 105–6, 112
"Garden of Righteousness," Yad Vashem, 285, 288
Gausachs, Luis, 199–200
Geneva: André's decision on ministerial job in, 269–70; André's illness in, 1–2, 19–21, 284; Magda's work in, 16, 273; Trocmés' retirement to, 16, 269, 271–73, 282; Vietnam Peace Conference, 263. *See also* Temple St. Gervais, Geneva
Geneva School of Interpreters, 273, 289
Geodesic Brigade, French army, 87–89
German prisoners, response to André's sermons, 216
Germany: André's ambivalence toward in WWI, 32; armistice with France, 99, 147, 159, 163, 168; economy following WWI, 91; eugenics policies, 156; French surrender to/collaboration with, 154, 161; invasion of France, 159;

invasion of Haute-Loire region, 203; invasion of St. Quentin, 30–31; pacifist groups in during and following WWII, 236; Service de Travail Obligatoire, xxvi. *See also* Vichy France

Gibert, Suzanne, 189

Giovine Italia (Young Italy) movement, 54–55

Goguel, Maurice, 84–85

"Great Conferences of St. Gervais," 272

Great Depression, 128–29

Grilli, Marguerite, 105, 119

Grilli di Cortona, Nelly Wissotsky (Magda's mother), 57–58, 60, 119, 298

Grilli di Cortona, Oscar, 54–56, 61–62, 105, 112, 249

Groupe Contact (discussion groups), 219–20

Guespy, La, children's home, Le Chambon, 166, 169–72

Guillon, Charles, 149

Gurs internment camp, 160, 170, 172

Hallie, Philip, 23, 137, 290, 305

Hatzfeld, Olivier, 156, 208, 209

Haute-Loire, France, 285

Haverford College (Haverford, PA), 22, 287

Heidelberg, Germany, 127

Herdt, René, 135

Heritier, Emily, 6

Hértier, Henri and Emma, 167, 184–86

Hewett, Nelly Trocmé: André's letters to, 244, 269; *Angels and Donkeys*, 47; birth, 123; childhood illness, 130; and father, 19, 142, 190; during Lamirand visit to Le Chambon, 182; Magda's letters to, 289–90; photo of, 130; pressure on Magda to write memoirs, 293; on Paul Trocmé, 42; on Piot Vernier's arrival at Le Chambon, 98–99;

Hilgenstock, Mrs., 68

Hippocratic Oath, 176, 211

Hitler, Adolf: eugenics and concept of Master Race, 156–57; handling of COs, xxiv; populism of, 127–28; rise of, 72, 92; 132; ultimatum to Laval, 176–77

Ho Chih Minh: peace mission to, 264; victory over French, 263–64

Hoefert, Mlle., 151

Hoffman, Hans, 184

Holocaust, 21–22

honeymoon, 119

Hôpital Cantonal de Genève, André's final illness in, 1–2, 19–21, 284

Hôtel des Roches, Le Chambon, 196–97

Huguenots: Camisards, 6; courage, 155; resistance activities in Cévennes region, 139–40; traditions taught in L'École Nouvelle Cévenol, 150. *See also* French Protestants

Hungary, conscription in, xxiii

IFOR (International Fellowship of Reconciliation): activities, xxv; admission of non-Christian members, 256; André and Magda's expansion of secretary role, 242–43; André on, 231–32; André's work for, 95–96, 221, 240, 268–69; Bartlett's leadership, 268–70; first postwar meeting (1946), 235–36; Magda's role in developing Italian constituency, 247–48, 269; March Through Europe, 127; MIR branches, xxii–xxiii; Roser's leadership of, 96; Sayre's postwar invitation to André, 217. *See also* MIR (Mouvement International de la Réconciliation)

India: espousal of nonviolence in, 97; Magda's trip to, 241–42; planned visit to, 80, 97, 105–6, 112. *See also* Gandhi, Mohandas
Instituto Superiore di Magistero, 65
instrumental pacificism, 93
International Christian Service for Peace, 263
International Civil Service (Switzerland), 227, 255
International Conference Against the Atom and Hydrogen Bombs, 264–65
International Fellowship of Reconciliation. *See* IFOR (International Fellowship of Reconciliation)
International Peace Conference, 263–64
International Protestant Loan Association, 187
International Rescue Committee (IRC), 164
International Secretariat of the MIR, 239
internment camps, Vichy France, 159–60, 164–65, 170–72, 174, 177, 188–90
IRC (International Rescue Committee), 164
Italy: IFOR branch, 247–48, 269; and Magda's ancestry, 52, 54–55, 297–98; Magda's childhood and education in, 53–65, 103, 118; pacifists in following WWII, 269; Swiss Reformed Church, 57, 61–62, 271–72
IWW (Industrial Workers of the World), 70, 85, 128–29

Jackson, Julian, 162
Jalla, Aimée, 103
Jaulmes, Antoine, 42
Jeanne (maid), 26–27
Jeannet, Marcel, 182
Jesus: and André's views on truth/lying, 11, 303; controversies about, 84
Jésus-Christ et la Révolution non violente (A. Trocmé), 303
Jesus the Nazarene: Myth or History (Goguel), 84
Jews: Darbyist commitment to sheltering, 141; internment of by Vichy government, 159; job quotas and other restrictions, 163; as refugees, 6, 17, 141, 160, 175, 226; registration requirement, 162–63; roundups and deportations, 173, 176–88, 191, 194, 197–98. *See also* City of Refuge; Le Chambon-sur-Lignon, France
Jispa (Alice Reynier): arrival at Le Chambon prebytère, 145; background, 17; death, 293; as "mother" in Trocmé family, 18; move to Paris with Magda, 22; photo of, 17; refurbishing of Versailles mill house, 244; return to Paris after André's death, 289; role in hiding Trocmé, 7; sixty-seventh birthday celebration, 273
Johnson, Tom, 156
John XXIII (Angelo Roncalli), xxii, 249–50
"Journal of a Chambonnaise in India" (M. Trocmé), 242
Journal of the War Years: 1914–1918 (Rolland), 92

Kaltenbach (pastor), 33–34
Kastler, Alfred, 266–67
Kebaili, M., 258
Kershner, Howard, 174
Kindler, Herr, 35–36, 76, 86
King, Martin Luther, Jr., xxii, 260–61

kitchen meetings, Sous-le-Bois, 120, 122, 139
Kokutai, Kozo Tanaka, 265

l'Abric children's home (Le Chambon), 172
L'Accueil Cévenol, 220–21
La Fayolle, France, 184–85
Lamastre, France, 7–8
Lambaréné, Gabon, 176
Lamirand, George, 181–83
Landowska, Wanda, 164, 305
La Rochelle, France, Protestant lycée at, 150
Latour, Amy, 283–84
Laubach, Frank, 278
Laval, Pierre, 161–62, 176–77. *See also* Pétain, Henri-Phillipe (Marshal Pétain); Vichy France
Lavondès, Antoinette, 151–52
Le Chambon-sur-Lignon, France: André's ministry in, 3, 134–35, 138–39, 146–47; 158, 189, 194; armed resistance in, 202–5; books about, 23; as City of Refuge, 99, 154–55, 166–69, 196; courage of people in, 6, 181–84; dominance of Protestants in, 137; as escape route to Switzerland, 186–88; as haven for refugee children, 137–38, 141, 149, 165–66, 175–76; honors/awards given to people of, 22–23; 284–85; Les Roches, 196–98; after liberation, 219; location, 134, 137; L'Oeuvre des Enfants à la Montagne, 166; Magda's social work and organizing activities, 145–46; movie theater, 45–46; peace activism in, 219–20, 237–38; population growth (1934–40), 137; presbytère in, 141–43; reorganization of team ministry in, 221, 224; resistance to Vichy demands, 168, 181–84; response to D-Day in, 206; response to roundups and deportations of Jews, 176–88, 197–98; rural lifestyle, 138; U.S. interest in, 251–52. *See also* City of Refuge; peace activism; *and specific individuals*
LeForestier, Danielle, 212
LeForestier, Roger: background, 176; capture and execution, 189–90, 211–12, 236; importance of in Le Chambon, 184, 203–4, 211; letter to A. Trocmé, Theis, and Darcissac, 189; rescue and escape missions, 179, 206, 211–12
Le Grillons children's home, Le Chambon, 196
Le Mazet-Saint-Voy, France, 139
Le Puy, France, 181, 214
Lespet, M., 7
Lest Innocent Blood Be Shed (Hallie), 23, 290, 305
Lewin, Jacob, 170–71, 178–79
Lewin, Martin, 178
liberated areas, students from, 75–76
liberty, Vinet's views on, 115–16
Lipschitz, Jacques, 305
literacy, as focus of peace efforts, 256–58
"Little Beast, The" (La Petite Bête) (A. Trocmé), 48
Louis XIV, Huguenot resistance to, 6, 139–40
Louvre Museum (Paris), 41
love, André's craving for, 42–44
Lowenson, James, 291–92
loyalty oaths, 192
Luquet farmhouse (Le Chambon), 225, 228–29
Lycée des Glières d'Annemasse, Magda Trocmé Faculty Lounge, 287–88

lying and truth-telling, André's views on, 11–15, 78. *See also* pacifism

Maber, Lesley, 151, 206
Macalester College (Minnesota), 246
Magri, M., 63
Mairesse, Simone, 205, 209, 285
Maison de le Réconciliation (Versailles): costs of maintaining, 269–70; "Mill of Peace" and "The Tower," 246; renovations/refurbishing of, 244
maisons d'enfants (children's homes), 137–38, 149, 169, 173, 187
Mantellate Sisters convent school, 62
Maquis (French armed resistance): arming of, 194; assassination of Praly, 202; and formation of Forces Françaises de l'Intérieur, 205; in Le Chambon, 7–8, 168, 194, 204–5; Martin's withdrawal from and rescue by, 95; in Plateau Vivarais-Lignon, 203; response to D-Day, 206; warning to André from, 4, 201
Marcoule, France, anti-nuclear protest, 266
Marie (maid), 26–27
Marseilles, France: Fayol's training in, 203; relief organizations in, 164
Martin, Jacques: André's friendship with, 95–96; commitment to nonviolent resistance, 97–98; pacifist stance, 80; refusal to serve in military, 95; role in hiding Trocmé, 10; time in prison, 98
Massacre of the Innocents, The (Breughel the Elder), 67–68
Master Race, 156
Maubeuge parish ministry, 121
Maury, Pierre, 240
Mazel, Christian, 119–20, 224
Mazel, Solange, 224

Mazzini, Giuseppe, 54–55
"Medal of the Just," Yad Vashem, 283–84
memoirs: Magda's, xix–xx, 24, 110, 121, 293, 304; André's, xix–xx, 16, 110, 121, 175, 283, 304
Memoirs (Rockefeller), 106
Mennonite Church, Moroccan work projects, 262
Menthon-St. Bernard, family holiday in, 144
Menut, George, 183
Mercy, Jean, 211
Meunier, Albert, 33
military service. *See* conscription/military service
Military Tribunal (Nuremberg, Germany), 21
Miller, Henry, 128–29
"Mill of Peace" (Maison de la Réconciliation), 238, 243–44, 246
Mind Widening Bank, 79
MIR (Mouvement International de la Réconciliation): activities, xxv; André's and Magda's service to, 230, 233, 235–36; *Cahiers de la Réconciliation*, 95, 234, 268; current activities, xxii; headquarters, 235; organizational needs, 240; principles, 233–35
Mise au point concernant mon attitude en temps de guerre (A. Trocmé), 157–58
Missionary Society, 96
Mohammed V of Morocco, 262
"Monsieur André" resistance group, 285
Montrouge-Clamart-Malakoff Church Council, 131
Morel, Tom, 287
Morocco: EIRENE project, 262–63; Geodesic Brigade in, 88–90; visits to after independence, 260–61; work camps in, 262

Moulin, Jean, 287
Mount Holyoke College, chaplaincy invitation, 269
Mouvement International de la Réconciliation. See MIR (Mouvement International de la Réconciliation)

National Congress of Christianisme Social (1933), 139
National Council, Vichy government, 163, 174
National Honor Diploma, 65
National Socialist German Workers Party, 92
Neunkirchen, Captain, 237
New York City: André in, 101–3; André's and Magda's meeting and courtship in, xiii, 110–14; Magda in, 103. See also Rockefeller, John D., Jr.; Union Theological Seminary (New York)
New York School of Social Work, 103
Niebuhr, Reinhold, 239–40
Niemöller, Martin, 22, 240, 264
Noble Peace Prize, 283
nonviolence: adhering to during war, 155–57, 160–61; André's and Magda's commitment to, 4–5, 112; Brémond's studies of, 97; Gandhi as model for, xxii, 97, 241–42; as matter of conscience, 126, 156, 235; MIR's commitment to, 234; Roser's commitment to, xiii, 80, 85, 96–98, 234–35; teaching of at L'École Nouvelle Cévenol, 154; training in, xxiii; U.S. Civil Rights movement, 259–60; versus violent resistance in Le Chambon, 204. See also pacifism; peace activism; reconciliation

North Africa, 256–57
nuclear arms race, 266–68

obedience to authority, 115–16. See also COs (conscientious objectors)
Occupied Zone, France, implementation of "Final Solution" in, 177. See also Free Zone (Unoccupied Zone), France; Vichy France
Oeuvre des Enfants à la Montagne, 166
Oeuvres de Secour aux Enfants (OSE), xxv–xxvi
Ombrages, Les, boarding house, Le Chambon, 203
Oratoire du Louvre (Paris): Mazel's appointment as pastor to, 224; R. Trocmé's wedding at, 78–79
Organisation de Secours aux Enfants (Organization for the Relief of Children), 283
Origen, on pacifism, 254, 255
OSE (Oeuvres de Secour aux Enfants), xxv–xxvi
"Oser Croire" (Audacity of Believing) (A. Trocmé), xiii, 3

pacifism: and accountability, 21; André's commitment to, 26, 28–33, 35, 67–68, 85, 97–98, 100 123, 156–58, 216; arguments in support of, 254–55; armed resistance versus, 204; conscience-driven, 96–97; as cowardly and treasonous, xxiv, 79, 97, 234–35; definitions and use of term, 97; discrediting of by Barth and Niebuhr, 239–40; economic violence and concentration of wealth, 36–37; education for, 154, 238; efforts to give Christian face to, 93;

pacifism (*cont.*)
and hiring difficulties, 131–32; history of, 304; imprisonment for, 98–99; instrumental as politically motivated, 93, 265–66; and nuclear disarmament, 266; as opposition to war, xxi, 92; as patriotic, 234–35; rejection of by Église Réformée and mainstream Protestant churches, 69, 79, 97, 132, 234, 240, 254–55; Roser's complete commitment to, 96; in Sweden, 236; in United States, 252–53; and WWI, 92. *See also* IFOR (International Fellowship of Reconciliation); nonviolence; peace activism; reconciliation

Pacifisme, Le (Faguet), 97

Paillot, Juliette, 15

"pale hooligan" image, 28–30

Paris: André and Magda's move to, 239; André's studies in, 77–78; André's trips to for MIR meetings, 237; evacuation of children from (1939), 157; experience of WWI, 75–76; students from liberated areas in, 75–76

Paris Regional Council (Église Réformée Évangélique), 131–32

Parks, Rosa, 287

Parrot, André, 101

Paxton, Robert O., 23, 290–91

peace activism: in Algeria, 256–59, 278; André's and Magda's efforts, 229, 236, 247–48, 254–59, 263–65, 273–74; anti-nuclear efforts, 265–68; "Consultations Fraternelles," 237–38; creating conditions for peace, 234–36; as hard work, 221; Indian model, 241–42; in Le Chambon, 231–32; in Morocco, 261–63; pragmatic approaches, 256–57; in United States, 251–53, 260–62; and

Vietnam, 263–64. *See also* nonviolence; pacifism; reconciliation

peace churches: as COs, xxiii–xxiv; participation in Moroccan work camps, 262

Pélissier family, 8–9

Pentecostalism, 130, 140

Perret, Jean: as André's supervisor at Sous-le-Bois, 117; ministry in Maubeuge parish, 121; pastoral visit at time of Nelly's birth, 124; personality, 121; reconciling with outer world, 3; takeover and destruction of kitchen meetings, 122–23

Pétain, Henri-Phillipe (Marshal Pétain): communications about Le Chambon, 168; cult of personality, 162; expressions of thanks to relief organizations, 174; focus on youth, 180; as incarnation of French patriotism, 161; *La Révolution Nationale,* 160–61; National Council, 163; photo showing, 153; popularity, 174

Petit-Lancy, Switzerland, Trocmé home in, 271, 282

Philip, Mireille, 170, 186–87, 198

Philippeville, Algeria, diesel school, 278–80

Phillip, André, 79, 151, 238

Pierre, Abbé (Henri Antoine Grouès), 247–48

Piton, Pierre, 186–87

Pius XII, 248

Plateau Vivarais-Lignon (Protestant Plateau): Armée de Salut, 140–41; attraction of Maquists to, 203; beauty, 139–40, 143; Christianisme Social, 139; Darbyists, 141; growth of armed resistance forces in after removal of A. Trocmé and Theis,

204; Pentecostalism, 140; response to roundups of Jews, 180; revenge activities in, 219; sheltering traditions, 166, 186
Poggio, Alexei (or Allesandro), 52, 54, 297, 298
Poggio, Osip-Giuseppe (or Joseph), 297
Poggio, Varia Alexandrovna. *See* Wissotsky, Varia Alexandrovna Poggio
politically motivated pacificism, 93
Politics of Repentance, The (Trocmé), 251
Pomeyrol, France, Protestant order in, 17
Pont, Lucy, 151
Pont de Mars, France, 216
Poujol, Jacques, 7
poverty: André's commitment to alleviating, 115; André's experience of in Belgium, 38–39; Magda's commitment to alleviating, 58–60; as spiritual path, 108–9
Praly, Leopold, 197, 202–3
Prasad, Rajendra, 241–42
prayers: African-American Presbyterian Church, 260; Catholic, 62; at Christian Union, 34; internment camps, 159; and Jean-Pierre's death, 210
presbytère, Le Chambon: histories about, 23; paying guests, 144; refugees sheltered in, 175–76; Trocmé family life, 46–47, 141–42, 144
presbytère, Sin-le-Noble, 124
presbytère, Sous-le-Bois, 119–20, 122
pretension, Magda's impatience with, 291
privilege: André's struggles with, 29, 36–37, 83–84, 94; duty and, 83; Magda's experience of and struggles with, xiii, 52, 59–60; Rockefeller children's, 107; Soviet approach to, 254
Protestant Plateau. *See* Plateau Vivarais-Lignon (Protestant Plateau)

Quakers: André's connections with, 164; financial support for Le Chambon refuge efforts, 169; Kershner's report to on French hospitality, 174; nomination of André for Noble Peace Prize, 283; ongoing work with refugees after WWII, 255; peace activism among, xxi; Pétain's expressions of thanks to for relief efforts, 174; support for Foyer Univérsitaire, 195–96. *See also* Chalmers, Burns
"Quatre Coups du Destin, Les" ("Destiny raps four times at your door," André), 275–76
Quétier, M. and Mme., 246–47
Queyroi, Captain, 88

Radio-Genève Suisse Romande, 274
Rajagopalachari, C., 242
Ranc family, 8
reconciliation: André's commitment to, 215–16, 246, 274–75; André's sermons on, 274–75; IFOR efforts on behalf of, 127; John XXIII's efforts toward, 250; revenge versus, 246; St. Paul on, 254–55; working for, 219, 221, 233, 237–38; after WWII, 254–55. *See also* pacifism
Réconciliation, 254–55
Reiter, Friedel, 170–71
religion, as sociological phenomenon, 85
religious and spiritual education: Christian Union, 33–35, 67–68, 78, 83–84, 94; contemporary religious controversies, 84–85; education for ministry, 69, 103–4; and experience of imprisonment, 56–57; Magda's, 33, 61–64; popularity of, 174; Roser's, 96; Union Theological Seminary, 97, 101–3, 116

Résistance, armed (French resistance, maquis). *See* Maquis (French armed resistance)
Reutlingen, German, 127–28
Révolution Nationale, 161–62. *See also* Vichy France
Reynier, Alice (Jispa). *See* Jispa
Ricoeur, Paul, 238, 294
Riou, Dr., 209–10
Rivesaltes internment camp, 160, 170–71
Robert Trent Lectures, Boston University, 251
Roches, Les (Quaker school, Le Chambon), 178, 195–200
Rockefeller, Abby Aldrich, 106–7, 113–14
Rockefeller, David, 106, 107, 113–14
Rockefeller, John D., Jr., 106–7, 109
Rockefeller, John D., Sr., 108
Rockefeller, Laurence, 107, 113–14
Rohr, Maurice, 5
Rolland, Romain, 92
Rollins, J. Metz, 259
Roman Catholic Church: conditional baptism, 63; defections from, 248; Église, xxvi; Magda's exposure to, 57, 62–64, 65, 105; in Sin-le-Noble, 125–26; as voice of state, 129
Roncalli, Angelo: elevation to papacy, 249; as Papal Nuncio to France, 248–49; work with MIR, 240
Roser, Henri: *Cahiers de la Réconciliation*, 95; at IFOR, 98, 268; imprisonment, 98–99, 240; leadership of MIR, 233–34; as model for André, 95–96; pacifism, nonviolence, xiii, 80, 85, 96–98, 234–35; rupture of friendship with, 99
Rosowsky, Oscar, 167, 186
Rostagno, Giovanni, 62–63
Rouiller, M., 272
Rudi-Weber, Hans, 255

Russia: Decemberist revolt (1815), 52–53, 305; dissidents in, 297–98; Magda's 1958 visit to, 253–54
Russian Orthodox Church, 57, 60

Saint Genis-Laval, France, 212–13
Saint-Paul d'Eyjeaux detention camp, 4, 8, 185, 188–93
Saint-Saëns, Camille, 92
Sangree, Carl and Florence, 225–26, 230
Sangree, Elizabeth, 226
Sauvage, Léopold and Barbara, 178–79, 184–85
Sauvage, Pierre, 6, 23, 137, 184–85
Sayre, Nevin, 217, 239, 251
Schmähling, Julius, 212, 215, 236
Schmidt, Charles, 149
Schnerb, Mme., 222
Schomer, Howard: activities assigned to, 219; and Collège Cévenol, 223–25; description of André, 6, 275; friendship with André, 282; "Icons and Mentors," 220; L'Accueil Cévenol, 220–21; in Le Chambon, 217–21; peace mission to North Vietnam, 22, 264
Schwab, Ernest, 271–72
Schwartz, Isaïe, 161, 164
Schweitzer, Albert, 176
Secours Suisse aux Enfants: activities in Le Chambon, 169; establishment of mission, 171–73; Weber's service with, 214
Service Civil International (SCI), xxvi
Siberia, exile of Wissotsky family to, 52
Sin-le-Noble, France: air pollution, 130; André and Magda's move to, 124; André's ministry in, 125–29; childcare classes, 145; as company town, 125; economic tensions, 128–29; presbytère in, 124

Smirnova, Larissa Andrevna, 298
Smith College (Northampton, MA), Magda speech at, 21
smoking, abstention from, 44–45, 78
Smotriez, Léopold. *See* Sauvage, Léopold and Barbara
socialist movements, 70–71, 128–29
Socialist Party, 120, 123
social justice: André's commitment to, 36–37, 130, 136; Magda's commitment to, 48–50, 56–57, 65, 136; socialist movements' call for, 71–72
social work training, 65
soldiers: behavior following Armistice, 69–70, 74; Russian POWs in St. Quentin, 35; soldiers without guns, 86, 89–90. *See also* conscription/military service; Kindler, Herr
Solomon, Hans, 197–98
Somme battlefield, 31
Sorbonne University (Paris): André's studies in, 77; response to Yellow Star mandate, 177
Sous-le-Boise, Maubeuge parish, 116–17, 119–20, 124
Spanish Civil War, 93, 160, 166, 171
Steckler, M., 178–79
St. Étienne, France, 219–20
St. Gervais church. *See* Temple St. Gervais, Geneva
St. Gervais-Philippeville project (Algeria), 278
St. Gobain, France: André's military service near, 86; Trocmé home in, 117
Stöhr, Hermann, 236
St. Paul, on reconciliation, 254–55
St. Quentin, France: bombed church in, 71, 72; Christian Union meetings, 84; impacts of WWI, 30–31, 37, 72; marriage of André and Magda in, 114; rebuilding of, 72–73; Trocmé family in, 26, 51, 117
Strong, Tracy, Jr., 144
Sunday School, Le Chambon, 146
Surrealist painters, 128
Swarthmore College Library, Peace Collection, Trocmé archive, 293
Sweden, neutral status during WWII, 159, 236
Swiss Red Cross, 172
Swiss Reformed Church, Florence, 57, 61–62, 271–72
Switzerland: escapes to, xv, 167, 175, 179, 186–87, 198; Hitler's view of as heroic, 92; International Civil Service, 255; Le Croix Bleue (Blue Cross), xxv; neutrality during WWII, 159; Secours Suisse aux Enfants, 171–72; sending of Nelly Trocmé to, 130. *See also* Geneva

Tagore, Rabinandrath, 97, 112, 241
Tallahassee, Florida, Magda's 1956 visit to, 259–61
Talloires children's home, 169
Temple, Le Chambon-sur-Lignon: André's first sermon at, 134; cultural activities, 137; engraving showing, 147; photo showing, 135; pulpit, 146; service during Lamirand's visit, 182
Temple St. Gervais, Geneva, contributions of André and Magda to, 2, 270, 272–73
Theis, Edouard: approach to teaching and preaching, 146–48; arrest and detention (1943), 188–89; assassination threat, 7, 201; awards and honors, 285; as CO, 97–98; commitment to nonviolent resistance, 4, 96–97, 148, 162; contributions to Le Chambon community, 45–46, 217, 224; descriptions of, 229;

Theis, Edouard (*cont.*)
  exemption from draft, 159; friendship with André, 96, 150; friendship with Trocmés, 96; fundraising by, 187; L'Accueil Cévenol, 221; at L'École Nouvelle Cévenol, 150–52; military service, 96; photos of, 153, 195; rescue and escape missions, 179, 186–87; retirement, 231
Theis, Jeanne, 229
Theis, Mildred, 151, 285
"There Was a Jew at the Door" (M. Trocmé), 252–53
Thonon-les-Bains, France, 133
Tolstoy, Leon, xxii
Torre Pellice, Italy, 149
Tour de Constance postcard, 168
Tower, The (Maison de la Réconciliation), 245
Treaty of Versailles, 91
Trocmé, André: *Angels and Donkeys: Tales for Christmas and Other Times*, 47; *bachot* exams, 75–76; childhood, 26–30, 33–34, 44–46, 94; concept of duty, 33, 43, 44–45; conflicts with authority, 68, 73, 83–84, 121–22, 155, 254, 269; connections with American Quaker and CIMADE relief organizations, 164; conscience, moral compass, 11–15, 44, 75, 78, 126, 155; contributions to Le Chambon community, 156, 165–66, 195–96, 224; courage, 6, 138, 162; courtship, 110–12; and cousin Daniel, 196, 201; death, 19–21; decision to go into hiding, 3–5, 7, 201; difficulties finding a parish, 131–33; diphtheria, 73; drawing skills, 48–49, 190–91; education for ministry, 69, 97, 101–4, 116; enduring wounds from/dialogues about, 290–91; energy, 2; "The Face of God on Earth: one sick person speaks to another," 1–2; final illness, 1–2, 17, 18–19; financial limits and struggles, 153, 222, 244, 269; first meeting with Sangrees, 226; first meeting with Schomer, 218–19; on handling loss, 276–77; on happiness at Le Chambon, 135–36, 138–39, 175; in hiding, 7–10, 12–15, 201, 204; honeymoon, 119; honors and awards, 22, 283–84, 286; humor, creativity, and playfulness, 46–49, 50, 142, 150, 155, 273; impact of mother's death, 26–28, 44, 74; initiation of St. Gervais-Philippeville project, 278; inner conflicts while in hiding, 10–11; internment camp experiences, 164–65, 188–90; language skills, 56; and l'Armée de Salut, 140–41; lectures and speaking engagements, 81–82, 251; love for art and beauty, 41, 44, 107, 109; love of language, 48–50, 273; and Maquis, 204–5; memoirs, papers, xix–xx, 16, 110, 121, 175, 283, 291–93, 304; memory, 15, 34, 111, 226; middle name, 110; military service, 85–88, 91, 94, 99–100; ministry in Geneva, 2, 270–73; ministry in Le Chambon, 3, 135, 158, 221–22; ministry in Sin-le-Noble, 125–29; ministry in Sous-le-Bois, 120–24; Mount Holyoke chaplaincy invitation, 269; movies, 45, 109, 224; nominations for Nobel Peace Prize, 283; organizing skills, 262, 277–78; "Oser Croire" (The Audacity of Believing), 3; others' response to, 19–20; "pale hooligan" image, 29–30; passion for social justice, 136; peace activism and reconciliation

projects, 229, 236, 247–48, 256–59, 263–65, 273–74; persuasive powers, 156, 277; photos of, 3, 27, 102, 195, 265; physical stature, 6, 224, 266, 275; planned trip India, 105–7; as refugee in Belgium, 37–39, 66–69, 73; relationship with brothers, 32, 41–42, 281; relationship with father, 42–44, 51, 102–3, 136; relationship with his children, 46–48, 142; relationship with Magda, 19, 25, 44, 50, 136–37; religious education, 80; rescue and escape missions, 186–87, 212; resistance to bullying, 32, 183; response to Barth, 240; response to failed projects, 280; response to sons' deaths, 210, 274; retirement, 2, 282; self-doubt, 6, 33, 67; sermons, 47, 57–58, 85, 147–48, 159, 215–16, 260, 274–76; sexual awakening, 45, 74–75, 77–78, 109–10; skills as student, 69, 77; as soldier without gun, 89–90; spiritual development and commitment, 4, 32–34, 51, 94–95, 101, 105–6, 110, 115, 120–21, 130, 140, 224, 276, 282–83; storytelling abilities, 47; as tutor to Rockefeller children, 106–8; understanding of privilege and class, 28–30, 36–37, 69–70, 83–84, 94, 107–8, 120; university studies and organizing activities, 76–82, 95; verse messages, 50, 273; Vinet as model for, 115, 123; on war and militarism, 28–29, 31–32, 204, 255; willingness to work with Red Cross, 159; WWI experience, 30–32, 37, 67, 70, 74–75. *See also* École Nouvelle Cévenol, Le Chambon; IFOR (International Fellowship of Reconciliation); Le Chambon-sur-Lignon; MIR (Mouvement International de la Réconciliation); pacifism; peace activism; reconciliation

Trocmé, Daniel (cousin): arrest, 5, 199–200; death, 136, 200–201; efforts to rescue, 192, 211, 305; at Les Roches, 190, 196; photo showing, 199

Trocmé, Daniel (son), 124, 130, 273–74

Trocmé, Étienne, 28–29, 74, 136

Trocmé, Eugène, 32, 40

Trocmé, Francis: assistance during Nelly's birth, 123; description of family, 42–43; on first meeting Magda, 117; funeral, 280–81; medical career, 40; openness to peace-making activities, 271; respect for André's preaching skills, 148, 281

Trocmé, Germaine Pacquement, 78

Trocmé, Jacques: on André and Abbé Pierre audience with John XXII, 250; birth in Sin-le-Noble, 124; care for Magda and Jispa, 289; drawing for, 48–49; memories of meals at Le Chambon, 141–42; photo showing (1934), 130; on Roncalli-Grilli di Cortona chess games, 249; visit with André at Perdyer, 11

Trocmé, Jean-Pierre: accidental death, 208–10, 274; birth in Sin-le-Noble, 124; drawing for, 48–49; love for poetry, 207; photos of, 130, 209

Trocmé, Leslyn, 289, 293–94

Trocmé, Louise, 74

Trocmé, Magda: during André's arrest, 189; André's courting of, 110–12; André's description of, 50; aspirations shared with André, 137; awards and honors, 65, 286, 287; baptism, 57; childhood, 58–65; children, 123; commitment to nonviolent resistance, 242;

Trocmé, Magda (*cont.*)
contribution to parish notes, 144; curiosity, 24–25; death, 293–94; on difference between Italian and Russian grandmothers, 55; educational ambitions, 65, 103; experience of WWI, 63–64; Falkenberg and, 103, 105; fear of death, 60, 64, 294; film interview (1984), 22; final letter, 291–92; on happiness at Le Chambon, 135–36; health problems, 113; honeymoon, 119; honors and awards, 285, 287, 299; household responsibilities, 124, 144–45; impact of mother's death, 57, 60; influence of Grandmother Wissotsky, 53; introduction to Trocmé family, 117–18; language/linguistic skills, 56, 61–62; in Le Chambon, 176; life after André's death, 25, 289, 291; marriage, 117; memoirs, 292–93; memory, 24; move to Paris, 22; move to Versailles, 244; need for freedom, 105; as oral historian, 23; organizing in Italy for IFOR, 247–48, 269; organizing skills, 145, 168, 258–59; papers and archives, 293; passion for social justice, 136; peace activism, 241, 256–58, 262, 263; personal statement of faith, 294; philosophical/moral conflicts with Catholic Church, 63–64; photos of, 104, 292; playfulness, 44, 144; pragmatism, 10–11, 256; relationship with André, 19, 25, 136; religious education, 61; religious heritage, 56–57, 62–63, 249; rescue efforts on behalf of German Jews, 175; response to André's death, 20–21; response to cousin Daniel's arrest, 199–200; response to failed projects, 280; response to grandmother's death, 103; response to sons' deaths, 210, 274; retirement plans, 282; Russian and Italian ancestors, 52, 54–55, 297–98; social work/organizing activities, 105, 144–45, 258–59; speaking engagements, 21, 251, 286; teaching and courses, 16, 145–46, 151, 273; travels to Greece, 289; trip to India, 241–42; on U.S. pacifists, 252–53; visit to André when in hiding, 9; visit to civil rights activists, 259–60; visit to Russia (1958), 253–54; visit with Martin Luther King, Jr., 260–61; work on André's papers and archives, 23–24, 291–92; work with IFOR, 247–48, 256. *See also* Jispa

Trocmé, Marie Album, 32, 41

Trocmé, Maurice, 32, 40, 73

Trocmé, Nelly. *See* Hewett, Nelly Trocmé

Trocmé, Paul: advice to Magda, 118; André's relationship with, 42–44, 102–3, 136; in Belgium, 66; bourgeois values, 115; church and business leadership, xxv, 40, 50–51; family identity and sense of duty, 40–42, 43–44; on first meeting Magda, 118; impact of remarriage on André, 73–74; importance of order to, 51; as patriarch, authoritarian, 42; photo of, 41; plans for André's and Magda's wedding, 116; relocation in Brussels, 66–67; response to André's engagement, 112–13; return to France, 69; return to St. Quentin, 94; sense of family identity, 33; strict morality, 44–45; successful careers of sons, 40–41; and Paula Troche's accident, 27–28

Trocmé, Paula Schwerdtmann: accident and death, 27–28, 44; André's memories of, 26–27; German origins, 32; photo showing, 27

Trocmé, Pierre, 30, 41–42, 75–76
Trocmé, Robert: André's relationship with, 32, 41; business success, 40, 94; influence and care for younger siblings, 41; letter to, about André's preaching, 148; marriage, 78; Mind Widening Bank, 79
truth: Absolutist view, 11; André's commitment to, 11–15, 78, 126, 155

Under Fire (Barbusse), 92
Union Theological Seminary (New York): André's studies at, 97, 101–3, 116; marginalization of André at, 252
United Nations, IFOR representatives at, xxii
United States: concern for refugees in, 227; COs in, xxiii–xxiv; Magda's visit to, 259–61; peace activism, 251–53
Universal Peace Congress, Glasgow, xxi
University of Geneva Interpreters School, 16, 273
University of Strasbourg, 136
Unoccupied Zone. *See* Free Zone (Unoccupied Zone)
U.S. Holocaust Memorial, 22–23

Valeri, Valerio, 248
Van Dusen, Henry ("Pit"), 252
Vassieux-en-Vercors, France, German reprisals in, 205
Vasto, Lanza del, 266–67
Vélodrome d'Hiver, Paris, roundup of Jews in, 177
Vernier, Philippe ("Philo"), 80, 98
Vernier, Pierre ("Piot"), 85, 98–99, 240

Versailles: MIR headquarters, 235; Trocmé home in, 242–43; Trocmés' decision to leave, 268
Vichy France: changing response to offering of refuge, 173; collaboration with Germany, 161; Commission on Jewish Questions, 186; enforcement of anti-Semitic regulations, 173, 177; Jewish Statute (Oct. 3, 1940), 162–63; military force allowed by Germany, 163; Papal Nuncio and, 248; role in pursuing Nazi racist policies, 23
Vietnam, division into North and South, 263–64
Villon, François (*Ballade des Pendus*), 207–8
Vinet, Alexandre: André's thesis on, 115; call for separation of church and state, 124–25; concept of complete, spontaneous individual, 123; linking of obedience and liberty, 116
Volkonsky, Sergei, 53, 297–29
von Bulow, Hans, 297–98

Waldensian Protestant Church, 57–58, 62–64, 145
war: as crime, 21–22; as just, 255. *See also* nonviolence; pacifism
Waziers housing project, Sin-le-Noble, 125
Weapons of the Spirit (movie, Sauvage), 186
Weber, Hans-Ruedi, 214, 216–17
West Cummington, Massachusetts, Jewish refugees in, 226
Wiesel, Elie, 22
Wilhelm II, Kaiser, abdication, 70
Wissotsky, Varia Alexandrovna Poggio: death, 105; family background, 298; importance of to Magda, 52–53, 61–62; photos of, 53–54; religious beliefs, 57

worker-priest movement, 97, 246, 248–49
World Council of Churches, Geneva, Trocmé archive, 293
World Pacifist Congress, India, 241

Yad Vashem: honors for people of Le Chambon, 285, 288; "Medal of the Just" nomination, 283–84; Righteous of the Nations recognition, 171, 186